The Land-Water-Energy Nexus

BIOPHYSICAL AND ECONOMIC CONSEQUENCES

This work is published under the responsibility of the Secretary-General of the OECD. The opinions expressed and arguments employed herein do not necessarily reflect the official views of OECD member countries.

This document and any map included herein are without prejudice to the status of or sovereignty over any territory, to the delimitation of international frontiers and boundaries and to the name of any territory, city or area.

Please cite this publication as:
OECD (2017), *The Land-Water-Energy Nexus: Biophysical and Economic Consequences*, OECD Publishing, Paris.
http://dx.doi.org/10.1787/9789264279360-en

ISBN 978-92-64-27933-9 (print)
ISBN 978-92-64-27936-0 (PDF)

The statistical data for Israel are supplied by and under the responsibility of the relevant Israeli authorities. The use of such data by the OECD is without prejudice to the status of the Golan Heights, East Jerusalem and Israeli settlements in the West Bank under the terms of international law.

Photo credits: Cover © Steve Quinlan/Shutterstock.com

Preface

This report presents the first comprehensive assessment of the global consequences of the land-water-energy nexus in the coming decades. It provides a global outlook to 2060 for the major impacts of nexus bottlenecks on regional biophysical and economic systems. It uses a detailed modelling framework that links The Netherlands Environmental Assessment Agency PBL's IMAGE model to the OECD's ENV-Linkages model to calculate regional and global consequences related to the nexus bottlenecks. Together, these provide a unique insight into the global and regional costs of emerging bottlenecks in the land, water and energy systems.

Interest in the land-water-energy (LWE) nexus in recent years has led to a growing appreciation that policies in each of these domains are inextricably linked and that to focus on just one bottleneck runs the risk of suboptimal outcomes whether in respect of effectiveness, efficiency or sustainability. A key question is the extent to which these interdependencies have repercussions at the macroeconomic and global level and thus support the urgency of promoting integrated policies for the nexus. An unambiguous positive answer cannot be drawn from the modelling evidence presented in this report. At the global level, the biophysical and economic bottleneck impacts are very moderate, and only a very small interaction effect emerges from the combined bottlenecks. In some world regions impacts of LWE nexus bottlenecks are much more severe, with implications for food security and public health exceeding the scale of macro-economic losses. This suggests that the notion of paying greater attention to the LWE nexus is better understood as an issue of hotspots and local disruptions.

Further degradation of the environment and natural capital can compromise prospects for future economic growth and human well-being. In order to assess the feedbacks from the environment on economic growth, modelling tools used for projecting future pathways of economic activity need to be able continually to assess how different environmental impacts affect various elements of the economic system. This has been the ambition of the OECD's "Costs of Inaction and Resource scarcity: Consequences for Long-term Economic growth" (CIRCLE) project. The modelling tools underlying this report contribute to this ambition by quantifying the full description of the biophysical and economic systems. This allows a much more elaborate quantitative assessment of the consequences of emerging nexus bottlenecks in the coming decades.

Significant uncertainties remain in the evaluation of the rate and geographical distribution of nexus impacts. Furthermore, some of the most severe consequences will materialise at finer spatial scales than can be investigated here. Further work on downscaling the modelling analysis to the level of water basins is therefore recommended. Nonetheless, policy-makers in countries and regions that are nexus hotspots have a lot to gain from more integrated policy approaches to assess and counter nexus challenges, building on the insights from the systems analysis presented here.

Simon Upton
OECD Director for Environment

Foreword

As part of the "Costs of Inaction and Resource scarcity: Consequences for Long-term Economic growth" (CIRCLE) project, this report was prepared jointly by Olivier Durand-Lasserve, Jean Chateau and Rob Dellink of the OECD Environment Directorate and Fritz Hellmann and Tom Kram of the Netherlands Environmental Assessment Agency PBL. Hester Biemans (Alterra) contributed to the modelling of groundwater depletion; Tarik El-Laboudy contributed to the integration between the modelling tools at OECD and PBL; Ton Manders led the PBL input during the inception phase of the project.

The OECD Environment Policy Committee (EPOC) was responsible for the oversight of the development of the report. In addition, the Joint Working Party on Agriculture and Environment (JWPAE) and the experts following the CIRCLE project reviewed earlier drafts. The work at PBL received financial support from the Dutch Ministries of Foreign Affairs, of Infrastructure and the Environment, and of Economic Affairs.

The project was managed by Shardul Agrawala, who also provided feedback on the modelling and earlier drafts. Marie-Jeanne Gaffard and Jacqueline Maher provided administrative and technical support; statistical and technical assistance was provided by François Chantret. This version also benefits from comments on earlier drafts by Guillaume Gruère, Xavier Leflaive and Simon Upton (all OECD), as well as Jeannette Beck, Pieter Boot, Frank Dietz and Ton Manders (all PBL).

Follow OECD Publications on:

 http://twitter.com/OECD_Pubs

http://www.facebook.com/OECDPublications

 http://www.linkedin.com/groups/OECD-Publications-4645871

 http://www.youtube.com/oecdilibrary

 http://www.oecd.org/oecddirect/

This book has...

StatLinks ⟪🎚⟫

A service that delivers Excel® files from the printed page!

Look for the *StatLinks* ⟪🎚⟫ at the bottom of the tables or graphs in this book. To download the matching Excel® spreadsheet, just type the link into your Internet browser, starting with the *http://dx.doi.org* prefix, or click on the link from the e-book edition.

Table of contents

Tables

Boxes

Acronyms and abbreviations

CCS	Carbon Capture and Storage
CES	Constant elasticity of substitution
CGE	Computable general equilibrium
EC-JRC	European Commission Joint Research Centre
EJ	Exajoule (energy unit)
EU	European Union
FAO	UN Food and Agriculture Organisation
GDP	Gross domestic product
GHG	Greenhouse gas
IEA	International Energy Agency
IPCC	Intergovernmental Panel on Climate Change
LWE	Land-water-energy
PBL	Netherlands Environmental Assessment Agency
REDD	Reducing Emissions from Deforestation and Degradation
UN	United Nations
USD	United States dollars
VOLL	Value of lost load

Executive summary

Almost all economic activities are supported by the use of scarce land, water or energy, either directly or indirectly. Nexus is a useful label to describe how these resources are closely interlinked. To avoid negative side effects and to create synergies through policy, efficient management of the nexus resources needs to account for the direct and indirect effects of changes in various resources within the full biophysical and economic systems.

The report addresses the following question: What would be the global and regional biophysical and economic consequences by 2060 because of policy inaction regarding the limited availability of land, water and energy, given their interlinkages? The most direct linkages in the nexus are at the biophysical level, such as in the production of crops; however, it is vital to look at the consequences of the bottlenecks on different economic activities and on different policy objectives: welfare, environmental quality, food, water and energy security.

This report focusses on a dynamic, integrated, and disaggregated analysis of how land, water and energy interact in the biophysical and economic systems. In the modelling analysis that combines the IMAGE and ENV-Linkages models, a set of carefully chosen scenarios reflects on bottlenecks in water supply, land supply and energy supply. The water supply bottleneck scenario examines the consequences of the depletion of selected deep groundwater reservoirs before 2060. The land bottleneck scenario considers the impact of increased urban sprawl and of expanded protected natural areas on the access to land for agriculture. The energy bottleneck focusses on reducing the reliance on increasingly scarce fossil fuels through a partial shift in energy supply towards biofuels. The combined bottlenecks scenario aims to show how the three bottlenecks interact and add-up. The report also examines the sensitivity to the changes in biophysical conditions from alternative assumptions of climate change. This report, a part of the "Cost of Inaction and Resource scarcity: Consequences for Long-term Economic growth" (CIRCLE) project, compares the system-wide performance with selected nexus bottleneck scenarios to a baseline projection without bottlenecks. The top-down assessment carried out in this report complements more fine-grained analysis of the nexus in specific hotspots and provides essential context for such hotspot analyses.

Key findings

- There is no clear evidence to suggest an absolute scarcity of land-water-energy (LWE) resources globally. The impacts from LWE bottlenecks, however, vary significantly across regions and time periods. Therefore the main problem is having the resources at the right time in the right place.

- The multiple nexus interactions imply that the impact of the combined bottlenecks in land-water-energy resources may significantly differ from the summed effects of the individual bottlenecks. In around half of the regions the key results for the combined scenario are close to the sum of the individual three bottlenecks. In the most fragile regions, the interactions from combining the bottlenecks are more pronounced; this suggests that adding an overarching nexus vision to policy making has clear benefits. The quantitative analysis illustrates how in some regions the exploitation of the least critical (or scarce) resource can overcome the negative economic consequences of the other resources.

- Bottlenecks appear to have a relatively modest negative welfare effects at the global level, depressing GDP and consumption levels somewhat below the baseline level. In contrast, countries that rely heavily on the scarce resources, such as India and the People's Republic of China (hereafter China), could be more severely impacted. Other countries, such as the ASEAN economies and countries in Latin America, might benefit from the changes in international competitiveness of countries.

- Although difficult to quantify, the increasing food prices from the three nexus bottlenecks suggest that the welfare of the poorest households may be particularly vulnerable.

- The nexus bottlenecks combined triple the loss of pristine forest cover from baseline projections driven by demographic and economic trends between 2015 and 2060. Many core environmental services provided by pristine forests are thus seriously affected.

- All bottleneck scenarios lead to deteriorations in food security, as reflected in increasing food prices and increased budget shares spent on food. Furthermore, in most regions the import share of food increases, indicating increased pressure on self-sufficiency. The consequences are especially pronounced in India. The combination of all bottlenecks further amplifies the increase in food prices, while climate change adds to rising food budget shares and reliance on food imports with aforementioned social repercussions in equity issues.

- Even though the projected increase in total irrigation water demand is very moderate, the depletion of non-renewable sources reduces future water security. The combined effect of increasing demand for non-agricultural uses, and depletion of aquifer stocks for irrigation, will have serious implications for water security in many regions and countries, including India, Middle East, North Africa, Mexico and the Caspian region and specific arid parts of other regions. This in turn can also affect food and energy security.

- The implications of the nexus bottlenecks for energy security are much less clear. While energy is a key resource with economic importance, the large traded volumes of energy and the availability of alternative energy sources imply that supply risks are fairly low. A bioenergy policy could improve energy security at the national level, but the quantitative analysis shows that this comes at a trade-off with the other nexus resources, especially land, and can thus threaten other policy objectives such as food security.

Key policy conclusions

- At the global level, the biophysical and economic impacts of bottlenecks in the LWE nexus are moderate. International trade can help spread the risks and limit the worst regional impacts.

- Negative economic consequences of the nexus bottlenecks tend to concentrate in hotspots: countries with strong bottlenecks in economic activities that cannot be substituted or imported, as well as regions with strong decreases in crop yields and higher production costs. North Africa, the Middle East and parts of Asia, not least India, are projected to suffer the most from bottlenecks in the LWE nexus. Policy-makers of these areas can potentially gain a lot from more integrated policy approaches.

- The LWE bottlenecks threaten food security in all regions and water security especially in already water-stressed regions; this could disproportionately affect the poor as their share of income dedicated to food, water and energy tends to be largest.

Chapter 1

The nexus between land, water and energy

This first chapter outlines the context for the global analysis of the nexus between land, water and energy. The chapter first introduces the main concepts of the land-water-energy bottlenecks. It then lays out the main research questions as well as the structure of the report, and how it fits with other recent OECD analysis that looks at nexus bottlenecks. This chapter next presents an overview of the main linkages between water, land and energy, and describes how these together provide a nexus. It then describes the main bottlenecks that can be envisaged as they relate to water use, land use and energy use, as well as the materials dimension of the nexus. Finally, it motivates why an integrated dynamic modelling approach is most suitable for investigating the interlinkages of the nexus bottlenecks.

1.1. Introduction

Almost all economic activities are supported by the use of scarce water, land or energy, either directly or indirectly. We need water to grow food and for energy production, we need energy to grow food and to pump and treat water, and we need land to produce bioenergy. Unsustainable use of these resources raises serious concerns about their looming scarcity. There may be constraints or bottlenecks regarding the quantity and quality of supply of each of these resources, including pollution and degradation, and regarding increased demand for them in a growing global economy.

There are strong linkages between land, water and energy in biophysical and in economic terms. Nexus is a useful label to describe the way that these resources are bound together and that the bottlenecks in one area are tightly linked to the other resources. Policies neglecting these interlinkages may be sub-optimal and can actually create or exacerbate problems instead of solving them; i.e. they might resolve a specific problem with one of these resources but at the same time impact the others and create additional (and unforeseen) problems. Therefore some activities can impact indirectly other activities by increasing the scarcity or changing the quality of the resource they use in common. In terms of policy analysis, it implies that efficient management of the nexus resources needs to take into account the direct and indirect effects of changes in the demand and supply of the various resources on the whole biophysical and economic systems, as this is the only means to avoid negative side effects and to create synergies. For example, implementation of hydropower for electricity production can conflict with irrigation requirements where hydropower release schedules do not match the timing of irrigation needs. Under more favourable conditions and adequate operational management, a dam and reservoir can provide a win-win situation with both hydropower and agricultural benefits (Hellegers et al., 2008). This shows that a careful, simultaneous consideration of the land-water-energy resources is needed when designing policies, as ignoring their interactions can present negative side-effects. Therefore an integrated approach is needed to assess whether policies adequately resolves bottlenecks in the whole nexus, or effectively shift stress from one resource to another.

As part of the CIRCLE project,[1] the scope of this report is to provide a broad assessment of the global and regional implications of some of the main bottlenecks in the land-water-energy (LWE) nexus, and project how the consequences of these "nexus bottlenecks" affect the biophysical and economic systems by 2060. More precisely, it aims to shed light on the main trade-offs and synergies between the different bottlenecks in the LWE nexus, and their interactions with the global biophysical and economic systems. The report also examines the sensitivity of these indicators to the changes in biophysical conditions stemming from alternative assumptions on the evolution of the underlying assumptions regarding climate change. In other words, it addresses the following question: **What would be the global and regional biophysical and economic consequences by 2060 of policy inaction to account for the limited availability of land, water and energy, given all the complex relations between these resources?**

A full quantitative assessment of the global and regional consequences for the LWE nexus would require detailed modelling tools that can represent the key linkages in resource use and economic activity at the local level. Many of the nexus bottlenecks will occur within specific water basins (see Box 1.1 on recent OECD analysis of water risk hotspots), and have widely varying effects in different geographical locations, depending on the availability of all three key resources, and distances to economic markets. For instance, the IEA (2015) shows that the cost of water shortages for coal power generation can be higher (albeit not very much) in water-stressed areas far from economic hubs such as in western China, than in regions that benefit from a local mix of abundant coal resources, water availability and nearby cities, such as northern India. But such a detailed bottom-up analysis is necessarily partial in scope. Therefore, specific insights can be drawn from a more top-down analysis of key interlinkages between land, water and energy in the global biophysical and economic systems. The current report hence does not aim to provide an exhaustive answer on the costs of inaction in all regions in the world. Rather, it limits itself to a top-down approach, by using large-scale global systems models to explore how major resource bottlenecks can affect the land use systems and economies of the major regions in the world.

Given the multi-faceted nature of the bottlenecks in the nexus, and their local nature, it is impossible to provide a full picture of the global economic consequences of all aspects of the nexus. Rather, insights are provided by investigating a carefully selected set of scenarios that are designed to illustrate the key bottlenecks: one scenario for each resource bottleneck, plus two scenarios that combine all bottlenecks, with and without an overlay of climate change. The different resource bottlenecks are quantified using specific examples of widespread trade-offs between different resources and policy objectives that are relevant from a macro perspective. Specifically, the water bottleneck investigated in this report concerns the use of unsustainable groundwater reserves, a key challenge for irrigated agriculture. The land bottleneck assesses the influence of nature conservation and urban sprawl to reflect the effects of reduced access to potentially very suitable land for agriculture. The energy bottleneck focuses on the feasibility and trade-offs in (partially) shifting away from reliance on imported fossil fuels, using an ambitious biofuel penetration scenario. As the precise timing of the bottlenecks is quite uncertain, the analysis focuses on the results in the longer run, in line with the larger CIRCLE project with a model horizon of 2060.

The core of the analysis of the consequences of the nexus for the costs of inaction is carried out by soft-linking two global dynamic systems models: a general equilibrium economic model with a detailed specification of sectoral and regional economic activity and their interlinkages (OECD's ENV-Linkages model; Chateau et al., 2014) and a spatially explicit biophysical model with detailed representation of resource use (PBL's IMAGE model; Stehfest et al., 2014). This systems modelling assessment is complemented by more generic anecdotal evidence of specific bottlenecks that can have significant impacts on local economies and on specific sectors, but that will likely not lead to significant changes in the macro economy.

The nexus bottlenecks are described in this report from the perspective of the natural resources that are needed to sustain economic activity. But these are clearly linked to the services they provide: land use allows agriculture to provide food, energy use provides heat, power and fuel, and water use provides water for irrigation, cooling, drinking, et cetera. Therefore the LWE nexus is effectively roughly the same as the food-water-energy nexus as discussed in the literature, with a different label and with a more explicit acknowledgement that other sectors than agriculture, not least energy production, also rely on scarce land resources. These links also make it clear that there are three specific economic sectors that are central to the analysis: agriculture, water production and energy production. But an essential part of the assessment in this report is to go beyond a partial investigation of direct impacts on these sectors. The report aims to highlight the sectoral linkages and indirect effects that the nexus bottlenecks have on the rest of the economy, and how bottlenecks in a certain region affect other regions.

Agriculture is central to the nexus analysis, as it relies heavily on water, land and energy as inputs, in fact agriculture is by far the most important driver of land-cover and land-use changes and irrigation is the biggest water consuming activity at the global scale and in many regions and countries. In terms of economic impacts, challenges posed by restricted availability of LWE resources on agriculture come primarily in the form of yield reductions and/or limited availability of suitable land. Such impacts can be assessed with the IMAGE model. In the CGE framework of ENV-Linkages these sectoral impacts are introduced as exogenous shocks, which in turn induces economic impacts throughout the economy, and on other economies, not least due to shifts in competitiveness between regions.

The challenge is to move beyond the nexus as a "slogan" and develop a methodology to assess quantitatively the biophysical and economic consequences of bottlenecks in the linked use of land, water and energy. By using a soft-linking of two major systems models, one for the biophysical aspects and the other for the economic system, a wide range of indicators of the negative and positive consequences of the nexus bottlenecks can be investigated. These include indicators for (economic) welfare, environmental sustainability, as well as food security, water security an energy security.

In line with the wider objectives of the CIRCLE project, and as part of the economic assessment, expressing the costs of inaction on the bottlenecks in the same terms as the usual indicator for economic growth, i.e. in terms of GDP losses, helps to communicate the importance of the nexus for economic policy making, despite its well-known drawbacks as a welfare indicator. But by embedding this indicator in a much wider set of indicators that capture different aspects of the multiple policy objectives, one can create clear insights into the major trade-offs and synergies in the feedbacks of the bottlenecks in the nexus on the biophysical and economic systems.

The land-water-energy nexus analysis in CIRCLE has several innovative aspects. Few studies have analysed linkages between land-water-energy simultaneously in an integrated framework and then translated the biophysical indicators into economic impacts. Despite the complexity of the modelling tools, and their suitability to explore future pathways of economic activity, environmental pressure and their interlinkages and feedbacks, this report contains only exploratory insights into the costs of inaction on the nexus. A limited number of scenarios are explored, with only a limited number of interlinkages between the nexus elements quantified. It is not a prediction of what will happen, nor a synthesis of the full literature on LWE nexus concerns. Some studies have looked at linkages and trade-offs between individuals pairs of the land-water-energy sectors (Bartos and Chester, 2014; Howells and Rogner, 2014; Dale et al., 2011; Hoff, 2011; Monaghan et al., 2007). Some other studies have looked at individual links between bottlenecks for a single resource and the economy (Berrittella et al., 2007; Veldkamp and Verburg, 2004). However, none of the above studies have adequately addressed all three aspects of the land-water-energy nexus together and their link with the economy. The analysis of the land-water-energy nexus in the CIRCLE project follows such an integrative approach, and is thus complementary to earlier and ongoing research efforts.

The report is structured as follows. The remainder of this chapter introduces the LWE nexus in more detail and explains how the different aspects interact. Chapter 2 describes the methodology used for the quantitative analysis, with a brief description of the modelling tools, and a brief explanation of the modelling scenarios. Chapter 3 introduces the baseline projection of economic activity and environmental pressure, while Chapter 4 presents the main results from the modelling analysis. Chapter 5 concludes.

Agriculture is expected to face increasing water risks in the future, ranging from water shortages, to floods and water quality risks. These risks could affect agriculture production, markets, trade and food security. Targeted policy action by defining hotspots, or localised agricultural productive region subject to acute water risks, can help increase the efficiency and effectiveness of efforts to mitigate these future water risks.

A comprehensive assessment of the water risk literature, combined with baseline projections on agricultural production in 2024 and 2050, was used to assess future water risk hotspots for agriculture. China, India and the United States lead the global production of major commodities, but they are also considered to be the most exposed of 141 countries to future water risks. More specifically, agriculture water risks are especially prevalent in the regions of Northeast China, Southwest United States and Northwest India.

The materialisation of agricultural water risks in hotspots can generate three levels of impacts: they can lead to falls in production in hotspot locations; affect agricultural markets and trading partners of the affected country; and lead to broader food security and socio-economic concerns in a larger set of countries. The evidence collected shows that these impacts can be significant including in the case of the three identified hotspot regions. In the absence of policy action, agriculture production in Northeast China, Northwest India and the Southwest United States will be significantly impacted by water quantity constraints. Activities generating low economic value per water use will be the first affected by these changes. A simulation of projected impacts of gradual increases in surface and groundwater irrigation stresses and droughts only in the three hotspot regions reduces global production and increases prices of major field crops – in particular maize, wheat and cotton, but also fruits and vegetables. National production in the three countries falls by a few to a dozen percentage points, affecting their trade balance. Partner countries' trade balances are also affected significantly. Some of these effects may intensify when climate change projections are taken into consideration. Acute agricultural water risks can also result in broader food security and socio-economic consequences, manifested for instance via foreign land purchases from water scarce regions that are sometimes detrimental to food and water security.

Responding to these risks effectively require considering three types of policy actions. As a priority, governments of countries facing water risks should focus their attention to hotspot regions, introduce targeted agriculture and water instruments, including information, extension services, technical and institutional measures in the area, and customise some of their key water and agriculture policies locally. As a complement, they should co-ordinate their efforts with that of active private companies and with other water users. Second, to limit market effect, these governments should work with trade partners to strengthen domestic and international market linkages. Third, at a broader level, all governments should engage into international collaboration to support the resilience of vulnerable countries to future water risks, exchange information to reduce the diffusion of indirect impacts, and increase their preparation and their resilience to unexpected indirect effects.

Source: OECD (2017).

1.2. Overview of the LWE nexus and interlinkages

Key interactions within the LWE nexus are shown in Figure 1.1, which indicates how the biophysical resources are linked to economic activities and – mostly indirectly – to a number of key policy objectives. Resources are often understood to be exhaustible, and attention tends to go to scarcity and depletion. But resources can also be renewable, such as fresh water supply from the hydrological cycle. Still, the supply can be constrained locally and/or seasonally, and also due to poor quality. In the first domain in Figure 1.1, the LWE resources represent a biophysical system, characterised both in terms of quantity (for instance, surface of land, energy equivalent of in situ oil, volume of aquifer water and rainfall) and quality (for instance the fertility of land, the accessibility of water supplies, and the access to oil fields). Concern over availability of adequate volume and quality of resources emerges from their vital role as inputs for economic activities; the second domain in Figure 1.1. These resources provide various goods and services that meet the needs of the population, including agriculture providing food (and biomass), energy transformation providing power and heat, and water supply providing clean water services and sanitation. Finally, the third domain transcends the sectoral scope and highlight how the resources in the nexus, through the economic services they provide, contribute to a range of policy objectives; obvious examples include "security of supply" for food, water and energy, welfare and environmental quality.

Figure 1.1. **Main linkages within the land, water and energy nexus**

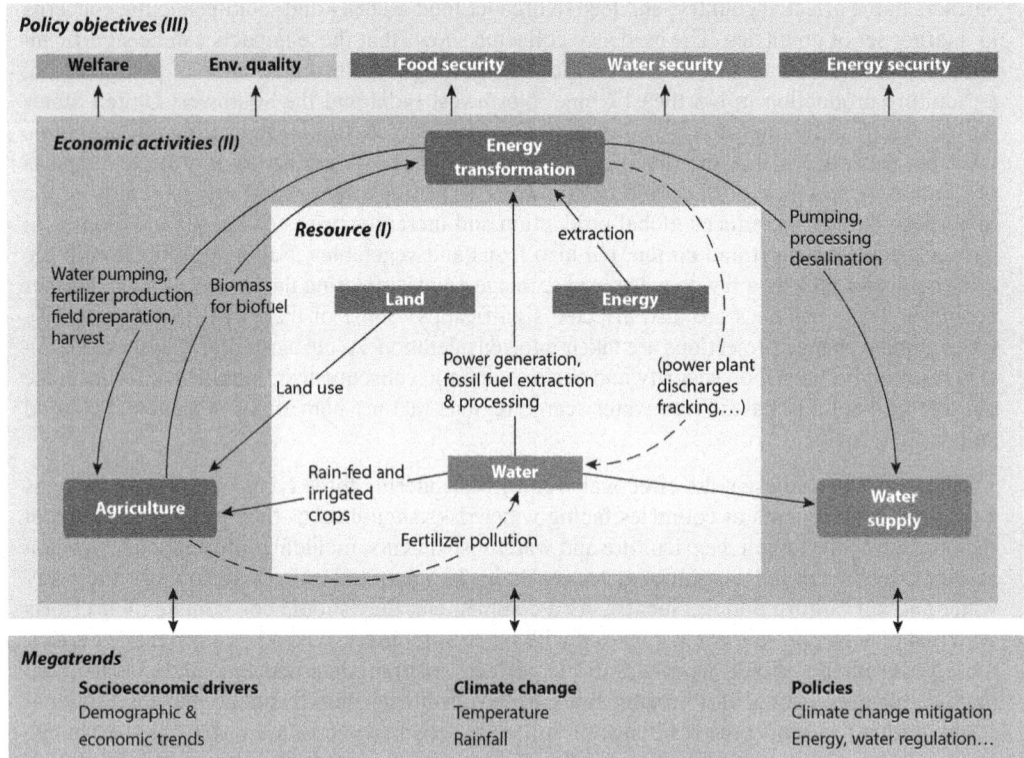

In a narrow sense, security of supply is met only when there is no physical or economic scarcity, but definitions often go beyond pure access and include notions of satisfaction or preferences. Food security is defined in the 1996 Rome Declaration on World Food Security as "when all people, at all times, have physical and economic access to sufficient, safe and nutritious food to meet their dietary needs and food preferences for an active and healthy life" (FAO, 1996). Similarly, the IEA defines energy security as "uninterrupted physical availability at a price which is affordable, while respecting environmental concerns" (Jewell, 2011). On water security, UN (2015) writes "The availability of an acceptable quantity and quality of water for health, livelihoods, ecosystems and production, coupled with an acceptable level of water-related risks to people, environment and economies (Grey and

Sadoff, 2007)". However, the broader connotation, i.e. a movement in the direction towards security, is more relevant for this report: do the bottlenecks in the nexus, and the policies that aim to address these, bring the world closer to the objectives of security of supply.

The food, energy and water aspects are not independent of each other. Agriculture depends on land and water resources, and also on the energy transformation sector. The energy transformation sector needs energy resources and water. In the case of biofuel developments, it will also interact with the agriculture sector. Water supply services require indeed water resources, but also energy services. Unsustainable use of one resource can hence affect the other resources. Firstly because some sector use the same resource and will thus rival for access in particular when the resource is under stress. This is for instance the case for agriculture and energy transformation which both use water. Hence, operations in the energy sector may affect the water availability for agriculture and therefore crop yields. Secondly, when the resource becomes scarcer and less accessible it may be overcome by using more of other resources (substitution). For instance, with depletion of conventional oil reserves, oil and gas resources require more water to be processed, which may put pressure on water resources. Lastly, resource scarcity may require redirecting the inputs or output of a sector towards other sectors in order to ensure security of supply. For instance, in the Middle East where water is scarce, a significant share of regional energy production is used for pumping, transporting and desalinating water. This is beneficial to the water security objective, but it represents a cost for the society in the form of lower national revenues from energy exports.

In general, the economic cost of bottlenecks through constraining production is not easy to assess. On the one hand, if bottlenecks are well managed and the change of resource availability is well anticipated, all the options available to limit the effect of scarcity will be implemented in a cost effective way. In that case, the cost of adjusting to the bottleneck is quite low for the economic system. On the other hand, if disruptions in key sectors cannot be avoided, they can be very costly. Therefore one needs to take into account the cost of investments to hedge systems against the risk of disruption, for instance by providing more back-up production capacity. Lastly, a major policy problem is that currently a large part of the world population has no access to electricity or clean water. Nexus bottlenecks can make the deployment of the necessary infrastructure more difficult, and thus hamper energy and water security.

The nexus interactions imply that a potentially large part of the cost of resource scarcity cannot be captured if not taking all the elements of the nexus together. It is also true for assessing the benefits of policy action. For instance, policies that favour biofuel, for climate policy of energy security (independence) reasons, can put pressure on land use and water resource and conflict with food security concerns.

The trade-offs and synergies within the land-water-energy-nexus and their impact on the economy are substantially influenced on the long run by a number of socio-economic and environmental "megatrends". The term "megatrends", which is further explained in Box 1.2, includes the consequences of demographic and economic growth, climate change and also climate change policies.

The next sections discuss in more detail how constraints in the quantity or the quality of these environmental resources can be a bottleneck for economic activities, and how economic competition for scarce resources affect the bottleneck. This discussion is grouped per bottleneck; i.e. each paragraph explains which factors and nexus linkages contribute to respectively land, water and energy bottlenecks, and highlights which economic activities are most affected by each bottleneck.

Box 1.2. **Megatrends and the LWE nexus**

There are a number of important trends that underlie this baseline projection.

Firstly, over the long run, there are important factors that influence the demand for goods and services, and therefore the demand for resources by the producing sectors. Population growth increases consumer demand for food, water and energy, thus increasing the pressure on the scarce resources, not least land, through agricultural production. It also exacerbates the competition for these scarce resources: more water is needed for final consumption, but also for agriculture. Similarly, income growth leads to stronger demand for high-quality commodities, often produced in ways that are more water and energy-intensive (a typical example is the shift in diet towards more meat-based food consumption). But the net influence of income growth is not a priori trivial. For example, it also means that people are more versatile in avoiding the negative consequences resulting from shortages or quality issues in the nexus. And it is often argued that people with higher income demand a higher quality of their environment, thereby increasing efforts to improve resource efficiency through re-use and recycling, and inducing governments to do more to protect the essential resources. Education and urbanisation influence both population and income levels (and are affected by them), but also the composition of sectoral demand.

Secondly, on the supply side, climate change is probably the most important megatrend. Climate change affects all aspects of the nexus directly and indirectly. IPCC (2013, 2014a,b) and others have shown that there are significant direct effects on land availability (not least due to land loss from sea level rise), water stress, and energy demand and supply. Not least, climate lchange influences the hydrological cycle, resulting in shifts in annual water availability in many regions, and also in more erratic precipitation patterns including extreme events such as droughts and excess rainfall. Reduced water availability can increase competition for water between sectors, as described above. Moreover, climate change is projected to have negative impacts on agricultural productivity in most regions, e.g. through loss of yields due to excess temperatures. Lower agricultural yields due to climate change means additional intensification and/or expansion of agriculture to meet the demand for agricultural products with implications for land and energy requirements. As all sectors are linked in the economic system, impacts on one sector in one region trickle through to other sectors and regions through changes in the allocation of production factors, changes in final demand and changes in trade patterns (OECD, 2015a). By using a multi-sectoral, multi-regional general equilibrium model, the economic analysis in this report picks up such indirect effects in the same way.

Thirdly, there are a number of megatrends that affect both demand and supply, but in opposite ways for the different resources in the nexus. As a prime example, substitution of fossil fuels by bio-energy reduces energy stress, but exacerbates stress levels for land and water. Large-scale biofuel crop cultivation negatively interacts with the other elements in the land-water-energy nexus. Considerable land areas are required for biofuels to supply a substantial share of the global energy demand, which raises concerns over competition with food production and higher prices. Moreover, if and where additional land for biofuel production goes at the expense of naturally vegetated land, this will affect the hydrological cycle. Additional water stress can result on irrigated land, and this competition over water between food and fuel crops can affect agricultural production in drought-prone regions and potentially lead to yield reductions.

1.3. Land-related bottlenecks

Agriculture is globally the most land-demanding human activity (see Box 1.3). Currently around 33% of the earth's surface (excluding Greenland and Antarctica) is used for crops and livestock farming (PBL, RIO+20). Projections indicate that agricultural land use is likely to increase even further in coming decades due to population and welfare growth.

Meeting an increasing demand for food can be met either by increasing exploitation of the land resource (extensification), or by increasing the inputs of other resources per unit of land (intensification). Evidently, intensive agriculture also requires substantial water and energy inputs and has therefore a clear link with the nexus.

Box 1.3. **Agriculture as a key driver of global land and water use**

Agricultural production has increased strongly over recent decades to meet rising food demand driven by both population growth and changes in diets. About 80% of the production increase has been achieved through higher yields from existing land, and about 20% through expanding agricultural land (Bruinsma, 2003). Between 1970 and 2010, the share of agricultural land use (crop and grazing land), expanded by about 4 percentage points, largely at the expense of forest area (OECD, 2012a: Figure 2.12). A somewhat lower pace of expansion has been observed over the last decade.

Figure 1.2. **Global land use, 1970 and 2010**

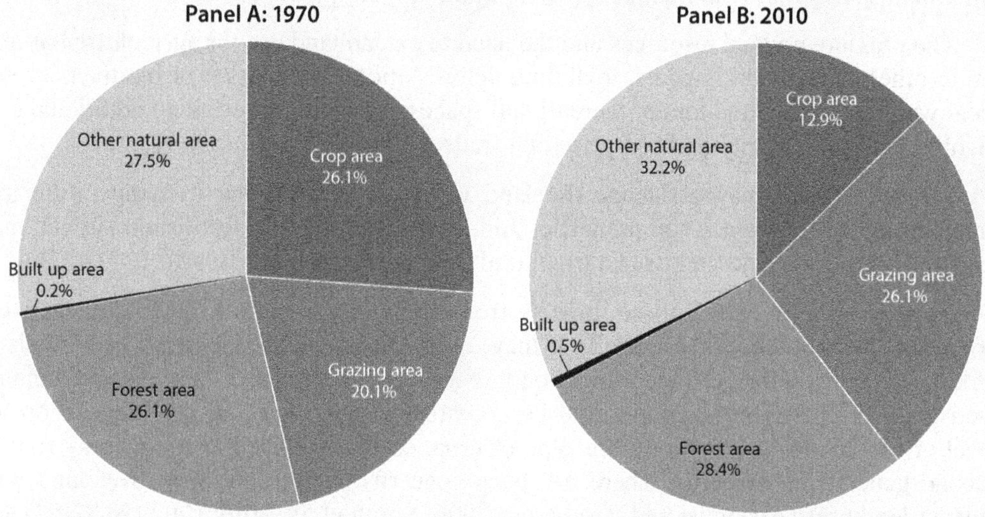

Panel A: 1970

Other natural area 27.5%
Crop area 26.1%
Built up area 0.2%
Forest area 26.1%
Grazing area 20.1%

Panel B: 2010

Crop area 12.9%
Other natural area 32.2%
Grazing area 26.1%
Built up area 0.5%
Forest area 28.4%

StatLink ⟰ http://dx.doi.org/10.1787/888933554582

Source: IMAGE model.

The *OECD Environmental Outlook* baseline projects that competition between agricultural land use and other land uses will intensify in the coming decade under current policies. This is also the conclusion of the *OECD/FAO Agricultural Outlook to 2020* (OECD/FAO, 2011). A converging GDP per capita and a growing population will both increase the demand for food, especially animal products. Moreover, policies that stimulate the use of biofuels also increase the demand for agricultural production and land area (Chapter 4). Given the limited supply of land, this means that in the short run deforestation will continue, although at slower rates than in past decades.

Source: OECD Environmental Outlook to 2050 (OECD, 2012a).

Various forms of renewable energy production require substantial land areas. Hydropower plants, biofuel plantations, solar and wind "farms", for example, require significant quantities of land, and sometimes even require relocation of existing activities and local communities (Bazilian et al., 2011). They often also interfere with existing hydrological flows and regimes. "Regular" coal or gas fired power plants also require land for their site locations, but their land claim is relatively minor.

The combined land claims of economic activities can result in a regional competition for land, and such a land bottleneck can impact certain economic activities such as agriculture. Land competition reduces the available land supply for agriculture and increases land rental rates. In turn, this results in an agricultural expansion onto marginal lands if possible, or agricultural intensification (Van Meijl et al., 2006). Agricultural production on marginal lands often leads to lower overall yields unless more inputs are used. Likewise, agricultural intensification necessitates higher input requirements (Van Meijl et al., 2006; Smith et al., 2010; Bazilian et al., 2011; Lal, 2013; Ringler et al., 2013). This implies not only more capital/labour inputs (Van Meijl et al., 2006), but also more energy/water inputs. Overall, land competition seems to imply lower yields or a higher input use, and can thereby result in higher production costs and a shift in the pressure on other nexus resources (Bazilian et al., 2011; Lal, 2013; Ringler et al., 2013).

The pressure on land resources and the need to extend land use for agriculture has also led to other detrimental impacts, including deforestation, degradation of biodiversity and local water pollution, and loss of recreational spaces which all represent an additional cost involved by land scarcity and comprise of a trade-off between the nexus resources.

Climate change may influence the land resource. The change in temperature and precipitation will influence soil properties and, apart from the CO_2 fertilisation effect, may lead to decreases in yields, a loss of agricultural land due to sea level rise, etc. (OECD, 2015a).

Climate policies reduce these impacts from climate change, but may also negatively affect the land bottlenecks, especially if they imply large scale development of biofuels in order to achieve climate change mitigation targets. The land claim of biofuels and biomass feedstock for energy production could be potentially very large, but will depend on the level of biofuel deployed and on the type of crop, especially whether it concerns first or second generation bioenergy. There has been concerns over competition over land with current land uses (Anderson and Fergusson, 2006; Smith et al., 2010; Cai et al., 2011) and the consequences for food security (FAO, 2012). Moreover, a need for additional agricultural land for bioenergy production – at the expense of naturally vegetated land – will increase water demand and affect hydrological cycles (Berndes, 2002; Rowe et al., 2009). Similarly, climate policies aimed at reducing the use of fossil fuels provide an incentive to increase the amount of hydro, wind and solar power, which may lead to increased land use, e.g. from flooded areas behind dams. Thus, both "renewable" power and large scale bioenergy production have substantial land claims and affect both water and energy, and thus interact within the land-water-energy nexus (Ringler et al., 2013).

An important final remark on this topic is that competition for land is currently mostly a regional phenomenon. At the global level, physical scarcity of land seems less of an issue; i.e. the world is not immediately running out of land as "only" 33% of global land is used for agriculture. But agricultural commodities are heavily traded internationally, implying that a shock to the agricultural system in one region will have spill-over effects on other regions, the sign of which cannot be determined a priori. Furthermore, the lack of global scarcity may evaporate over time. Restrictions may be put on the use of land for agriculture, for instance because of biodiversity concerns. Under more stringent environmental restrictions, land competition may become increasingly important in the future. In combination with the socioeconomic developments (see the description of megatrends), this can put a significant strain on the available land resources, and may eventually lead to global scarcity, price increases and lower welfare.

1.4. Water-related bottlenecks

Many economic activities, including agriculture, require extensive water consumption, with impact on the quantity and the quality of water resources.[2] The energy industry requires water for power generation and also for fossil fuel extraction and processing, adding pressure to the resources. If trends in food consumption outpace increases in agricultural productivity, the bottlenecks and competition for access to water will increase, in particular between (irrigated) agriculture and energy. In addition, in regions with severe water stress, it may be necessary to use large amounts of energy for groundwater pumping and transporting water to consumption areas.

Agriculture is globally the most important water user; i.e. around 70% of all global water withdrawals are for irrigated agriculture, which provides 40% of the world's food supply (Figure 1.3). Irrigated areas and subsequent water withdrawals differ significantly between regions (Siebert et al., 2010). For irrigation water, some regions rely mainly on surface water withdrawals, whereas others rely more heavily on groundwater withdrawals. In some regions, concerns of groundwater overexploitation have emerged due to large groundwater withdrawals in combination with limited natural recharge (Wada et al., 2012). Projections by e.g. FAO and Wada et al. (2012) and confirmed by OECD (2012a, 2015b), indicate that irrigated agriculture and groundwater withdrawals will increase even further in coming decades, which means that irrigated agriculture will remain a great user of both surface and groundwater.

Figure 1.3. **Projected water withdrawals by sector**
(Cubic kilometres)

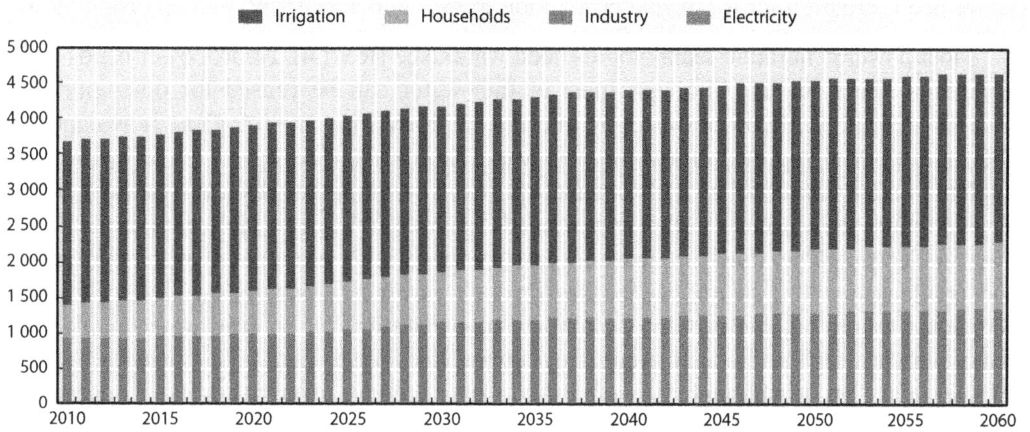

Source: IMAGE model.

While not the only sector responsible for water pollution, agriculture also has an impact on water quality through the release of excess nutrients and micro-pollutants into surface water and groundwater (OECD, 2012b). Excess nutrient availability in surface and groundwater can lead to eutrophication problems, and make water unsuitable for human uses such as drinking and bathing. Such deterioration in water quality can thus also cause a water bottleneck by constraining the amount of water that is suitable for other uses. Municipal wastewater treatment at the intake can be used to manage water quality for most end users, but this requires energy.

These combined claims on the available water have the potential to constrain the quantity and/or quality of remaining water, and such a water scarcity can seriously impact certain economic activities. There is a clear reason why water scarcity particularly affects irrigated agriculture: irrigated agriculture is the largest global water user, while non-agricultural sectors often place a higher economic value per litre water than the agricultural sector. This makes it often the residual claimant in case of water scarcity (OECD, 2015b). Water scarcity can directly impact irrigated agriculture; i.e. less available irrigation water can lead to yield reductions during droughts and thus result in regional production losses (Berndes, 2002; De Fraiture et al., 2008; Havlik et al., 2011). But water scarcity and competition can also indirectly impact irrigated agriculture by compelling it to use alternative water sources (groundwater extraction, desalinisation, etc.). Such alternative water resources necessitate a higher energy use (e.g. diesel for pumps), which ultimately translates into higher production end costs (Bazilian et al., 2011; Ringler et al., 2013). Furthermore, the investments needed for improving water quality or consumption efficiency link this to the rest of the capital market, and therefore to the entire economy.

In the context of the land-water-energy nexus, it is also important to note that lower agricultural yields due to water scarcity could induce agricultural intensification and/or expansion onto natural lands to compensate for production losses and to still meet the regional demand for agricultural products. In turn, this requires more inputs and can increase land competition (Ramankutty et al., 2002; Godfray et al., 2010; Smith et al., 2010; Lal, 2013). This is discussed in more detail in Section 1.3.

Even though the energy sector uses less water than agriculture at the global level (15% vs. 70% of withdrawal in 2010; IEA (2016), FAO (2012)), the energy sector's share in overall water use can nonetheless be significant in some countries. The share of water used for energy production is projected to increase in the next decades (IEA, 2016; King et al., 2013). Water needs are high for fossil fuel production, power generation and biofuel production.

Most power generation technologies need water (see Box 1.4). Hydropower needs water to activate the turbines. Although most of this water can be reused for other purposes such as agriculture, hydropower does interfere with existing hydrological flows and can alter hydrological regimes due to higher evaporation rates. Moreover, naïve hydropower implementation can conflict with other purposes as hydropower release schedules do not always match the timing of other water needs such as irrigation (Hellegers et al., 2008). Thermoelectric plants (nuclear, coal, oil gas fire) need large amounts of water for cooling and condensation the steam that passes through turbines. Globally, electric production depends strongly on this type of technology and therefore on cooling water availability. Water withdrawals for this technology are growing fast (Feeley et al., 2008; Roy et al., 2012; Ringler et al., 2013). Although this water use is largely non-consumptive, it can nonetheless have consequences for water quality (e.g. thermal pollution) and availability for other uses during droughts (Feeley et al., 2008; Bazilian et al., 2011; Ringler et al., 2013).

The energy sector might respond to sustained events of water scarcity and competition by switching to alternative cooling techniques for power plants such as wet-tower or dry-cooling (see Box 1.4). These cooling techniques require less water volume as input and their water withdrawal is therefore lower. A disadvantage is that their capital costs are higher, and that their water consumption is higher than regular cooling (i.e. although they withdraw less surface water, they actually evaporate a larger share of this water before returning it; IEA, 2016). Moreover, dry-cooling is less efficient and can affect power plant performance. Another response of the energy sector to sustained water scarcity could be to locate new plants along the coast so they can use sea water for cooling, although land-locked countries do not have this option.

Box 1.4. **Water use by type of power plant**

The water requirements for operating different types of power generation technologies differ markedly (Figure 1.4). Hydroelectric plants produce electricity from water that passes through turbines. The water is mostly discharged with no change of quality (the temperature is the same). But for hydropower with reservoir water storage (as opposed to run-of-the-river hydropower), water is consumed through evaporation. The consumption intensity, which depends on the weather condition and on the shape of the reservoir, can be higher than for the other power generation technologies (IEA, 2016; Mekonnen and Hoekstra, 2012). Thermoelectric power plants (i.e. plants where power is produces by steam that passes through a turbine) use large amounts of water for cooling. In these types of plants, that can be fuelled by coal, oil, gas biomass or nuclear energy, water cycles into a circuit where it is boiled to activate turbines, and then condensed. For this purpose, cooling water (mostly surface water) is passed through a steam condenser and where its temperature increases as it receives discharge of the heat of the steam. There are technologies that are much less water intensive. Open cycle power plants need less cooling, because the heat produced by the combustible is passed to the turbine directly and no steam condensation is needed. But the cost of such plants is high. Renewable technologies solar and wind consume almost no water. Concentrating solar power, where solar energy created steam to activate a turbine can be more water intensive. The more efficient the plant is, the less waste heat per unit of electricity produced has to be cooled and thus the lower the water requirement. Because they are the less efficient, coal power plants use in general more water. But water intensity also depends on the cooling techniques.

Figure 1.4. **Water use for energy technologies**

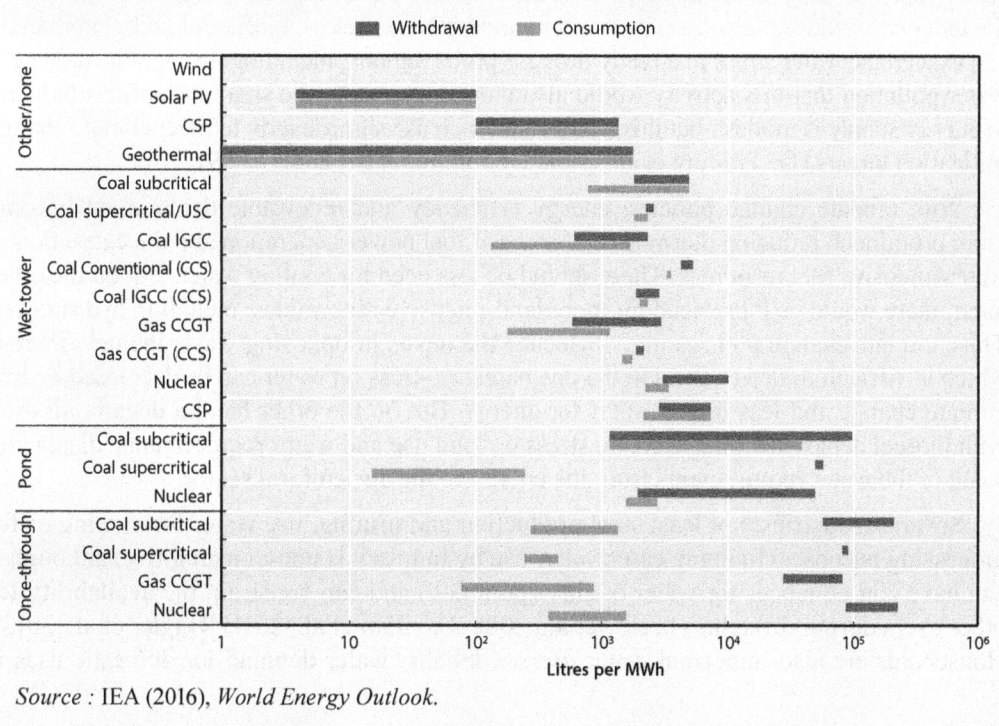

Source : IEA (2016), *World Energy Outlook.*

Box 1.4. **Water use by type of power plant** *(continued)*

Once through systems: water passes through a steam condenser. The capital costs systems are low and the water consumption (evaporation) is small. But the withdrawal is high and the discharge is at a high temperature which detrimental to aquatic life and ecosystems. This is why permitting requirements for these systems have become more stringent, for instance in the United States, and they are being gradually phased out.

Wet re-circulating systems: the water passed through the steam condenser is cooled in a wet tower or a pond. Water not consumed by evaporation is returned to the steam condenser for reuse. This reduces the water withdrawals and exposure to risks posed by constrained on water resources and environmental impacts. But compared with once-through systems water consumption is higher and installation is more costly (40% higher than for once-through systems; NETL, 2008) and requires more land.

Dry cooling systems: instead of water this system uses air flow through a cooling tower to condense steam. Water requirements are very limited. Their cost is about 3-4 times higher than for re-circulating systems and they can reduce power plant efficiency. In addition, they may not suffice during warm periods.

Fossil resource extraction, processing and transportation also require water. For instance, water is injected in oil wells for increasing the reservoirs' capacity, or used to remove dust from coal. The water intensity of fuel exploitation depends heavily on the type of resource used (IEA, 2016). The exploitation of non-conventional fuel resources which are abundant in some regions can be very water-intensive compared with "conventional" resources (this will be discussed in Section 1.5).

Biofuels and biomass also have water requirements, but their water use depends enormously on the type of bioenergy crop and whether these crops are irrigated or rainfed. In the latter case, additional water use is often modest. Nonetheless, biofuel/biomass production can exacerbate water stress in already drought-prone regions, including through the increased water pollution that this activity would also induce. Presently the share of biofuels/biomass in energy supply is modest, but this share could increase significantly to meet climate change mitigation targets (De Fraiture et al., 2008; Dominguez-Faus et al., 2009).

With climate change policies, energy efficiency and renewable deployment become more prominent, reducing thermodynamic fossil fuel power generation and the extraction of water-intensive fuel resources. There should be less need for cooling water. But on the other hand, there would be more need for more land-intensive renewables, including hydropower. Thus, climate change policies may influence the nexus in opposing ways, the net effect of which is difficult to determine. On the one hand the stress on water can be decreased by less climate change and less use of water for energy. But on the other hand a decarbonisation with biofuel deployment mays create stress on land use and water requirements, displacing some of the water requirements from the energy to the agricultural sector.

Several industries, not least steel production and mining, use water for cooling or for processing purposes. In many cases water use by industry is non-consumptive, although it can have consequences for water quality (pollution) and can constrain the availability for other users during droughts (Feeley et al., 2008; Bazilian et al., 2011; Ringler et al., 2013). Households are also important water users. Globally, water demand for domestic uses is modest, but projections indicate a substantial increase due to factors including population growth, higher sewer connectivity levels (OECD, 2012b).

Large quantities of energy are used for supplying clean water to the populations and industries. According to IEA (2016) which provides a global assessment of energy consumption from the water sector, in 2014, the water sector represented around 4% of world electricity consumption. This electricity was used mostly for extraction (40%) and then for waste water treatment and water distribution. The water sector is also a large consumer of thermal energy; for pumping in agriculture and for desalination (IEA, 2016). In the United States, energy use in the residential, commercial, industrial sectors (including agriculture but excluding power) for direct water and steam services was in 2010 approximately 6.3%[3] of the primary energy consumption (Sanders and Webber, 2012). When surface water is abundant there is limited need for pumping and thus for energy use. But energy consumption will increase when water is scarce and needs to be pumped from deeper aquifers, or transported from other locations. In extreme cases, such as in parts of the Middle East, desalination and reuse of wastewater can be used, which in general has a high energy intensity compared with "conventional water" (Ghaffour et al., 2013).

However it is very difficult to evaluate the energy consumption of water. Firstly, a large part comes from individual pumping in agriculture which is not well monitored. Secondly, the energy consumption of water supply largely depends not only on the volume of water consumption, in particular in the agricultural sector, but also on the availability of the water resources in the regions considered, and the distance from the place of consumption.

As with global land supply, water is not physically scarce at the global level. The global total quantity of freshwater is more than sufficient to meet current demand, but its uneven distribution makes water a scarce resource in some regions and watersheds. Moreover, part of the water reserves may be reserved for ecosystem functioning in order to maintain ecosystem services and biodiversity values. Under those environmental restrictions, water can already be considered a scarce resource in many regions and may become so in many more regions and watersheds as indicated by environmental outlooks (e.g. OECD, 2012a).

1.5. Energy-related bottlenecks

Energy is a key driver of economic activity. But energy resources are limited. For instance fossil fuel resources, including coal, oil and gas, decrease with extractions, and they become less and less accessible. The issue of depletion is not a matter of absolute depletion, but rather of the need to use a more diverse and more complex and thus more costly set of technologies to get them.

Over the last decade, instead of depletion there has been an increase in the use of costly technologies for exploration and productions. Most notably the booming shale oil and shale gas production has substantially increased the scope of fossil fuel resources. Shale gas and oil production require hydraulic fracturing (fracking) which consumes a lot of water and large quantities of water are needed for releasing and processing bitumen. At the global level, there is way less water used for fossil fuel extraction than for power generation (IEA, 2016), but this part of the nexus can be crucial for many reasons.

Firstly because due to resource depletion, the share of non-conventional sources in fossil fuel supply is projected to increase steeply. Therefore, the water intensity will be pushed up and in the absence of water regulation it might significantly increase water withdrawals and consumption from the fossil fuel sector, although IEA (2016) argues that water consumption may not have to increase.

Secondly, in some regions, water intensive extraction activities and potentials are located in water stressed areas. When the resource is exploited, water stress becomes very high. For instance, if water for hydraulic fracturing is 1% of US water withdrawal, it is 20-30% in some counties of Texas that are semi-arid (Reig et al., 2014). The Monterey shale play in California, which is projected to contain the biggest shale oil reserve in the United States (EIA, 2011), is located is an area where water is scarce, and therefore, if large-scale production starts, water stress will be high in these regions. In the case of China, the regions where shale resources are abundant are arid and therefore the competition for water is high according to IEA (2016).

Thirdly, there is not only an issue of water quantity but also of reduced quality (Kuyama et al., 2013; Allen et al., 2011). Even in regions where water is abundant, there can be problems because water effluents are polluted. The effluents need to be treated and stored by industrial and municipal facilities, which can have a high cost. In addition, there can be leakages and local pollution before and during clean-up. In areas where water regulation is not enforced, polluted water might be released and damage ecosystems. The water quality impacts are not well known for the moment, but can be significant.

Climate change policies may influence the energy resource bottleneck and thus the nexus. A reduction in CO_2 intensity would involve less fossil fuel consumption, and therefore less depletion and less need to develop very water intensive non-conventional resources. Therefore, one of their co-benefits would be to limit the energy and water bottlenecks. On the other hand, as outlined above, increased reliance on bioenergy may aggravate the competition for scarce land.

In the sense of the nexus, the energy resources bottlenecks are less stringent than the land and water bottlenecks, because the dependence of the services provided by energy on availability of local resources is less strong. Firstly, energy can be relatively easily transported and traded (compared with water and land). In addition, there are several options to produce energy from natural resources and various possibilities of substituting one fuel for another. Lastly, markets for energy products and services tend to be functioning better than those for land and water, thus helping to co-ordinate the supply and the demand and prioritise access for the most efficient uses. The notion of energy scarcity is therefore more one of increasing costs of supply rather than absolute scarcity, and its role in the nexus is primarily one of essential interlinkages with water and land resources.

1.6. The materials aspects of the land-water-energy nexus

An important link between the economy and the land-water-energy nexus not covered in the modelling analysis comes from the interactions with materials; together, they form the resource fundament of economic activity. For instance, agricultural yields rely on the material fertilisers nitrogen, phosphor and potassium; most energy is produced from the fossil resources coal, oil and gas. Mining, beneficiation, and processing activities make considerable claims on energy and water; future output expansion in the metal sector, most likely utilising lower grade ores, will tend to increase pressures on these resources. On the output side, the wastes generated by mineral and metal production can have negative consequences for the quality of land and water resources, and therefore for the economic productivity of sectors that utilise these as inputs. All extraction of materials requires inputs of land, water or energy, and often at least two of these.

Like the nexus resources, material resources represent the physical basis for economic growth. They are essential for the global economy and future economic and social development depends on their continued supply (Coulomb et al., 2015). Like land, water and energy, minerals are in finite supply. Their distribution within the Earth's crust is highly geographically clustered, more so than land, water and energy. This makes security of supply a potential risk – no country is completely self-reliant across the entire range of materials. For a number of mineral commodities, the depletion of higher grade ores in industrialised countries has exacerbated this issue; global supply has become more dependent on the political stability of a small number of resource rich countries. At the same time, increasing demand from emerging markets, the emergence of low-carbon technologies that require significant quantities of rare minerals, the lack of substitutes for metals with particular properties, and currently low rates of recycling have all made economies more vulnerable to potential supply bottlenecks or disruptions.

Raw materials can serve to ease, or aggravate, bottlenecks within the land-water-energy nexus. Finite carbon budgets, and the need to transition a low carbon energy system, will lead to greater claims on a number of speciality metals. In a similar way, the limited availability of new arable land will mean that increased food demand will have to mostly be met though yield improvements which, in many cases, will place additional claims on mineral fertilisers. The availability of these materials, or lack thereof, will determine to a significant extent the costs of meeting these constraints. Mineral and metal production can also influence bottlenecks in the land-water-energy nexus through their effect on resource quality. Emissions to land, water, and the atmosphere from mining and mineral processing activities are well documented and serve to lower the availability and productivity of these resources.

Increased resource efficiency and a transition towards a circular economy can reduce the threat of materials scarcity. An economic analysis of such a transition is left for future study.

1.7. The need for an integrated and dynamic analysis

The linkages in the nexus are complex. It is hard to say which link is most important or deserves most attention. Bottlenecks resulting from resource scarcity are time and place specific. The linkages with water deserve special attention. Projections show that over time limited supply and increasing demands will lead to increasing water stress. The OECD Environmental Outlook to 2050 projects that the number of people living in severe water stressed basins will threefold in the next decades to 4 billion in 2050 (OECD, 2012a). Competition for this scarce resource will increase. Depending on how scarce water is allocated among different users, lack of water may lead to lower agricultural yields, high energy costs or both. The water-agriculture link may currently be the most relevant, with a majority of global water withdrawals for agricultural use. However, the water-energy link may become more relevant in the future with rapidly increasing water withdrawal by non-agricultural users (households, industry, and electricity). Also the links between agriculture, land-use and energy may become increasingly important in the future. Biofuels only play a limited role in baseline scenarios. However, most climate mitigation pathways rely heavily on the input of biofuels. Whether biofuel production competes with food production for scarce water and land depends on the production technology, i.e. whether it is rainfed or irrigated, whether it concerns food crop land or abandoned land. Population growth, income growth and climate change, all affect the demand and supply of the nexus resources in different ways, and has the potential to shift pressures from one side of the nexus to others. This calls for a dynamic analysis that takes changing trends into account to paint a plausible picture of how the situation may look by 2060.[4]

This section showed that there are large interactions between the different resources in the land-water-energy nexus, and intricate connections to sectoral economic activity; increasingly strong links between economic sectors and between regions further spread the bottlenecks in the nexus to other parts of the global economic system. This calls for integrated analysis. An integrated systems approach is needed to shed light on how bottlenecks in the nexus affect the various aspects in the biophysical and economic systems.

In addition, physical scarcity may be less of an issue at the global level: the global economy is not running out of its most important resources any time soon. But the uneven distribution over space and time and often limited transferability make resources scarce in specific regions in specific periods. The global megatrends are also not manifesting themselves equally across the globe: population growth and income growth are projected to vary widely between OECD and non-OECD countries, climate change impacts primarily affect countries in Asia and Africa, etcetera. Therefore, tensions are more manifest on a disaggregated level. This calls for an analysis at a disaggregated level.

Notes

1.   CIRCLE stands for Costs of Inaction and Resource scarcity: Consequences for Long-term Economic growth.

2.   Water consumption is not the same as water withdrawals. For instance in cooling of power plants, a large part of the water intake is given back to the system, leading to high withdrawals but relatively small consumption. However, non-consumptive withdrawals of water may affect the quality of the water resource (such as an increase of water temperature which may be detrimental to the functioning of aquatic ecosystems) and therefore still represent a water use.

3.   And 12.6% if including power which is 49% of the withdrawal.

4.   While the modelling tools are all recursive-dynamic in nature and calculate a full path of the evolution of the biophysical and economic systems between 2010 and 2060, the transitional dynamics of the scenario shocks are somewhat less clear; therefore, the modelling results presented in this report largely focus on the situation in 2060.

References

Allen, L. et al. (2011), "Fossil Fuels and Water Quality", in The World's Water, pp. 73-96, edited by P. Gleick, Island Press/Center for Resource Economics publisher.

Anderson, G.Q.A. and M.J. Fergusson (2006), "Energy from biomass in the UK: sources, processes and biodiversity implications", *Ibis* 148, pp. 180-183.

Bartos, M. and M. Chester (2014), "The Conservation Nexus: Valuing Interdependent Water and Energy Savings in Arizona", *Environmental Science and Technology* 48(4), pp. 2139-2149.

Berrittella, M. et al. (2007), "The Economic Impact of Restricted Water Supply: A Computable General Equilibrium Analysis", *Water Research* 41(8), pp. 1799-1813.

Bazilian, M. et al. (2011), "Considering the energy, water and food nexus: Towards an integrated modelling approach", *Energy Policy* 39(12), pp. 7896-7906.

Berndes, G. (2002), "Bioenergy and water – the implications of large-scale bioenergy production for water use and supply", *Global Environmental Change* 12, pp. 253-271.

Bruinsma, J. (ed.) (2003), *World Agriculture Towards 2015/2030: An FAO Perspective*, FAO Publishing, Rome.

Cai, X. et al. (2011), "Land Availability for Biofuel Production", *Environmental Science and Technology* 45(1), pp. 334-339.

Chateau, J., R. Dellink and E. Lanzi (2014), "An Overview of the OECD ENV-Linkages Model: Version 3", *OECD Environment Working Papers*, No. 65, OECD Publishing, Paris, http://dx.doi.org/10.1787/5jz2qck2b2vd-en.

Coulomb, R. et al. (2015), "Critical Minerals Today and in 2030: An Analysis for OECD Countries", *OECD Environment Working Papers*, No. 91, OECD Publishing, Paris, http://dx.doi.org/10.1787/5jrtknwm5hr5-en.

Dale, V.H. et al. (2011), "The land use–climate change–energy nexus", *Landscape Ecology* 26(6), pp. 755-773.

De Fraiture et al. (2008), "Biofuels and implications for agricultural water use: blue impacts of green energy." *Water Policy* 10(S1), p. 67.

Dominguez-Faus, R., S.E. Powers, J.G. Burken and P.J. Alvarez (2009), "The Water Footprint of Biofuels: A Drink or Drive Issue?", *Environmental Science & Technology* 43 (9), 3005-3010.

EIA (2011), *Review of emerging resources: U.S. shale gas and shale oil plays*, US Department of Energy, Washington.

FAO (1996), *Rome Declaration on World Food Security*, FAO, Rome.

FAO (2012), "Impacts of Bioenergy, on Food Security, Guidance for Assessment and Response at National and Project Levels", *Environment and Natural Resources Working Paper* No. 52, FAO, Rome.

Feeley, T. J. et al. (2008), "Water: A critical resource in the thermoelectric power industry." *Energy* 33(1), pp. 1-11.

Ghaffour, N., T. Missimer and G. Amy (2013), "Technical review and evaluation of the economics of water desalination: Current and future challenges for better water supply sustainability", *Desalination*, No. 309, pp 197-207.

Godfray, H. C. et al. (2010), "Food security: the challenge of feeding 9 billion people", *Science* 327(5967), pp. 812-818.

Grey, D. and C.W. Sadoff (2007), "Sink or swim? Water security for growth and development", *Water Policy* 9, 545-571.

Havlík, P. et al. (2011), "Global land-use implications of first and second generation biofuel targets", *Energy Policy* 39(10), pp. 5690-5702.

Hellegers, P. et al. (2008), "Interactions between water, energy, food and environment: evolving perspectives and policy issues", *Water Policy* 10(S1), pp. 1-10.

Hoff, H. (2011), *Understanding the Nexus*. Background Paper for the Bonn 2011 Conference: The Water, Energy and Food Security Nexus. Stockholm Environment Institute, Stockholm.

Howells, M. and H. Rogner (2014), "Water-energy nexus. Assessing integrated systems", *Nature Climate Change* 4, pp. 246-247.

International Energy Agency (IEA) (2016), *World Energy Outlook 2016*, OECD publishing, Paris, http://dx.doi.org/10.1787/weo-2016-en.

International Energy Agency (IEA) (2015), *World Energy Outlook 2015*, OECD publishing, Paris, http://dx.doi.org/10.1787/weo-2015-en.

IPCC (2014a), *Climate Change 2014: Impacts, Adaptation, and Vulnerability. Part A: Global and Sectoral Aspects*, Contribution of Working Group II to the Fifth Assessment Report of the Intergovernmental Panel on Climate Change [Field, C.B., et al. (eds.)]. Cambridge University Press, Cambridge, United Kingdom and New York, NY, USA, 1132 pp.

IPCC (2014b), *Climate Change 2014: Mitigation of Climate Change*, Contribution of Working Group III to the Fifth Assessment Report of the Intergovernmental Panel on Climate Change [Edenhofer, O. et al. (eds.)]. Cambridge University Press, Cambridge, United Kingdom and New York, NY, USA.

IPCC (2013), *Climate Change 2013: The Physical Science Basis*, Contribution of Working Group I to the Fifth Assessment Report of the Intergovernmental Panel on Climate Change [Stocker, T.F et al. (eds.)]. Cambridge University Press, Cambridge, United Kingdom and New York, NY, USA, 1535 pp.

Jewell, J. (2011), "The IEA model of short-term energy security (MOSES): primary energy sources and secondary fuels", IEA Working Paper.

King, C. et al. (2013), "Coherence between Water and Energy Policies", *Natural Resources Journal* 53, pp. 117-215.

Klein Goldewijk, K. and G. van Drecht (2006), "HYDE 3: Current and Historical Population and Land Cover", in Bouwman, A.F., T. Kram and K. Klein Goldewijk (eds), Integrated Modelling of Global Environmental Change. An Overview of IMAGE 2.4. Netherlands Environmental Assessment Agency, Bilthoven.

Kuwayama, Y., S. Olmstead and A. Krupnick (2013), "Water resource and unconventional fossil fuel development", *Resource For the Future Working Paper*, RFF DP 13-34.

Lal, R. (2013), "Climate-strategic agriculture and the water-soil-waste nexus", *Journal of Plant Nutrition and Soil Science* 176(4), pp. 479-493.

Mekonnen M.M. and A.Y. Hoekstra (2012), "The blue water footprint of electricity from hydropower", *Hydrol. Earth Syst. Sci.* 16, pp. 179-187.

Monaghan, R. M. et al. (2007), "Linkages between land management activities and water quality in an intensively farmed catchment in southern New Zealand", *Agriculture, Ecosystems & Environment* 118, pp. 211-222.

National Energy Technology Laboratory (NETL) (2008), *Estimating Freshwater Needs to Meet Future Thermoelectric Generation Requirements*, NETL, Pittsburgh.

OECD (2017 forthcoming), *Water risk hotspots for agriculture*, OECD Publishing, Paris.

OECD (2015a), *The Economic Consequences of Climate Change*, OECD Publishing, Paris, http://dx.doi.org/10.1787/9789264235410-en.

OECD (2015b), *Drying Wells, Rising Stakes: Towards Sustainable Agricultural Groundwater Use*, OECD Studies on Water, OECD Publishing, Paris, http://dx.doi.org/10.1787/9789264238701-en.

OECD (2012a), *OECD Environmental Outlook to 2050: The Consequences of Inaction*, OECD Publishing, Paris, http://dx.doi.org/10.1787/9789264122246-en.

OECD (2012b), *Water Quality and Agriculture: Meeting the Policy Challenge*, OECD Studies on Water, OECD Publishing, Paris, http://dx.doi.org/10.1787/9789264168060-en.

OECD/FAO (2011), *OECD-FAO Agricultural Outlook 2011*, OECD Publishing, Paris, http://dx.doi.org/10.1787/agr_outlook-2011-en.

Ramankutty, N. et al. (2002), "The global distribution of cultivable lands: current patterns and sensitivity to possible climate change", *Global Ecology & Biogeography* 11, pp 377-392.

Reig, P., T. Luo and J. N. Proctor (2014), "Global Shale Gas Development, Water Availability and Business Risks", World Resource Institute Report.

Ringler, C. et al. (2013), "The nexus across water, energy, land and food (WELF): potential for improved resource use efficiency?" *Current Opinion in Environmental Sustainability* 5(6), pp. 617-624.

Rowe, R., N. Street and G. Taylor (2009), "Identifying potential environmental impacts of large-scale deployment of dedicated bioenergy crops in the UK", *Renewable and Sustainable Energy Reviews* 13, pp. 271-290.

Roy S.et al. (2012), "Projecting Water Withdrawal and Supply for Future Decades in the U.S. under Climate Change Scenarios", *Environmental Science & Technology* 46(5), pp 2545-2556.

Sanders, K and M. Webber (2012), "Evaluating the energy consumed for water use in the United States", *Environmental Research Letters* (7), pp. 1-11.

Siebert, S. et al. (2010), "Groundwater use for irrigation: a global inventory", *Hydrology and Earth System Sciences* 14, pp. 1863-1880.

Smith, P. et al. (2010), "Competition for land", *Philosophical Transactions of the Royal Society of London, Series B, Biological Sciences* 365(1554), pp. 2941-2957.

Stehfest, E. et al. (2014), *Integrated Assessment of Global Environmental Change with IMAGE 3.0. Model description and policy applications*, PBL Netherlands Environmental Assessment Agency, The Hague.

United Nations (2015), *Water for a sustainable world*, UN World Water Development Report.

Van Meijl, H. et al. (2006), "The impact of different policy environments on agricultural land use in Europe." *Agriculture, Ecosystems & Environment* 114(1), pp. 21-38.

Veldkamp, A, and P. H Verburg. (2004), "Modelling Land Use Change and Environmental Impact." *Journal of Environmental Management* 72(1–2), pp. 1-3.

Wada, Y. et al. (2012), "Nonsustainable groundwater sustaining irrigation: A global assessment", *Water Resources Research* 48.

Chapter 2

A framework for assessing the land-water-energy nexus

This chapter presents the methodology used in this report to calculate the biophysical and economic consequences of the nexus bottlenecks. This methodology is based on soft-linking the IMAGE model with its detailed, grid-level projections of the global biophysical system with the ENV-Linkages model, which describes the sectoral and regional economic system. The chapter describes how both models are linked. The chapter ends with a description of the scenarios used in the modelling analysis in subsequent chapters.

2.1. A multi-model framework

Quantifying the costs of inaction is achieved through linking a comprehensive model that represents the global biophysical system (IMAGE) with a comprehensive model of the economic system (ENV-Linkages), see Figure 2.1. The economic model provides baseline projections for sectoral and regional economic activity (based on exogenous projections of the socioeconomic drivers), and the biophysical model translates this into grid-cell projections for the use of land, water and energy resources.

Figure 2.1. **Modelling framework**

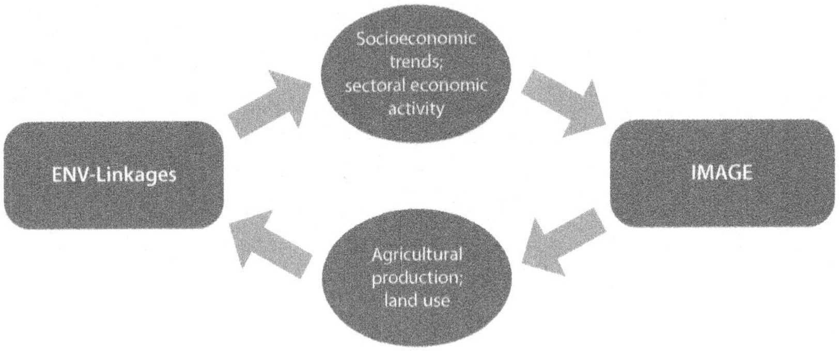

Making use of endogenously modelled processes, the biophysical model can identify how the different elements in the nexus (land, water, energy) affect each other and what impact a bottleneck for a nexus resource has on the availability and quality of the other nexus resources, and on the productivity of the land system. These changes in resource availability and land productivity (i.e. crop yields) can then be used an input for the economic model to assess the economic impacts of the LWE nexus resource bottlenecks.

More precisely, this multi-model framework is applied in two steps to provide insights into the costs of inaction. In a first step, the linked modelling framework is used to run a baseline. In a second step, counterfactual scenarios are run with the biophysical model in which a specific bottleneck (or a set of bottlenecks) is imposed or released. The IMAGE model provides detailed information on the availability of the nexus resources (e.g. water supply) and their efficiency (e.g. in sustaining crop yields) under a consistent set of assumptions on future developments. These are fed back into the ENV-Linkages model as revised assumptions on exogenous trends (e.g. land productivity by crop sector) to calculate the consequences for economic activities. Together, the baseline and counterfactual scenarios provide insights into the consequences of the nexus.[1]

The ENV-Linkages model developed by the OECD Environment Directorate is a global dynamic computable general equilibrium (CGE) model that describes how economic activities are linked to each other across sectors and regions; the model is described in more detail in Chateau et al. (2014). The model has considerable detail regarding the structure of production and the flows of factors and produced goods and services across the economy and international trade flows between economies. Sectoral production is represented through a production function, which allows for a detailed representation of environmental feedbacks on the different drivers of economic growth. Land as an input to agriculture is explicitly modelled as a primary factor for agricultural production, and, like other production factors, is in limited supply. The energy system is also represented in detail. However, the model in its current form does not explicitly capture water use; rather, it relies on implicit assumptions on future water use in agriculture through the specification of crop yields as provided by IMAGE.

IMAGE is a comprehensive integrated modelling framework of interacting human and natural systems; Stehfest et al. (2014) provides a comprehensive overview of the model. The IMAGE model is suited to large scale (global and regional) and long-term (up to the year 2100) assessments of interactions between human development and the natural environment, and integrates a range of sectors, ecosystems and indicators. IMAGE contains detailed representations of processes governing water and land use as well as a detailed description of the energy sector. It does not only model the relevant processes for each separate sector but also their interactions. IMAGE is characterised by relatively detailed biophysical processes, a wide range of environmental indicators (including water, energy and land), and spatial explicitness where many calculations are performed at the grid level. Each grid cell is characterised by its climate (e.g. temperature, precipitation), soil, topography, and land cover (natural or anthropogenic). Because of this spatial explicitness, IMAGE can account for variability within and between regions and provide regional inputs for the economic analysis with ENV-Linkages (i.e. region-specific estimates of land supply and yields).

The regional aggregation of both models have been harmonised to 23 regions encompassing the world. For presentational purposes, these 23 regions are sometimes further aggregated into eight macro regions, as shown in Table 2.1.

Table 2.1. **Overview of the regional aggregation of the modelling analysis**

Macro region	Model countries and regions	Most important comprising countries and territories
OECD America	Canada	Canada
	Mexico	Mexico
	United States	United States
OECD Europe	OECD EU	France, Germany, United Kingdom, Austria, Belgium, Czech Republic, Denmark, Estonia, Finland, Greece, Hungary, Ireland, Luxembourg, Netherlands, Poland, Portugal, Slovak Republic, Slovenia, Spain, Sweden
	Other OECD	Israel,[1] Switzerland, Norway, Turkey, Iceland, Liechtenstein
OECD Pacific	Australia & New Zealand	Australia, New Zealand
	Japan	Japan
	Korea	Korea
Rest of Europe & Asia	China (People's Republic of)	China (People's Republic of) and Hong Kong (China)
	Non-OECD EU	Cyprus,[2] Latvia, Lithuania, Malta, Bulgaria, Croatia, Romania
	Russian Federation (hereafter "Russia")	Russia
	Caspian region	Kazakhstan, Kyrgyzstan, Armenia, Azerbaijan, Georgia, Tajikistan, Turkmenistan, Uzbekistan
	Other Europe	Albania, Belarus, Ukraine, Republic of Moldova, Andorra, Bosnia and Herzegovina, Gibraltar, Former Yugoslav Republic of Macedonia, Montenegro, San Marino, Serbia

Table 2.1. **Overview of the regional aggregation of the modelling analysis** *(continued)*

Macro region	Model countries and regions	Most important comprising countries and territories
Latin America	Brazil	Brazil
	Other Latin America	Argentina, Bolivia, Chile, Colombia, Ecuador, Paraguay, Peru, Uruguay, Venezuela, Guyana, Suriname, Costa Rica, Guatemala, Honduras, Nicaragua, Panama, El Salvador, Belize, Antigua and Barbuda, Bahamas, Barbados, Cayman Islands, Cuba, Dominica, Grenada, Haiti, Montserrat, Saint Kitts and Nevis, Saint Lucia, Saint Vincent and the Grenadines, Turks and Caicos Islands
Middle East & North Africa	Middle East	Oman, Bahrain, Islamic Republic of Iran, Kuwait, Qatar, Saudi Arabia, United Arab Emirates, Iraq, Lebanon, Syrian Arab Republic, Yemen
	North Africa	Egypt, Morocco, Tunisia, Algeria, Libya, Western Sahara
South & South-East Asia	ASEAN 9 (excl. Indonesia)	Cambodia, Lao People's Democratic Republic, Malaysia, Philippines, Singapore, Thailand, Viet Nam, Brunei Darussalam, Myanmar, Timor-Leste
	Indonesia	Indonesia
	India	India
	Other Asia	American Samoa, Cook Islands, Fiji, Guam, Kiribati, Marshall Islands, Federated States of Micronesia, Nauru, New Caledonia, Niue, Northern Mariana Islands, Palau, Papua New Guinea, Pitcairn, Samoa, Solomon Islands, Tokelau, Tonga, Tuvalu, Vanuatu, Wallis and Futuna Islands, Mongolia, Democratic People's Republic of Korea, Bangladesh, Nepal, Pakistan, Sri Lanka, Afghanistan, Bhutan, Maldives
Sub-Saharan Africa	South Africa	South Africa
	Other Africa	Cameroon, Côte d'Ivoire, Ghana, Nigeria, Senegal, Benin, Burkina Faso, Guinea, Togo, Cabo Verde, Gambia, Guinea-Bissau, Liberia, Mali, Mauritania, Niger, Saint Helena, Ascension, and Tristan da Cunha, Sierra Leone, Central African Republic, Chad, Republic of the Congo, Equatorial Guinea, Gabon, Sao Tome and Principe, Angola, Democratic Republic of the Congo, Ethiopia, Kenya, Madagascar, Malawi, Mauritius, Mozambique, United Republic of Tanzania, Uganda, Zambia, Zimbabwe, Rwanda, Burundi, Comoros, Djibouti, Eritrea, Mayotte, Seychelles, Somalia, Sudan, Botswana, Namibia, Lesotho, Swaziland

Notes: 1. The statistical data for Israel are supplied by and under the responsibility of the relevant Israeli authorities. The use of such data by the OECD is without prejudice to the status of the Golan Heights, East Jerusalem and Israeli settlements in the West Bank under the terms of international law.

2. Note by Turkey: The information in this document with reference to "Cyprus" relates to the southern part of the Island. There is no single authority representing both Turkish and Greek Cypriot people on the Island. Turkey recognises the Turkish Republic of Northern Cyprus (TRNC). Until a lasting and equitable solution is found within the context of the United Nations, Turkey shall preserve its position concerning the "Cyprus issue".

Note by all the European Union Member States of the OECD and the European Union: The Republic of Cyprus is recognised by all members of the United Nations with the exception of Turkey. The information in this document relates to the area under the effective control of the Government of the Republic of Cyprus.

The complementarity between ENV-Linkages (with its detailed production structure for economic activities) and IMAGE (with its detailed biophysical modelling framework) makes these combined models an appropriate toolkit for studying the land-water-energy nexus. Nonetheless, not all of the linkages relevant for the nexus analysis can be captured in IMAGE or ENV-linkages. In soft-linking IMAGE and ENV-Linkages, there is no perfect match. The level of sophistication with which nexus issues can be included depends on model features and data availability. Table 2.2 gives an overview, and highlights which elements are captured in the models, which can only be assessed outside the modelling frameworks through anecdotal evidence, and which are entirely absent from the analysis in this report.

Table 2.2. **Overview of the nexus linkages and how they are captured in the analysis**

Nexus linkages	Type of impact	Treatment in this report
Land bottlenecks	Impact on water resource	Modelled in IMAGE through effect of agriculture on water quantity and quality
	Direct impact on agricultural and forestry sectors	Modelled in IMAGE and ENV-Linkages
	Impact on energy resource	Modelled in IMAGE and ENV-Linkages through endogenous bio-energy production
	Indirect impact on rest of the economy	Modelled in ENV-Linkages
Water bottlenecks	Direct impact on water sector	Not modelled
	Impact on land resource	Modelled in IMAGE through effect on agricultural yields
	Impact on energy resource	Anecdotal evidence on water for electricity
	Indirect impact on rest of the economy	Only indirect consequences of changes in crop yields
Energy bottlenecks	Impact on water resource	Anecdotal evidence on desalination
	Impact on land resource	Indirectly modelled in ENV-Linkages through agricultural energy use
	Direct impact on energy sectors	Modelled in ENV-Linkages
	Indirect impact on rest of the economy	Modelled in ENV-Linkages
Cross-cutting trends	Climate change	Modelled in IMAGE (water availability and use; yields) and in ENV-Linkages (effects through land availability and energy demand)

2.2. Assessing the biophysical impacts with IMAGE

Modelling water resources

The water bottleneck has been incorporated by looking at regional water scarcity. To assess this, IMAGE includes the hydrology model LPJml that calculates water demand and water availability at high spatial and temporal resolutions. Water quality as a bottleneck is yet not modelled in IMAGE.

Total water demand is the sum of the demand for agriculture/irrigation, livestock, electricity production, manufacturing and domestic demand. The demand in each grid cell is calculated as the product of crop irrigation demand and a country-specific irrigation efficiency factor that reflects the type and efficiency of prevailing irrigation systems

(Rost et al., 2008). Irrigation water is extracted from rivers and lakes in the grid cell or a neighbouring grid cell. If these local surface water sources cannot meet total demand, water is extracted from nearby (large) reservoirs – if available – or from groundwater reservoirs. The latter can be a limited or an unlimited source of water, which can be interpreted as non-sustainable groundwater.

The water demand for other sectors is calculated separately from LPJml:

- For the electricity sector, the type of power plant (e.g. standard steam cycle, combined steam cycle) determines the demand for cooling capacity (Davies et al., 2013; Bijl et al., 2016). In addition, the type of cooling facility determines the quantity of water required. Once through cooling systems use large volumes of surface water that are returned almost entirely to the water body from which they were extracted, albeit at an elevated temperature. Wet cooling towers exploit the evaporation heat capacity of water and thus require lower water volumes. However, a significant part of the cooling water evaporates during the process and does not return to the original water body. Estimates are based on Bijl et al. (2016).

- Livestock water demand is not included in the CIRCLE scenario projections.

- For household and manufacturing sectors, data and algorithms are derived through the methodology of Bijl et al. (2016). Both household and manufacturing water demand is a function of population size, corrected for structural and efficiency changes that relate to increases in regional income (GDP).

- The current version of IMAGE does not take into account the water needs of natural ecosystems, or of other uses such as shipping and recreation.

Largely reflecting existing water allocation rules (OECD, 2015b) and given the often observed difference in bargaining power and the economic losses incurred from interrupted water supply, meeting the demand from the electricity, household and manufacturing sectors receives priority in IMAGE over water withdrawal for irrigation.

Water stress has different impacts on the different sectors in IMAGE. For agriculture, the IMAGE model simulates lower production levels – especially in irrigated areas – due to limited water availability (Biemans, 2012). Under such conditions, the distribution of crops over the available land may change, new areas could come into production to meet regional crop demand (expansion) and management practices might need to intensify (intensification).

Water availability results in IMAGE from changes in various endogenous water flows. Firstly, there is surface water. This is in each grid cell the result of the net precipitation in a grid cell (i.e. gross precipitation minus interception of the land cover and evapotranspiration from soil and land cover), the net change in water storage in a grid cell (e.g. through snow melt), the inflow from surrounding grid cells using a routing algorithm (Rost et al., 2008), and a runoff into surface water storage in the cell, and subsequently flows downstream. Secondly, the IMAGE model includes three types of large reservoirs that could supply water in case local surface water sources are insufficient to cover the demand in a grid cell. The three types differ in the level that the water is used for irrigation or for other purposes, varying from primarily use for irrigation to not used for irrigation at all (Biemans et al., 2011). These reservoirs are included because about 50% of the river systems are regulated (Nilsson et al., 2005). Finally, groundwater formations can supply water to cover the demand (e.g. three out of the five water basins on the Indian subcontinent strongly rely on groundwater resources to meet irrigation water demand). Some of these formations are very large and use can be seen as sustainable, for others this is not the case.

Thus, IMAGE assumes groundwater withdrawals to be sustainable as long as they do not exceed the annual groundwater recharge. If the withdrawal demands exceed the annual groundwater recharge, it assumes that water is not available and demand is not met, unless the demand is at a location where there is an aquifer according to the WHYMAP dataset (BGR/ UNESCO, 2015). At those locations the remaining demand is fulfilled from that aquifer. Groundwater recharge is contributing to river baseflow. The relation between groundwater recharge and river baseflow is implemented as a linear reservoir with a uniform release coefficient of 1/100, meaning that the average residence time of groundwater is around 100 days. Therefore there is a direct link between groundwater and surface water, and a direct link between upstream water use and downstream availability. If water is withdrawn from groundwater, it decreases the downstream baseflow and therefore surface water availability.

Modelling land resources

One of the important features of the IMAGE model is the explicit consideration of different types of land use and cover. The land-use categories are:

- Agricultural (irrigated and non-irrigation) and grassland areas to meet the demand for food and fodder.

- Other crop area to cover the demand for cash crops, such as fruits and fibres.

- Bioenergy area to meet the demand for biofuels.

- Built-up areas, which are assumed to be excluded from other biophysical applications in IMAGE

- Forest areas – including plantations established by humans – to cover the demand for timber (i.e. paper/pulp, sawlogs and traditional biomass for energy); and newly established forests for carbon storage (afforestation/reforestation under the climate convention).

- Other areas covered by natural vegetation to include areas that are not (strongly) affected by humans. These areas could be taken into human production in future, with the exception of protected areas and unsuitable areas such as deserts and ice.

Human activities affect many of these land-use categories, transforming natural areas to human dominated landscapes, changing ecosystem structure and species distribution, and water, nutrient and carbon cycles. Natural landscape characteristics and land cover also affect humans, determining suitable areas for settlement and agriculture, and delivering a wide range of ecosystem services. As such, land cover and land use in IMAGE results also from the interplay of natural and human processes, such as crop cultivation, fertiliser input, livestock density, type of natural vegetation, forest management history, and built-up areas.

Changes in different land-use purposes drive, among others, the land demand and supply in IMAGE for food, fodder, grassland, biofuels and timber. The demand is derived from economic activities and demographic information, like changes in income, income elasticities, commodity prices, etc.as provided by the ENV-Linkages baseline projection.

Land cover and land use are also the basis for the land availability assessment in IMAGE. In principle, the different land-use categories are allocated to grid cells in an iterative process until the regional demand is met. First, it is determined whether the supply from land-cover and land-use maps of the previous time step can meet the different demands. Yield changes over time are possible due to climatic and technological changes. If the production is lower than the demand, the area for the particular land-use form needs to become expanded, most often at the cost of natural vegetation. In contrary, when production exceeds the demand, land can become abandoned.

In determining the location of land expansion in a region, all grid cells are assessed and ranked by suitability, based on an empirical regression analysis. Suitability, in turn is determined by climate, atmospheric conditions like ozone, terrain characteristics (soil, slope) and two socio-economic variables (i.e. population density and accessibility). Additionally, a few other rules are applied in determining the suitability of a grid cell. For instance, agricultural expansion is not permitted in protected areas, and in areas otherwise protected, such as in assumed REDD (reducing emissions from deforestation and degradation) schemes. Finally, optionally a small random factor can be included to account for inherent uncertainty and non-deterministic behaviour of land-use change processes, allowing the emergence of new patches.

In IMAGE the specification of land competition, i.e. the allocation of the different land-use forms in the regions is done through a hierarchical land allocation mechanism. First, urban built-up areas and infrastructure is allocated. Second, the area for food/fodder (including other crops) is allocated, followed by the area for biofuels. Fourth, forests become productive and/or forest plantations are established to meet the regional demand for timber, and fuelwood, using different forest management systems. Finally, when a grid cell is not used to meet one of the demands, it is assumed to be covered by natural vegetation. These areas are very relevant as they play an important role in the global carbon cycle and as such in future climate change. Such a hierarchy can lead to simulations where, for example, built-up areas expand into very productive agricultural areas, resulting in additional demand for agricultural land elsewhere. Note that this effect is small compared to other drivers of agricultural land-use change.

In IMAGE, land use and land competition directly affect the other nexus resources:

- Different land uses have different water demands and thereby affect hydrology.

- Land suitability, degradation and competition affects the potential for biofuel production in a region and as such the energy supply.

- Climate change and atmospheric conditions (including ozone concentrations) affect land uses differently, and as such the land competition.

Modelling energy resources

Energy (demand and supply) is a central component of the IMAGE model and covers all major relevant aspects of the energy system; the focus in this section is on parts that are relevant for the land, water and energy nexus.

Energy interacts in multiple ways with water and land in IMAGE:

- Energy production is an important source of greenhouse and other gasses. Resulting changes in climate and atmospheric composition affects productivity of the different land-use types and as such in land demand.

- Different ways to produce energy have different demand for water. This can be cooling water in thermal power plants, or the water availability for hydro power and biofuels.

- Biofuels also compete with other demand for land, an interaction where water availability is included.

The IMAGE specification of the energy system is not used for the analysis, as this sector is sufficiently covered in the ENV-Linkages model.

Modelling feedbacks in IMAGE

These biophysical relationships in IMAGE have multiple dimensions that have an effect on the socio-economic dimensions as used in ENV-Linkages. Land productivity, for example, can change over time (e.g. due to climate and atmospheric changes, land degradation/overexploitation, agricultural intensification), affecting the land demand in a region. Likewise, land competition can result in changes in land demands (e.g. the expansion of built-up areas at the cost of high productive agricultural land). These feedbacks are relevant because of the assumption in IMAGE that most productive areas are used first, implying that expansion and relocation lead to the use of less productive regions with increasing operational costs. At the same time, information from ENV-Linkages (e.g. on agricultural management) is relevant for determining land production and land competition.

IMAGE represents a unified biophysical representation of linked land/water/atmosphere processes, including feedback such as changes in agricultural productivity due to climate change, or impacts of land-use change on the hydrological cycle, subject to human activities. Also interactions between the energy sector and land-use are accounted for, e.g. in the case of bio-energy production and use. Some feedbacks are not included in the current IMAGE model, such as additional energy use to sustain agricultural intensification (e.g. for fertiliser production and mechanisation).

2.3. Linking biophysical impacts to economic damages with ENV-Linkages

Modelling economic activity in ENV-Linkages

The detailed representation of economic activity in ENV-Linkages makes it especially suited for studying how environmental feedbacks affect the economy (as OECD, 2015a, shows for the feedbacks from climate change).

ENV-Linkages is a global dynamic computable general equilibrium (CGE) model that describes how economic activities are linked to each other between sectors and across regions. The version used for the current analysis contains 35 economic sectors and 25 regions, bilateral trade flows and has a sophisticated description of capital accumulation using capital vintages, in which technological advances only trickle down slowly over time to affect existing capital stocks.[2] It also links economic activity to the use of natural resources and to environmental pressure, specifically to GHG emissions, and contains feedbacks from climate change impacts on the economy.

Production in ENV-Linkages is assumed to operate under cost minimisation with perfect markets and constant return to scale technology. The production technology is specified as nested Constant Elasticity of Substitution (CES) production functions in a branching hierarchy. This structure is replicated for each output, while the parameterisation of the CES functions may differ across sectors. The nesting of the production function for the agricultural sectors is further re-arranged to reflect substitution between intensification (e.g. more fertiliser use) and extensification (more land use) of activities; or between intensive and extensive livestock production. The structure of electricity production assumes that a representative electricity producer maximises its profit by using the different available technologies to generate electricity using a CES specification with a large degree of substitution. Non-fossil electricity technologies have a structure similar to the other sectors, except for a top nesting combining a sector-specific natural resource with all other inputs. This specification acts as a capacity constraint on the supply of these electricity technologies. The model adopts a putty/semi-putty technology specification, where substitution possibilities among factors are assumed to be higher with new vintage capital than with old vintage capital. This implies relatively smooth adjustment of quantities to price changes. Capital accumulation is modelled as in the traditional Solow/ Swan neo-classical growth model.

The energy bundle is of particular interest for analysis of nexus issues. Energy is a composite of fossil fuels and electricity. In turn, fossil fuel is a composite of coal and a bundle of "other fossil fuels". At the lowest nest, the composite "other fossil fuels" commodity consists of crude oil, refined oil products and natural gas. The value of the substitution elasticities are chosen as to imply a higher degree of substitution among the other fuels than with electricity and coal.

Household consumption demand is the result of static maximisation behaviour which is formally implemented as an "Extended Linear Expenditure System". A representative consumer in each region – who takes prices as given – optimally allocates disposal income among the full set of consumption commodities and savings. Saving is considered as a standard good in the utility function and does not rely on forward-looking behaviour by the consumer. The government in each region collects various kinds of taxes in order to finance government expenditures. Assuming fixed public savings (or deficits), the government budget is balanced through the adjustment of the income tax on consumer income. In each period, investment net-of-economic depreciation is equal to the sum of government savings, consumer savings and net capital flows from abroad.

International trade is based on a set of regional bilateral flows. The model adopts the Armington specification, assuming that domestic and imported products are not perfectly substitutable. Moreover, total imports are also imperfectly substitutable between regions of origin. Allocation of trade between partners then responds to relative prices at the equilibrium. Market goods equilibria imply that, on the one side, the total production of any good or service is equal to the demand addressed to domestic producers plus exports; and, on the other side, the total demand is allocated between the demands (both final and intermediary) addressed to domestic producers and the import demand.

Modelling environmental feedbacks in ENV-Linkages

The sectoral and international trade representation in computable general equilibrium (CGE) models is particularly suited to modelling the economic consequences of the modelled biophysical shocks. The biophysical shocks lead to changes in the equilibrium prices and supply of primary factors, which are unevenly spread across sectors and regions. The specification of international commodity markets in the CGE model allows projection of how demand, supply and trade patterns in all sectors and all regions adjust to minimise economic damages and maximise opportunities. These adjustments that take place in the model can be considered as market-driven adaptation, which already diminishes the level of damages imposed. For instance, a change in land productivity in a region will trigger substitution responses by agricultural producers that alter not only their use of land but also uses of other inputs, and substitution responses by consumers that may shift away to foreign producers of the commodity and to other commodities.

The production function approach that was used for studying the costs of inaction on climate change (OECD, 2015a) is also adopted to investigate the economic consequences of the nexus bottlenecks. In general terms, the production function approach specifies how nexus bottlenecks affect key elements in the sectoral production functions. Parameters capturing the level of productivity, biased technical change and changes in use of primary factors can be modified to reflect these bottlenecks. Similarly, changes in the households' demand system can be used to reflect consumption-related impacts. Finally, impacts on the supply of primary factors are important because they affect producers' input demands and output supplies as well as consumers' income and expenditures, which in turn lead to shifts in the equilibria in markets for factors and commodities.

In the illustrative set of scenarios analysed for this report, the impacts of the bottlenecks on the agricultural and land systems are passed from IMAGE to ENV-Linkages.[3] Specifically, IMAGE outputs for changes in crop yields and agricultural land use are used as input shocks in ENV-Linkages. Thus, the parameters that are affected in ENV-Linkages are agricultural productivity and land supply. Furthermore, the impacts of the energy bottleneck on the energy system are reproduced in ENV-Linkages through increased biofuel supply.

While other links between the environmental and economic systems can easily be imagined and quantitatively described, no other shocks are implemented in the scenarios in this report. The main reason for this is that insufficient data is available to provide robust quantitative assessments of these additional shocks, and the difficulty in teasing out such additional impacts from the ones that are quantified via the link with IMAGE.

2.4. Overview of the modelling scenarios

The combination of the IMAGE and ENV-Linkages modelling tools can illustrate the systemic effects of bottlenecks in the nexus: they provide a wide representation of global economic activity and their links to the biophysical system. However, there are significant data gaps that prevent a full inclusion of existing and potential nexus bottlenecks in the baseline projection provided by the models. More fundamentally, many of the consequences of the bottlenecks in the nexus operate on very specific local scales, both in terms of time and space. For instance, a drought will have serious short-term consequences within that particular area, but if the disruption is limited in time and geographical scale, it may not affect annual GDP much. But for wider scale bottlenecks, there are systemic effects that transcend the local community. The purpose of the modelling analysis is to shed light on these systemic effects, and illuminate the key mechanisms at play that are fundamental to the nexus. In order to do so, the modelling scenarios are constructed in a consistent, but stylised manner. Regarding the timing of the different bottlenecks, much is uncertain. Therefore, this report focuses on results by 2060, assuming the bottlenecks will have reached their full impact before then. This long-term horizon helps to shed light on the major permanent consequences of the nexus, but the analysis inherently remains more limited in describing the adjustment process.

A dynamic, disaggregated, integrated systems analysis of the combined costs of all the bottlenecks outlined in Chapter 1 can be considered to reveal the costs of inaction on the nexus. This refers to a scenario of inaction, in which policies remain absent for reconciling economic growth with resource preservation. A complexity in quantifying the consequences of the nexus lies in the interdependencies between land, water and energy resources. These resources are intricately linked, and many economic activities can substitute one of these resources with the others. A bottleneck in the availability of one resource can hence result in a higher demand for the other resources. Identifying how the different elements in the nexus (land, water, energy) affect each other and what impact the demand for one nexus resource has on the availability and quality of the other nexus resources is therefore important when quantifying the biophysical and economic consequences. The general concept behind CIRCLE's analysis is therefore to compare the system-wide performance of scenarios with selected nexus bottlenecks to a baseline projection without bottlenecks. A systems approach also allows illuminating how the consequences of combined bottlenecks are determined by specific interactions, and to what extent the various bottlenecks amplify or dampen each other.

A major complexity is that the costs of the various bottlenecks cannot be simply added up to determine an overall nexus-wide impact, given the strong internal linkages in the nexus. Therefore, the consequences of the nexus are first assessed for each individual counterfactual ("bottleneck") scenario. An illustrative scenario is designed for each of the three domains, based on an assessment of their significance and suitability for combination. A second step then consists of investigating an integrated scenario where multiple bottlenecks are addressed simultaneously, to provide deeper insights into the interaction effects between the different bottlenecks. A final third step is then to overlay this integrated scenario with changes in the climate system, to illustrate the role of the underlying megatrends that affect baseline projections between now and 2060.

Baseline projection: No bottlenecks

The baseline projection reflects the "business as usual" developments that are projected by the modelling tools in the absence of feedbacks from the nexus bottlenecks. The modelled baseline reflects a continuation of current socio-economic developments, including demographic trends, urbanisation and globalisation trends. The baseline reflects a continuation of current policies; it excludes new policies and feedbacks from air pollution and climate change impacts on the economy. This corresponds to the "no-damage baseline projection" in the CIRCLE analysis of the consequences of climate change (OECD, 2015a) and "no-feedback baseline projection" in the analysis of the consequences of outdoor air pollution.

Thus, the baseline projection resembles a hypothetical projection that ignores feedbacks from land, water and energy scarcity on the biophysical and economic system. The logic of this approach is not to deny that the nexus is already affecting these systems, but rather to be able to measure the consequences of the bottlenecks. The baseline projection describes the pressures that economic activity puts on the environment, by linking economic activity to the biophysical system. The bottleneck scenarios take this baseline projection to calculate the biophysical impacts of the bottleneck, describe how these feed back to the economy and project the resulting changes in economic activity, and calculate a range of specific indicators. The difference in indicators between the two projections reflects the consequences of the bottleneck.

Water bottleneck scenario: Limiting groundwater extraction

This scenario explores the effect of reductions in the availability of groundwater for agricultural production, used in many world regions to supplement inadequate supplies of surface water to sustain crop growth (see Box 2.1). In several cases, however, the continued supply of sufficient groundwater is not guaranteed. In the baseline, by assumption any differences between water demand for irrigation and surface water supply is always met by extraction of groundwater, i.e. ENV-Linkages and IMAGE assume no limits on the continued supply of groundwater available for irrigated land, ignoring potential groundwater scarcity issues in their calculations. The counterfactual analysis in this scenario explores what the impact would be of an emerging depletion of groundwater in specific reserves. In some regions, groundwater reserves and recharge rates are quite large and their depletion is by no means imminent, but groundwater extractions in other regions exceed recharge rates and depletion of these groundwater resources is a real possibility. Note that only withdrawal demands exceeding the annual groundwater recharge is restricted in the counterfactual scenario (see Box 2.1).

Box 2.1. **Sources of agricultural water supply**

Water use in agriculture draws from both surface water and groundwater. The modelling framework models the annual hydrological cycle including groundwater recharge; i.e. annual groundwater recharge flows are explicitly modelled and groundwater withdrawals reduce these recharge flows, which in turn reduces base flow downstream. These groundwater recharge flows are referred to as "renewable" groundwater in this report.

Some aquifers have lower recharge rates and are more vulnerable for unsustainable groundwater use, with groundwater withdrawals becoming higher than recharge rates (Figure 2.2). Such unsustainable groundwater use is captured in the modelling framework through a different "non-renewable" groundwater fraction. The modelling framework can restrict the use of this additional "non-renewable" groundwater fraction when an aquifer is "depleted" in the groundwater limitation scenario.

Although the labelling of renewable and non-renewable groundwater is technically not entirely correct, this terminology is shorthand for the more complex representation of water flows in the modelling framework.

Figure 2.2. **Overview of affected aquifers**

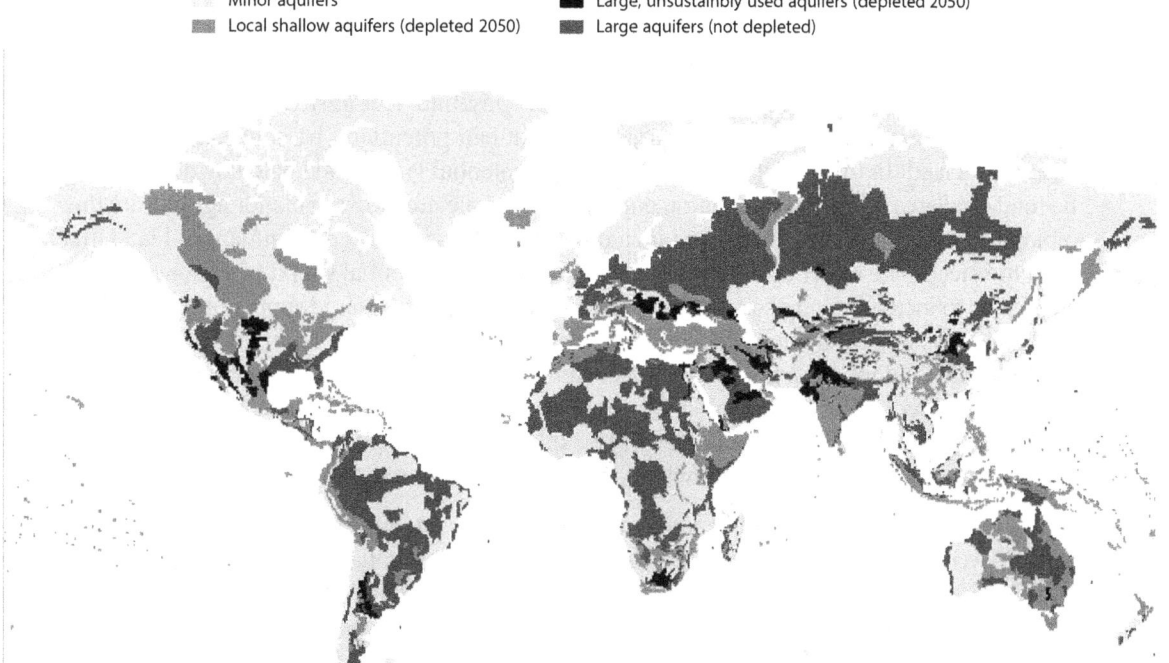

Source: IMAGE model based on WHYMAP (BGR/UNESCO, 2015) and Gleeson et al. (2012).

The specification of the depletion rates of aquifers in the model suite is based on the approach in a global analysis by Gleeson et al. (2012) to identify which groundwater aquifers are possibly used unsustainably. In the analysis, unsustainable use is associated with the groundwater "footprint", i.e. the area required to receive sufficient precipitation, given the local intensity, to sustain groundwater use and groundwater-associated ecosystem services. The larger the ratio between the water-collecting surface area and the area covered by the aquifer, the bigger the risk that extraction will exceed influx and thereby gradually exhaust the reservoir.

Unfortunately, insufficient and incomplete information exists to date that would make it possible to realistically assign depletion risks to all aquifers (although a number of ongoing research projects use Grace satellite data to improve on this). Therefore, the ad-hoc assumption is made that aquifers for which the water-collecting surface area exceeds five times their geographic area are depleted by 2055 and will become unavailable for irrigated agriculture from that year onwards. Hence, no attempt is made to model a smooth adjustment of groundwater extraction over time to minimise the impacts, but one source of water for irrigation is discontinued. Obviously, groundwater from aquifers that are not considered at risk of depletion remains available for irrigation. Additionally, groundwater from local aquifers is also assumed to become depleted by 2055. This does not mean that the entire aquifer is depleted, but that withdrawals from the non-renewable part are no longer available. In conformity with Wada et al. (2012), groundwater irrigation is assumed to be absent in all locations with very limited groundwater resources – both in the baseline and in the counterfactual scenario. The consequences of this bottleneck on water availability for water use by region is shown in Section 4.1, but Figure 2.2 shows the substantial regional differences in how aquifers around the world are affected.

Land bottleneck scenario: Urban sprawl and protection of natural areas

This scenario explores the effect of increased land competition and reduced potential agricultural land supply. Agricultural land supply (covering food and fodder crops, intensive and extensive grazing) can in most regions be further expanded beyond current levels, and in many cases also beyond the projection made in the baseline. But agricultural land supply is limited by the amount of currently unused land that can potentially be converted for use as agricultural land. In the modelling framework, this potential land is calculated by determining the total land area of each world region and subtracting the area unsuitable for agriculture due to biophysical or other restrictions and includes e.g. managed forests and unmanaged land that is not too steep. The closer agricultural land use gets to this potential supply, the more difficult it becomes to increase land use.[4] The rationale behind this is that a large supply of suitable land results in low land rental rates and a high price elasticity, and vice versa. In the baseline, best-guess default assumptions are used to project land that is unsuitable for agricultural production and thereby directly limit regional land supply. In this counterfactual scenario, the effects of the agricultural land supply bottleneck will be explored, by adding two further land conversion restrictions: *(i)* increased urban sprawl, and *(ii)* increased nature conservation.

Urban sprawl, i.e. the rapid expansion of low-density and non-contiguous development, or in IMAGE modelling terms the increase in urban land area, has been a significant cause of reduction of highly productive agricultural land in the past (OECD, 2017). Although the relationship between urban areas and agriculture is complex and extends both ways, urban sprawl generally reduces the availability of fertile land and thus reduces agricultural productivity.[5] Cities are historically mostly built on very fertile land and thus urbanisation takes away highly productive agricultural land; furthermore, cities compete with surrounding agriculture for water and other resources, which further limits agricultural production near urban areas.[6] In many regions, urbanisation is projected to continue in the coming decades (Jiang and O'Neill, 2017). The baseline projection uses the database of Klein-Goldewijk and Van Drecht (2006) to project urban land (see also Section 3.3). However, it is not straightforward to accurately measure which partially built-up land is still available for agriculture and which should be accounted for as urban land. Therefore, the influence of urban land expansion on the amount of land available for agriculture is unclear and alternative projections of urban land as discussed in Potere and Schneider (2007) suggest much larger areas than assumed in the baseline.

In the bottleneck scenario, the assumption is made that urban sprawl leads to a significant increase in urban land compared to the baseline. Due to regional differences in driving forces as well as in model parameters, the increase in urban area by region ranges from 2.6 to 6.7 times the baseline. For the world as a whole, the built-up area is relatively small in the baseline: 0.6% of the terrestrial surface, but for regions the percentage varies widely between 0.1% for vast sparsely populated countries (Canada and Russia), and around 4% for densely populated countries. With the land constraint in place, the percentage built-up area is around 3.7 times bigger, ending up at 2.3% for the world with a range of 0.3% to 15% between the regions.

The urban sprawl assumption is complemented with a projected increase in nature conservation. Based on the Aichi biodiversity targets as laid out in the Convention on Biological Diversity (UNCBD, 2012), specifically target #11, the assumption is made that 17% of all major natural ecosystems or biomes are protected from 2020 onwards, and are deemed unavailable for conversion to agricultural land from that year The additional protected areas are made geographically explicit, similar to existing nature reserves (percentages) of grid cells are excluded from conversion to agricultural land.

Together, these two assumptions constrain the possibilities for land use change in agriculture, with consequences for productivity and agricultural land expansion compared to the baseline.

Energy bottleneck scenario: Ambitious global biofuel targets

In the energy bottleneck scenario, the policy ambition to increase energy security and reduce reliance on fossil fuels is being pursued by an ambitious increase in biofuel production around the world.[7] This will relieve the pressure on fossil energy resource scarcity, but may have significant consequences for the other nexus resources land and water. Thus, there can be important trade-offs between policy objectives in this scenario. Increasing bioenergy supply is one of the very few options available in the short run to substitute away from fossil fuels, without requiring massive changes in the fuel delivery infrastructure, such as engine design. Especially in transport there are relatively few alternatives.

The scenario implementation assumes that global production of (second generation) biofuels, measured as input for conversion, will gradually increase to 220 EJ (5250 Mtoe) per year by 2060. This reflects an ambitious but technically feasible target (EMF, 2017). Production is spread across countries and regions based on the availability of land. To reduce conflicts between biofuels, nature conservation and agricultural production, regional production volumes are projected by looking at how much non-forest and non-agricultural land is available. However, there is no hard constraint on land allocation, and the increased land prices from the additional activity may endogenously lead to some competition with nature conservation and food production. Together, these assumptions reflect an ambitious policy that is not completely ignorant of other policy objectives.

As implemented in the IMAGE model, production of (second generation) feedstock for biofuel production is restricted to rainfed areas, hence there is no impact on water withdrawals. However, conversion of natural land to bio-energy crop land may alter the local water supply due to changes in water holding capacity, evapo-transpiration and run-off.

The increased biofuel production is assumed to enter the economy as substitutes for refined oil, and may lead to crowding out effects on oil markets, given that overall fuel demand is not exogenously adjusted.

Combined bottlenecks scenario

In this scenario, the individual water, land and energy bottleneck scenarios of limiting groundwater availability, urban sprawl and protection of natural areas, and ambitious biofuel targets are combined, to investigate whether there are significant interaction effects between these various bottlenecks. If there are, then indeed the LWE nexus is not just a combination of land, water and energy bottlenecks, but a true nexus.

Climate change scenario

The impact of climate change on the biophysical system, including water availability and regional temperature change are captured in the IMAGE model and translated into shocks on crop yields. The impact of elevated levels of CO_2 concentration in the atmosphere, referred to as the CO_2 fertilisation effect, is not included as its magnitude is very uncertain (see Box 2.2). These crop yield shocks are mimicked in ENV-Linkages. To ensure consistency, these climate change impacts have been scaled to the emission projection of the CIRCLE baseline, which leads to levels of radiative forcing that are between RCP6.0 and RCP8.5 (see Van Vuuren et al., 2012, for more details on these representative concentration pathways), albeit closer to the latter.

Box 2.2. **Influence of the CO_2 fertilisation effect on climate change damages in agriculture**

The projections in this report exclude an effect of higher carbon concentrations in the atmosphere on crop growth (the CO2 fertilisation effect, for which the basic idea is that increased concentrations of CO_2 can boost photosynthesis and dry weight of harvested crops). The CIRCLE report on the economic consequences of climate change (OECD, 2015a) presents a detailed analysis of the sensitivity of the economic analysis to this effect. That analysis provides at least tentative insights into the influence of the assumptions on CO_2 fertilisation for the bottlenecks in the nexus. The magnitude of the CO_2 fertilisation effect in agricultural practice is very uncertain, as plants require a range of other conditions to support enhanced growth and CO_2 is often not the primary constraining factor. Therefore crop models show diverging responses to CO_2 concentration.

The analysis in OECD (2015a) clearly shows that the impacts of climate change on crop yields varies widely between crops. Generally, the effect of CO_2 fertilisation on yields is quite strong and positive and can limit some of the major negative consequences in agriculture. The effects of CO_2 fertilisation on the economy is more limited. According to the simulations in OECD (2015a), the CO_2 fertilisation effect amounts to 0.2 percent-points of GDP by 2060, i.e. agricultural damages are a little less than 0.6% of GDP rather than a little less than 0.8%.

Figure 2.3, also reproduced from OECD (2015a), puts this result into perspective, by also varying the underlying crop model (LPJmL instead of DSSAT) and the underlying climate model (IPSL instead of HadGEM). The figure highlights the regional differences: for some regions, especially OECD Europe and OECD Pacific, the range of the projections of the four model combinations under scenarios of CO_2 fertilisation and no CO_2 fertilisation is very small, with minor impacts projected in all scenarios. For other regions, the range is much wider. The simulations with alternative crop and climate models all provide similar global gains from CO_2 fertilisation, between 0.2 and 0.3 percent-points, respectively. For a more detailed analysis of these results see OECD (2015a).

Box 2.2. **Influence of the CO₂ fertilisation effect on climate change damages in agriculture** *(continued)*

Figure 2.3. **Range of regional agricultural damages from climate change for alternative scenarios (including CO₂ fertilisation)**

(Percentage change in GDP in 2060 from baseline)

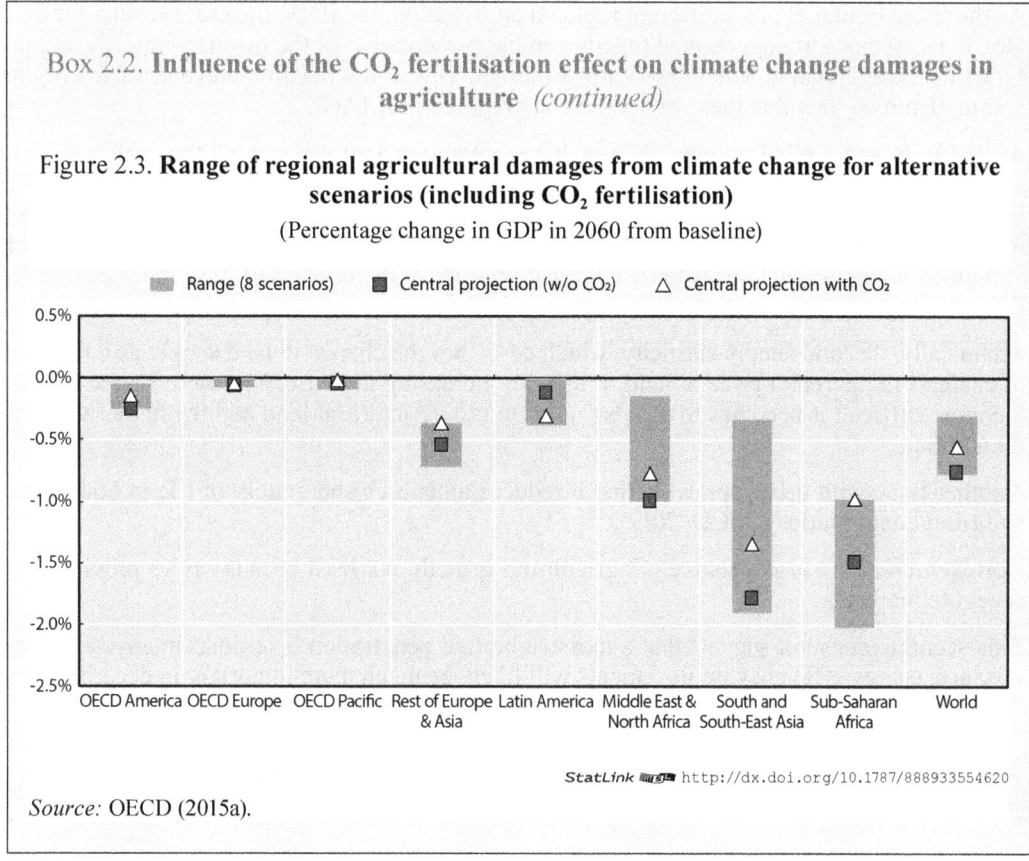

Source: OECD (2015a).

This scenario is not intended to by itself shed light on the LWE nexus. Rather, it allows a comparison of the feedbacks from the nexus with those from climate change, and provides the relevant starting point for the comprehensive combined bottlenecks with climate change scenario.

Combined bottlenecks with climate change scenario

The combined bottlenecks scenario is coupled with the climate change scenario, to explore how climate change affects nexus scarcity projections, and the associated economic consequences. This scenario provides the most comprehensive assessment of the biophysical and economic consequences of the nexus.

Notes

1.   In principle, the changes in economic activity as calculated by ENV-Linkages should feed back into the IMAGE model through a change in e.g. food demand. This iterative procedure is, however, very computationally expensive, and only relevant when the second-order effects of such a feedback are significant. Given the price-inelasticity of food demand, this is unlikely, and these feedbacks are ignored.

2. As the IMAGE model has a different regional aggregation, the ENV-Linkages results for both OECD EU regions are aggregated together in the presentation of the results; similarly, results for Chile are aggregated with Other Latin America. This re-aggregation prevents false insights coming from the fact that these regions are aggregated in IMAGE.

3. As IMAGE and ENV-Linkages do not have matching aggregations of the different crop sectors, some ad-hoc assumptions are made to translate the IMAGE outputs into inputs for ENV-Linkages. These assumptions aim to provide the best fit for representing the changes in yields for the crop sectors in ENV-Linkages and use FAO data on land use and production quantities for individual crops to disaggregate the IMAGE results and then re-aggregate for ENV-Linkages input.

4. Technically, the land supply elasticity, which describes the change in land supply as a function of changes in the rental price of land, falls with increasing land use. The more scarce land is, the more difficult it becomes to convert new land to agricultural land and the higher the land rental price.

5. Another issue with urban sprawl is that it reduces amenities and quality of life in both urban and rural communities (OECD, 2017).

6. However, cities are also a source of agricultural growth, not least because cities provide easy access to markets.

7. This scenario does not suggest that a massive biofuel penetration is optimal in any sense; for instance, energy efficiency improvements will likely be much more important in decarbonising the energy system.

References

BGR/UNESCO (2015), *WHYMAP*, www.whymap.org.

Biemans, H. et al. (2011), "Impact of reservoirs on river discharge and irrigation water supply during the 20th century", *Water Resources Research* 47(3).

Biemans, H. (2012), *Water constraints on future food production*, PhD thesis, Wageningen University and Research Centre, The Netherlands.

Bijl, D.L. et al. (2016), "Long-term Water Demand for Electricity, Industry and Households", *Environmental Science and Policy* 55(1), pp. 75-86.

Chateau, J., R. Dellink and E. Lanzi (2014), "An Overview of the OECD ENV-Linkages Model: Version 3", *OECD Environment Working Papers*, No. 65, OECD Publishing, Paris, http://dx.doi.org/10.1787/5jz2qck2b2vd-en.

Davies, E.G.R., P. Kyle and J.A. Edmonds (2013), "An integrated assessment of global and regional water demands for electricity generation to 2095", *Advances in Water Resources* 52, pp. 296-313.

Energy Modelling Forum (EMF) (2017), "Bio-energy and Land Use", *Energy Modelling Forum Working Group 33*, Stanford.

Gleeson, T. et al. (2012), "Water balance of global aquifers revealed by groundwater footprint", *Nature* 488(7410), pp. 197-200.

Jiang, L. and B. O'Neill (2017), "Global urbanization projections for the Shared Socioeconomic Pathways", *Global Environmental Change* 42, pp 193-199.

Klein Goldewijk, K. and G. van Drecht (2006), "HYDE 3: Current and Historical Population and Land Cover", in Bouwman, A.F., T. Kram and K. Klein Goldewijk (eds), Integrated Modelling of Global Environmental Change. An Overview of IMAGE 2.4. Netherlands Environmental Assessment Agency, Bilthoven.

Nilsson, C. et al. (2005), "Fragmentation and flow regulation of the world's large river systems", *Science* 308(5720), pp. 405-408.

OECD (2017 forthcoming), *Urban sprawl patterns in OECD urban areas*, OECD Publishing, Paris.

OECD (2015a), *The Economic Consequences of Climate Change*, OECD Publishing, Paris, http://dx.doi.org/10.1787/9789264235410-en.

OECD (2015b), *Water resources allocation: sharing risks and opportunities*, OECD Studies on Water, OECD Publishing, Paris, http://dx.doi.org/10.1787/9789264229631-en.

Potere, D., and A. Schneider (2007), "A critical look at representations of urban areas in global maps", *GeoJournal* 69, pp. 55–80.

Rost, S. et al. (2008), "Agricultural green and blue water consumption and its influence on the global water system", *Water Resources Research* 44(9), pp. W09405.

Stehfest, E. et al. (2014), *Integrated Assessment of Global Environmental Change with IMAGE 3.0. Model description and policy applications*, PBL Netherlands Environmental Assessment Agency, The Hague.

United Nations Convention on Biological Diversity (2012), *Resourcing the Aichi Biodiversity Targets: A first assessment of the resources required for implementing the strategic plan for biodiversity 2011-2020*, Report of the High-level Panel on Global Assessment of Resources for Implementing the Strategic Plan for Biodiversity 2011-2020, old.unep-wcmc.org/medialibrary/2012/10/17/3707b6c4/hlpgar-sp-01-01-report-en.pdf.

Van Vuuren, D.P. et al. (2012), "A proposal for a new scenario framework to support research and assessment in different climate research communities", *Global Environmental Change* 22(1), pp. 21-35.

Wada, Y. et al. (2012), "Nonsustainable groundwater sustaining irrigation: A global assessment", *Water Resources Research* 48.

Chapter 3

Trends that drive the land-water-energy nexus

This chapter outlines the main biophysical and socioeconomic trends that are projected to emerge in absence of feedbacks from the nexus bottlenecks. It describes trends for sectoral and macroeconomic activity, and the corresponding trends in agricultural production and land use. Together, these baseline projections form the reference for investigating the consequences of the nexus bottlenecks in the next chapter.

3.1. Macroeconomic trends

In ENV-Linkages, baseline developments of sectoral and regional economic activities are projected for the medium- and long-term future, up to 2060, based on socio-economic drivers such as demographic developments, macroeconomic growth and sector-specific trends (see also the discussion on megatrends in Chapter 1).[1] The baseline projection for the most important elements in the ENV-Linkages model, and the associated land use and water use projections from IMAGE, are presented here; further baseline projections from ENV-Linkages are described in Annex A.

The regional projections of GDP indicate that the slowdown in population growth projected in the coming decades (see Annex A) does not imply an equivalent slowdown in economic activity. While long run economic growth rates are gradually declining, Figure 3.1 shows that GDP levels in the no-damage baseline are projected to increase more than linearly over time. The largest growth is observed outside the OECD, especially in Asia and Africa, where a huge economic growth potential exists. The share of the OECD in the world economy is projected to shrink from 64% in 2010 to 38% in 2060. These projections are fully aligned with the OECD Economic Outlook (OECD, 2014) and include the main effects of the recent financial crisis as they emerged until 2013 and are consistent with the central scenario of the OECD@100 report on long-term scenarios (Braconier et al., 2014).

Figure 3.1. Trend in real Gross Domestic Product (GDP), baseline projection
(Billions of USD, 2005 PPP exchange rates)

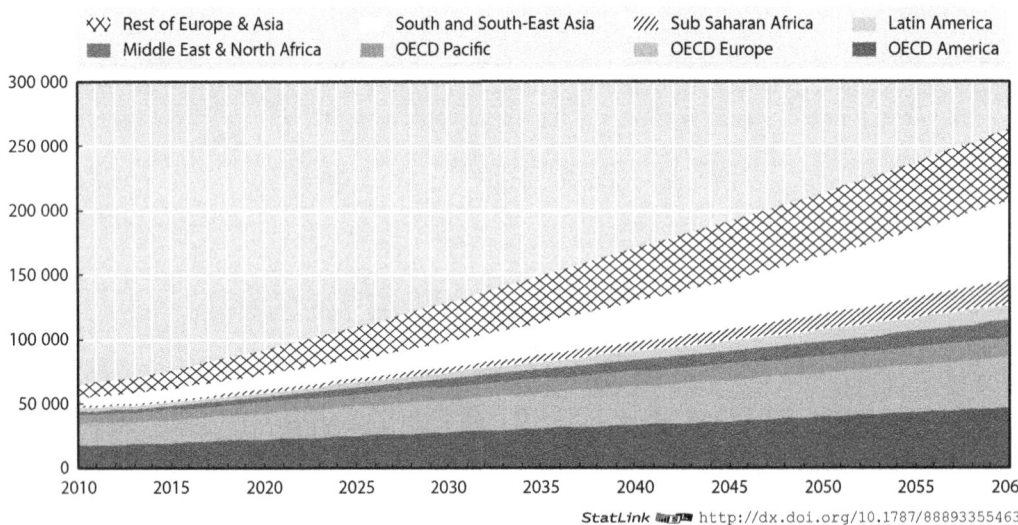

StatLink http://dx.doi.org/10.1787/888933554639

Source: OECD (2014) for OECD countries and ENV-Linkages model for non-OECD countries.

3.2. Energy trends

Baseline energy projections until 2035 are calibrated to be in line with the Current Policies scenario of the International Energy Agency's World Energy Outlook (IEA, 2015), and extrapolated to fit the macroeconomic baseline projections thereafter. In fast-growing economies such as China, India and Indonesia, the need to support economic growth with cheap energy drives an increased use of coal, which is abundant and cheap in the absence of carbon pricing. In OECD regions, however, energy use is projected to switch towards more gas, not least in the United States. Furthermore, in the OECD region, energy efficiency improvements dominate and imply a relative decoupling of energy use and economic growth. The resulting effects on energy production by fuel and region are given in Figure 3.2.

Figure 3.2. **Energy production, baseline projection**

Panel A. Evolution over time (million tonnes of oil equivalent)

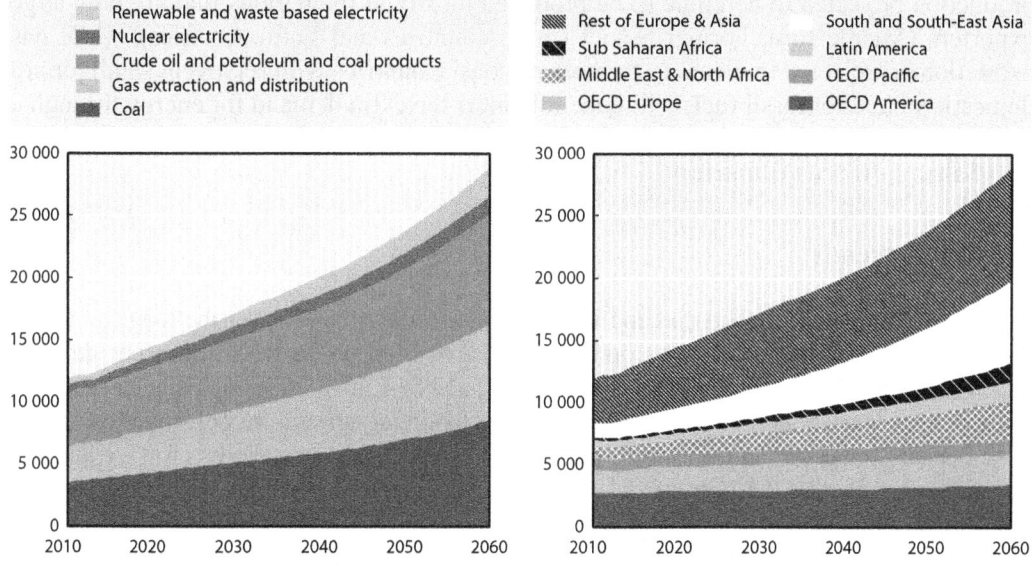

Panel B. Average annual growth rate (2015-60)

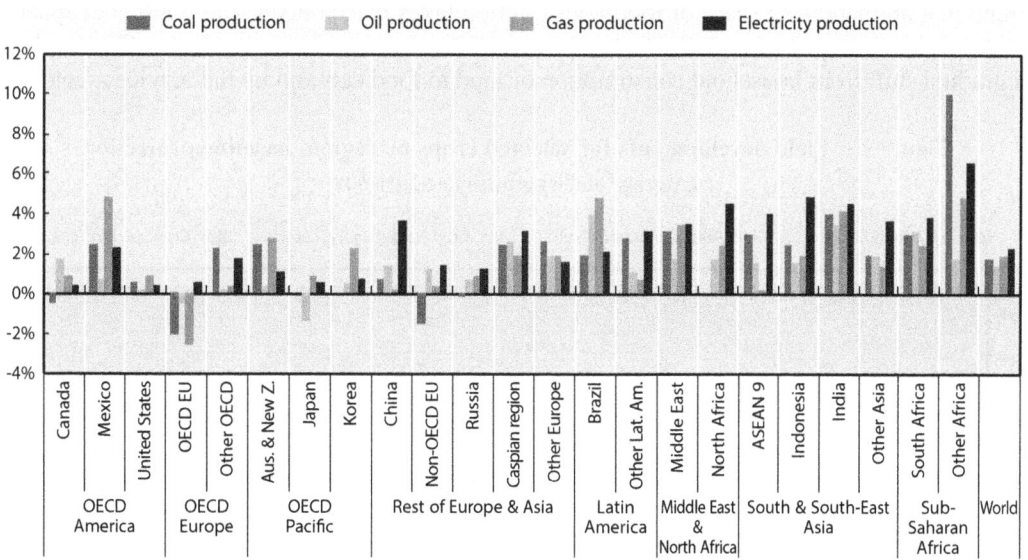

StatLink http://dx.doi.org/10.1787/888933554658

Source: ENV-Linkages model based on IEA (2015), *World Energy Outlook* projections.

The examination of the projected energy trends helps to identify the second possible potential bottleneck of the LWE nexus. Figure 3.2 shows that, in line with the macroeconomic developments, the increase in future energy demands are projected to be strongest in rapidly developing economies (Sub-Saharan African countries and India, followed by other Asian countries, China excepted). Moreover, despite a growing share of renewables in electricity production, the increase in fossil-fuel energy demand is almost in line with the increase in total energy demand. Under current policies, both fossil-fuel extraction and fossil-fuel based power generation are projected to grow in the coming decades, and these activities are very water-consuming.

Liquid fossil energy resources are unevenly distributed across countries, with oil production projected to continue to be produced mostly in the regions that are now large exporters (Middle East, Former Soviet Union countries and Latin America), while gas extraction is projected to diversify to more regions. Countries with relatively small (or no) domestic sources of fossil fuels will generally meet the extra demand for energy through a substantial increase in electricity generation (this applies to all Asian countries as well as Sub-Saharan African countries).

3.3. Agricultural trends

It is well-known that food demand is difficult to model robustly over the long run as the underlying megatrends affect development and income growth affects consumer demand (e.g. Valin et al., 2014). The baseline construction in ENV-Linkages pays particular attention to modelling household preferences and therefore food and agriculture consumption trends in a plausible manner. Furthermore, agricultural trends, and especially crop yields, are harmonised with the IMAGE model, to ensure consistency between both models. The projections on demand for crops as represented in the ENV-Linkages baseline are built on dedicated runs with the International Food Policy Research Institute (IFPRI)'s IMPACT model (Rosegrant et al., 2012) using the socioeconomic baseline projections from ENV-Linkages and excluding feedbacks from climate change on agricultural yields. Notice also that the trend that an increasing share of food consumption takes place outside the household sphere but in restaurants and other collective or private outlets is projected to continue. This implies a gradual shift from household consumption of food to food demand by the services sector.

Figure 3.3. Yield developments for selected crops by region, baseline projection

(Average annual growth rate 2011-60)

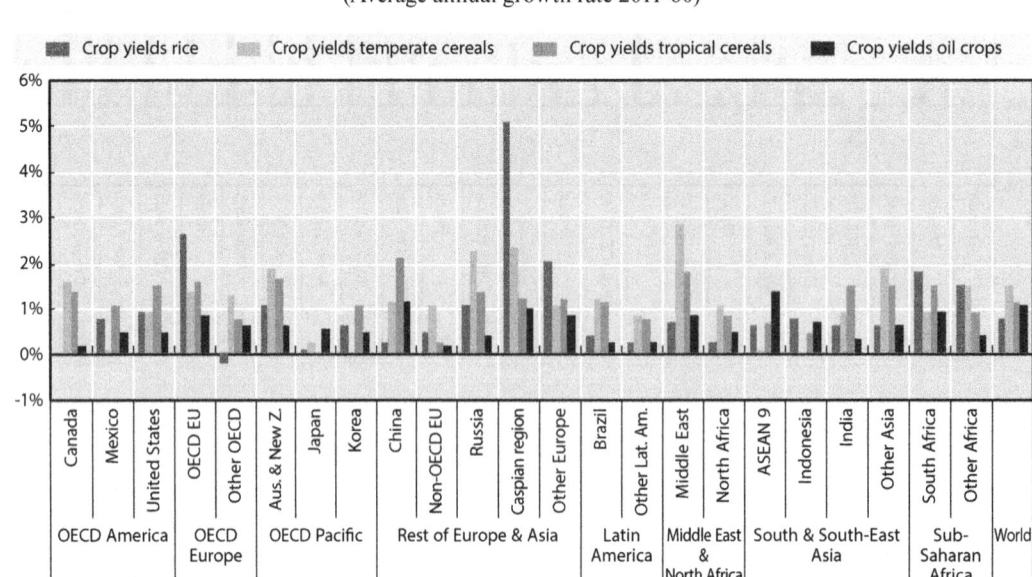

Source: IMAGE model.

Figure 3.3 summarises the assumed yield growth rates in various regions, according to the baseline projection. In line with historical trends, yields are projected to continue to grow, but the pace of growth is slowing. Most regions in Africa and Latin America still have ample room for yield growth, as agricultural management practices will be more and more modernised to catch-up to the most advanced countries' levels. In contrast, yields in North America and EU countries are substantially higher in the short run, but projected to not improve much more.

Figure 3.4. **Relative size of the agricultural sector by region, baseline projection**
(Percentage of total)

Panel A. Share of regional agricultural production in global production

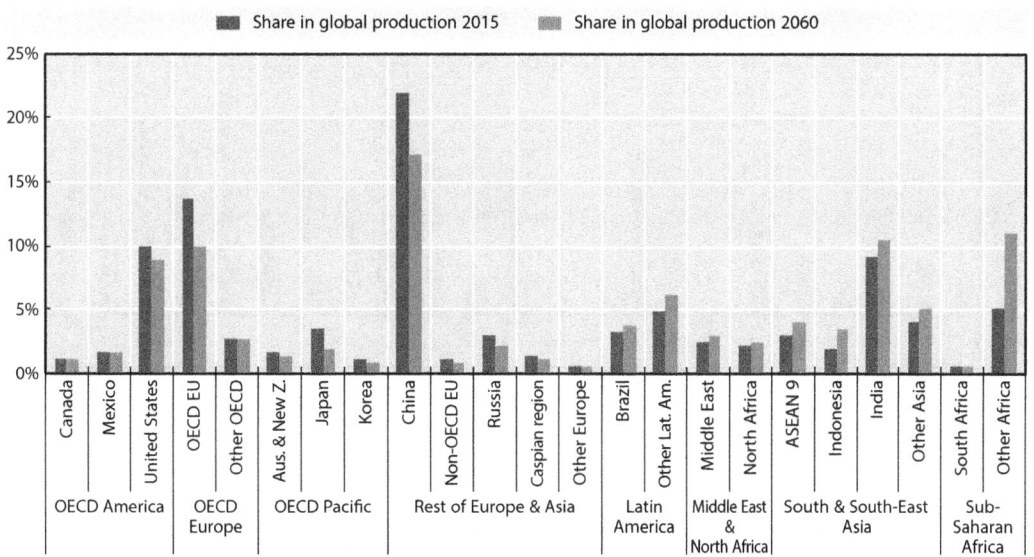

Panel B. Share of agriculture in regional total value added

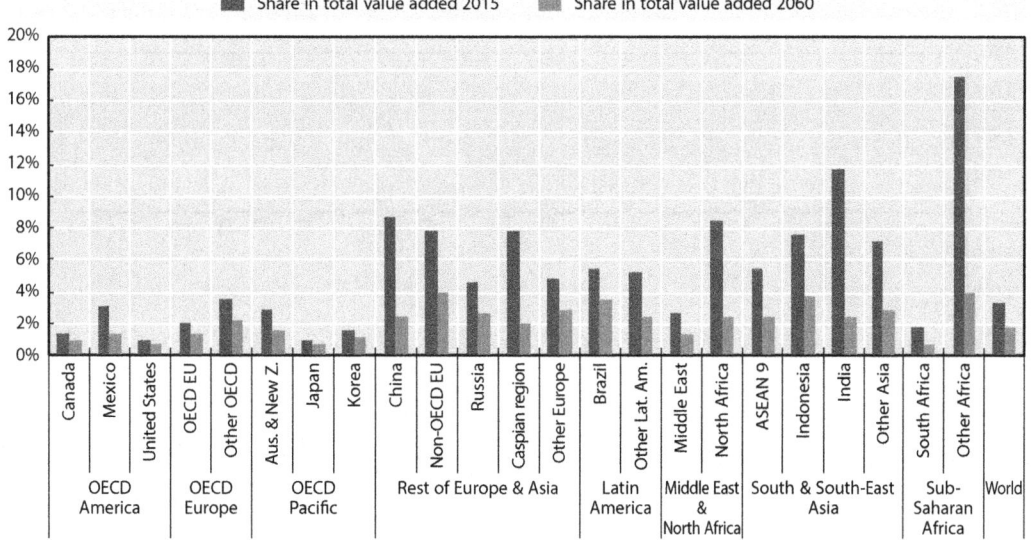

StatLink ⬛📈 http://dx.doi.org/10.1787/888933554696

Source: ENV-Linkages model.

The agricultural trends in the baseline scenario show that agriculture production (defined as the sum of real gross output over crops and livestock sectors) will increase in all regions between now and 2060. From 2011 to 2060, world agricultural production shifts away from less rapidly growing countries, including mostly OECD countries and China whose share in world agricultural output declines (Figure 3.4, Panel A), to less-developed but faster growing countries. The increase in agricultural production is closely related to the increase in food demand (Figure 3.5). Nonetheless, as Panel B of Figure 3.4 shows, the share of the agricultural sector is projected to decline in all regions, and converge across

Figure 3.5. **Growth in the agricultural sector and land use change, baseline projection**

Panel A. Share of regional agricultural production in global production (average annual growth rate)

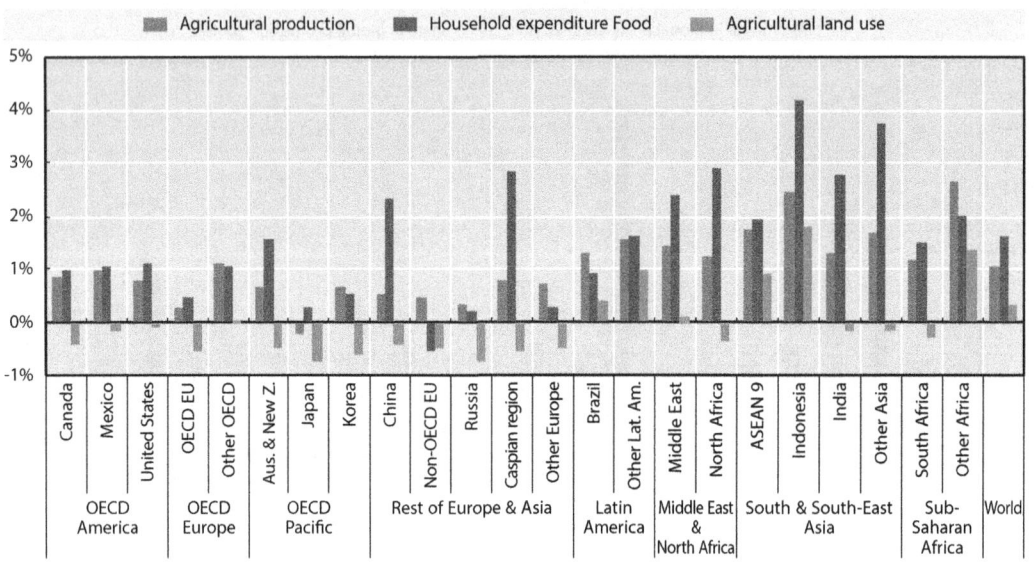

Panel B. Land use change (change between 2015 and 2060 in thousand square kilometres)

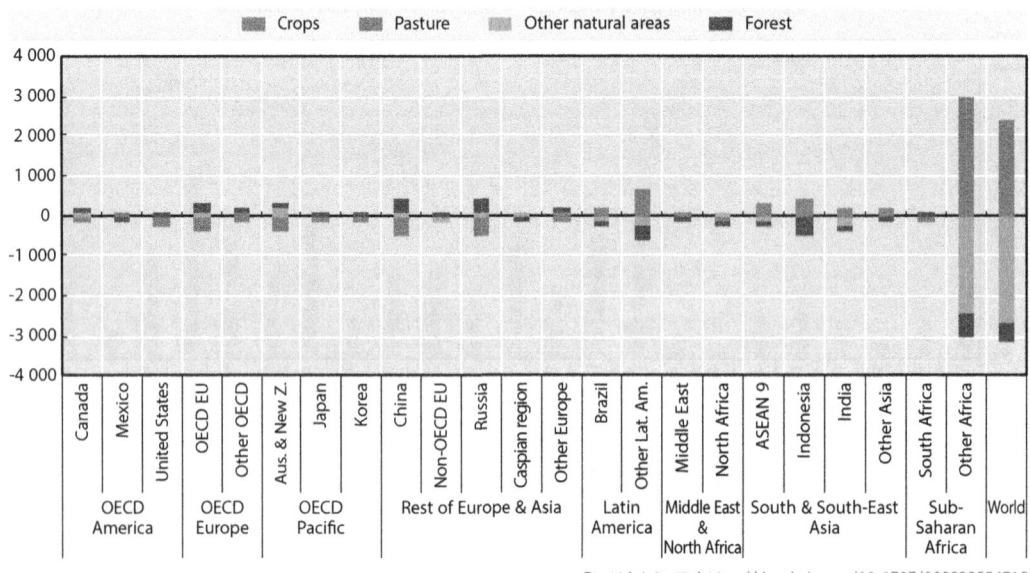

StatLink ⬛⬛⬛ http://dx.doi.org/10.1787/888933554715

Source: panel A: ENV-Linkages model; panel B: IMAGE model.

countries, i.e. fall sharpest in the regions that now have the highest share (the African regions, India, China and the Caspian Region).

The increase in demand for agricultural products puts upward pressure on agricultural land use, as indicated in Figure 3.5, to cover the extra needs for food production. But increasing yields imply that in some regions production increases can be met while simultaneously reducing agricultural land use. Agricultural production is still projected to increase because of the lower-than-historical but continued increase in yields assumed in the baseline (driven by better land efficiency and better total factor productivity in the crop sectors).

Based on the baseline projections of economic activity, the associated land use patterns are presented in panel B of Figure 3.5 and Table 3.1.

Table 3.1. **Land potentially available for agriculture in 2015**

		Agricultural land (thousands km²)	Remaining potential land supply (thousands km²)	Total potential land supply for agriculture (thousands km²)	Current land use (% of total)
OECD America	Canada	675	491	1 166	58%
	Mexico	1 075	391	1 466	73%
	United States	4 148	1 319	5 467	76%
OECD Europe	OECD EU	1 677	879	2 556	66%
	Other OECD	465	302	767	61%
OECD Pacific	Australia & New Zealand	4 624	869	5 494	84%
	Japan	51	0	51	>99%
	Korea	19	0	19	>99%
Rest of Europe & Asia	China	5 563	752	6 315	88%
	Non-OECD EU	272	126	398	68%
	Russia	2 155	1 224	3 379	64%
	Caspian region	2 927	137	3 064	95%
	Other Europe	630	187	817	77%
Latin America	Brazil	2 636	1 764	4 400	60%
	Other Latin America	3 491	2 085	5 576	63%
Middle East & North Africa	Middle East	2 164	151	2 315	93%
	North Africa	1 008	37	1 045	96%
South & South-East Asia	ASEAN 9	672	902	1 574	43%
	Indonesia	478	722	1 200	40%
	India	1 802	419	2 221	81%
	Other Asia	2 185	406	2 591	84%
Sub-Saharan Africa	South Africa	996	96	1 092	91%
	Other Africa	9 272	5 386	14 658	63%

StatLink http://dx.doi.org/10.1787/888933555304

Source: IMAGE model.

3.4. Water use trends

The associated regional irrigation water use profiles are shown in Figure 3.6; see also Figure 1.3 in Section 1.4 for the baseline projection of total water demand. Temperature and precipitation are characterised by substantial inter-annual variability, and the combined impact on crop growth and water requirements, and by implication irrigation water withdrawals, is highly non-linear. To capture this, the LPJmL module in IMAGE simulates each year many times with varying climate data, derived from 30 year historical time series, rather than averaging the weather upfront. The model reports for each year the moving average of the 30 simulations, which explains the irregular pattern over time in Figure 3.6. In relatively small agricultural areas, the inter-annual variability plays out more strongly than for larger areas which typically experience different weather conditions in the same year that dampens the impact. This is illustrated in Figure 3.6 by the results for Japan and Korea.

Total world water demand, that is the amount of water withdrawn from freshwater sources, increases 23% between 2015 to 2060 in the baseline from 3 790 to 4 670 km³. The increase is less than population and far less than GDP, so the water use intensity per capita and per unit of GDP drops. In 2015 irrigation is the dominant user (61%), followed by electricity production (15%), municipal use (14%) and industry (10%). Water for irrigation does not increase much until 2060, as the irrigated area is not projected to grow much in future. Hence the other sectors account for the overall growth in water use: electricity +46%, industry +38% and municipal +71%. As a consequence, the share of irrigation drops to 40% by 2060. Of the global total irrigation water demand in the baseline in 2060, around 40% is supplied from non-renewable groundwater sources; the volume and share vary strongly between regions. At some future point in time, these supplies cannot be continued as they are bound to become depleted.

Figure 3.6. **Water supply for irrigation from different sources, baseline projection**
(Cubic kilometres)

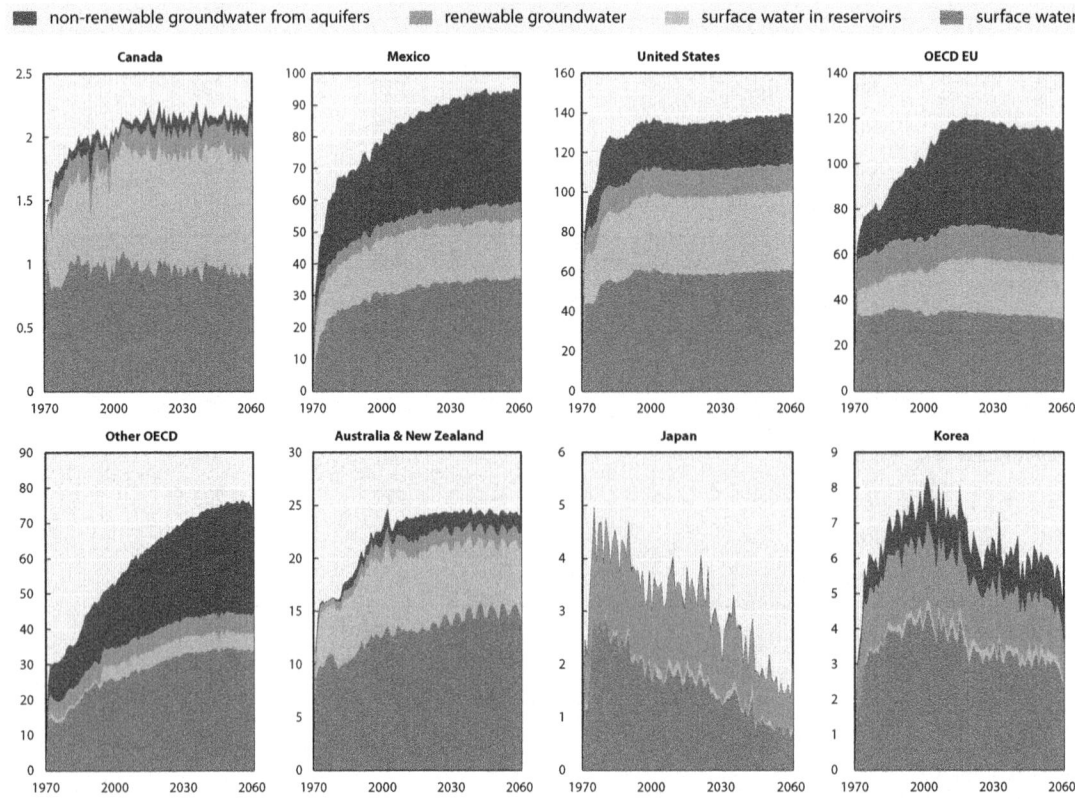

Figure 3.6. **Water supply for irrigation from different sources, baseline projection** *(continued)*

■ non-renewable groundwater from aquifers ■ renewable groundwater ■ surface water in reservoirs ■ surface water

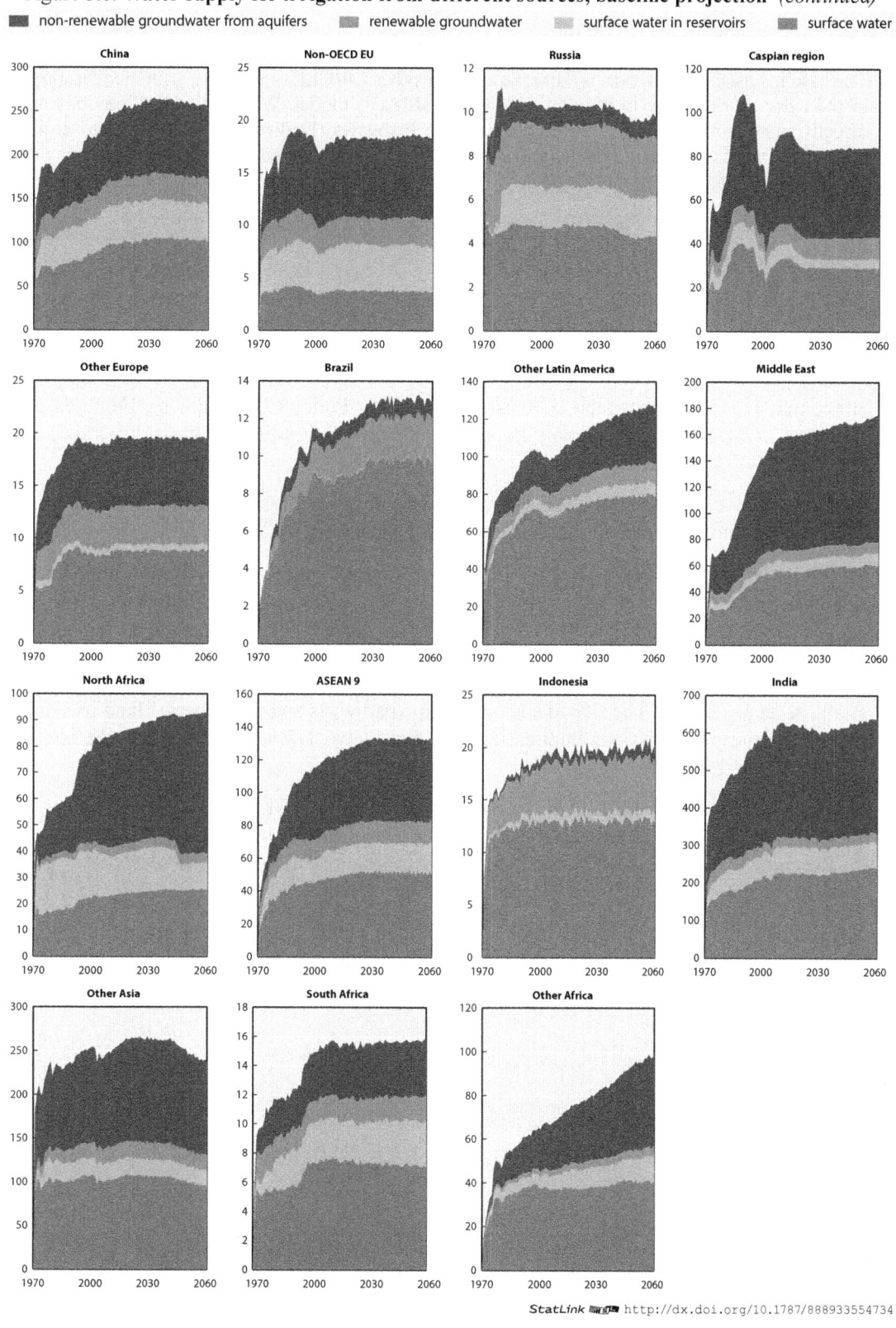

StatLink ᘛᖇᔿᔭ http://dx.doi.org/10.1787/888933554734

Note: Annual fluctuations stem from the variability in rainfall, as projected in the LPJmL model, and from changes in land use.

Source: IMAGE model.

Note

1. The baseline used in this report is the same as in the other CIRCLE reports, but with modifications in the agricultural sector to harmonise with the IMAGE model. While this baseline does not directly match any of the Shared Socioeconomic Pathways (Dellink et al., 2017; Riahi et al., 2016), it is based on the same methodology as the SSP projections, and follows the philosophy of the "middle of the road" scenario SSP2.

References

Braconier, H., G. Nicoletti and B. Westmore (2014), "Policy Challenges for the Next 50 Years", *OECD Economic Policy Papers*, No. 9, OECD Publishing, Paris, http://dx.doi.org/10.1787/5jz18gs5fckf-en.

Dellink, R.B. et al. (2017), "Long-term economic growth projections in the Shared Socioeconomic Pathways", *Global Environmental Change* 42, pp. 200-214.

International Energy Agency (IEA) (2015), *World Energy Outlook 2015*, OECD publishing, Paris, http://dx.doi.org/10.1787/weo-2015-en.

OECD (2014), *OECD Economic Outlook, Volume 2014 Issue 1*, OECD Publishing, Paris, http://dx.doi.org/10.1787/eco_outlook-v2014-1-en.

Riahi, K. et al. (2016), "The shared socioeconomic pathways and their energy, land use, and greenhouse gas emissions implications: an overview", *Global Environmental Change* 42, pp. 153-168.

Rosegrant, M.W. et al. (2012), *International Model for Policy Analysis of Agricultural Commodities and Trade (IMPACT) Model Description*, International Food Policy Research Institute, www.ifpri.org/publication/international-model-policy-analysis-agricultural-commodities-and-trade-impact-0.

Valin, H. et al. (2014), "The future of food demand: understanding differences in global economic models," *Agricultural Economics* 45, pp. 51-67.

Chapter 4

Biophysical and economic consequences of the nexus bottlenecks

This chapter presents the main results from the modelling analysis. It details the biophysical consequences of the individual and combined nexus bottlenecks as calculated with the IMAGE model as well as the economic consequences, as simulated with ENV-Linkages. Finally, it investigates the sensitivity of the modelling results for the underlying assumptions on climate change.

4.1. Results for the water bottleneck scenario

Biophysical consequences

The IMAGE model is used to project the impacts of non-renewable groundwater depletion on agricultural yields, and thereby on land use, before endogenous adjustment in the economic system takes place. Impacts vary widely between regions and crop types (Table 4.1) for two main reasons. First, in many regions the precipitation volume and temporal pattern are such that agriculture is predominantly rain fed, so it does not depend on irrigation. Where precipitation is insufficient to sustain plant growth over the growing season, irrigation is called upon to make up for the deficit. Where sufficient supply of renewable water from surface waters (rivers, lakes and reservoirs) is available, this, extraction from groundwater bodies is not necessary. In all these cases no, or only negligible impacts are bound to occur if water supply from non-renewable groundwater

Table 4.1. **Changes in crop yields in 2060 in the water bottleneck scenario**

(Percentage change from baseline)

		Temperate cereals	Rice	Maize	Tropical cereals	Pulses	Roots & tubers	Oil crops
OECD America	Canada	0%		0%	0%	0%	0%	0%
	Mexico	-28%	-23%	-3%	-3%	-12%	1%	-6%
	United States	-1%	-15%	-1%	-2%	-3%	-6%	0%
OECD Europe	OECD EU	-1%	-1%	-3%	0%	-26%	-20%	-1%
	Other OECD	-2%	6%	-20%	-2%	-23%	-16%	-1%
OECD Pacific	Australia & New Zealand	0%	0%	0%	0%	0%	0%	0%
	Japan	0%	0%			0%	0%	0%
	Korea		0%	0%	0%	0%	0%	0%
Rest of Europe & Asia	China	-4%	-7%	-3%	-6%	-8%	-4%	-8%
	Non-OECD EU	0%	0%	0%	0%	-2%	-2%	0%
	Russia	0%	-10%	-2%	0%	1%	-1%	0%
	Caspian region	-5%	-10%	-12%	0%	-16%	-15%	-11%
	Other Europe	0%	-2%	-2%	-1%	-4%	-1%	-1%
Latin America	Brazil	0%	0%	0%	0%	0%	0%	0%
	Other Latin America	0%	-1%	-1%	0%	-1%	0%	0%
Middle East & North Africa	Middle East	-24%	-37%	-2%	-25%	-6%	-16%	2%
	North Africa	-2%	-34%	-22%	-52%	-12%	-5%	-2%
South & South-East Asia	ASEAN 9	0%	1%	1%	0%	1%	0%	0%
	Indonesia		0%	0%	0%	-1%	0%	0%
	India	-21%	-25%	-23%	1%	-16%	-2%	0%
	Other Asia	-14%	-5%	-8%	-15%	-10%	-2%	-3%
Sub-Saharan Africa	South Africa	-5%	0%	-1%	-6%	-3%	0%	0%
	Other Africa	-1%	-1%	0%	0%	0%	0%	0%

StatLink http://dx.doi.org/10.1787/888933555323

Note: Averages over irrigated and rainfed production are shown. Temperate cereals comprise wheat, rye, oats and barley. Empty cells reflect situations where no significant production of those crops takes place.

Source: IMAGE model.

becomes constrained. If groundwater is used, the estimated volumes stored in large groundwater reservoirs may be so large compared with annual withdrawals, that depletion is not a constraining factor in the timeframe considered. Significant impacts can only occur in regions where non-renewable groundwater sources become constrained and plant growth is affected by the associated water limitation.

In the water bottleneck scenario, less irrigation water is used as some non-renewable groundwater sources become unavailable from 2050 onwards. Total water demand for irrigation in 2060 decreases by around 350 km³, 12% of total irrigation water, and 37% of the supply from non-renewable groundwater sources in the baseline. As mentioned in Section 2.4, the assumed supply reduction in the scenario is stylised and uncertain, but it illustrates that in the long run substantial shares of current irrigated land may become less or not productive in many parts of the world, with implications for food security.

Canada, Brazil and other Latin American countries, and Russia are countries and regions relying (almost) exclusively on rainfed agriculture and are thus not directly affected by groundwater limitations. The relatively small irrigated areas they have are amply supplied through surface water. As agricultural yields in these regions are hardly affected by the imposed water bottleneck, land use and agricultural production subsequently also differ little between baseline and counterfactual scenario. Figure 4.1 (which can be compared to Figure 3.6 in Chapter 3 which describes the baseline projection) confirms that these regions have sufficient water resources; i.e. they mainly use surface water for irrigation both in the baseline and counterfactual scenario. In these regions, groundwater availability does not seem to be a pressing aspect of the nexus.

Figure 4.1. **Irrigation water withdrawal from non-renewable aquifers in 2060 in the baseline and water bottleneck scenario**

(Cubic kilometres)

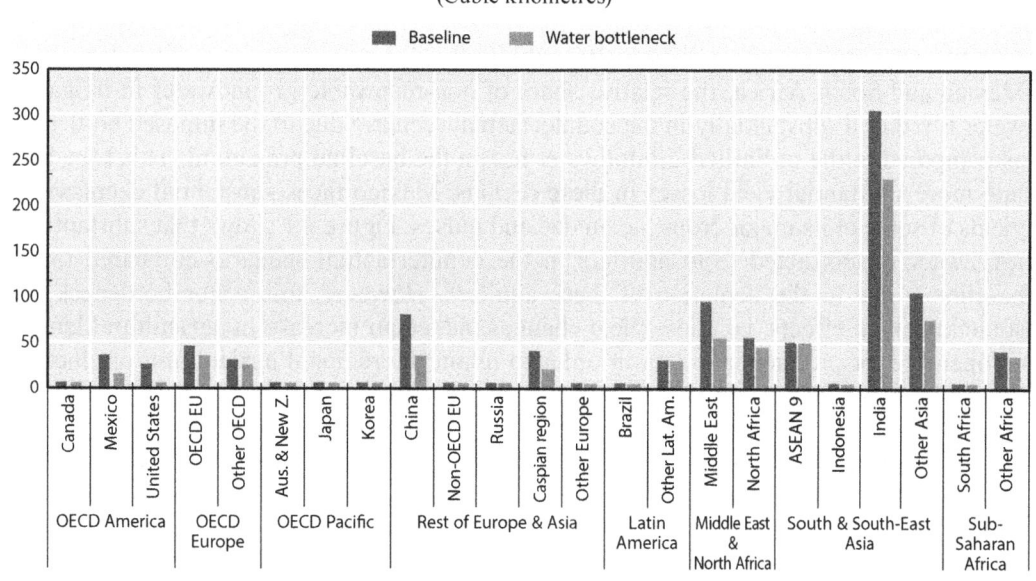

StatLink ⟨☶⟩ http://dx.doi.org/10.1787/888933554753

Source: IMAGE model.

In arid parts of Africa, agricultural output may well be constrained by water limitations, but irrigation is often not affordable, and the baseline assumption is that irrigation areas are not increasing over time. Hence the reliance on groundwater remains very limited and depletion is not imminent in the baseline; the impact on crop yields is therefore also very small.

Countries such as Japan, Korea, and Indonesia do have substantial areas of agriculture under irrigation, in particular paddy rice fields, but availability of renewable water from surface sources and annually renewed groundwater is sufficient to sustain growth. These countries rely on surface water plus renewable groundwater and not much on non-renewable groundwater withdrawals. Therefore introducing the groundwater bottleneck hardly affects these regions. This is clearly shown by comparing Figure 4.1 to Figure 3.6: both in the baseline and the counterfactual scenario, surface water and renewable groundwater are the largest sources of irrigation water in these regions. These figures also confirm that these regions have few non-renewable groundwater withdrawals. As agricultural yields are hardly affected by the imposed water bottleneck, agricultural production and land use are subsequently also little affected. Likewise agriculture in Australia relies heavily on irrigation, but surface water and reservoirs are by far the dominant sources.

The United States has some agricultural areas (such as California Central valley, High Plains aquifers) which rely heavily on non-renewable groundwater withdrawals. Non-renewable groundwater withdrawals account for 10% of all irrigation water withdrawals in the baseline, but this is reduced to 1-2% in the counterfactual scenario due to the introduced bottleneck. Although the groundwater bottleneck is imposed upon certain agricultural areas, the impact of the bottleneck does not become apparent in the overall results for the United States as a whole, as local yield losses remain relatively minor and other parts of the United States are not affected. Agricultural yields show only minor decreases, and subsequently agricultural production and land use is hardly affected. The exception is rice, which is dominated by irrigation and the productivity suffers from the lower availability of groundwater. The loss in output from irrigated fields is compensated by expansion of rainfed production with lower yields. The impact on the total food crop land area remains limited, as rice is grown on 1.2% of harvested land only in the baseline. Figures 3.6 and 4.1 show that the United States relies heavily on rivers, lakes and reservoirs for provision of irrigation water, and only to a lesser extent on groundwater.

Other regions are affected more strongly by the imposed groundwater bottleneck. In Mexico and South Africa, the relative share of non-renewable groundwater in irrigation water is reduced substantially in the counterfactual scenario due to the imposed bottleneck as compared to the unlimited groundwater use in the baseline projection. This translates into more substantial yield losses in these regions. Mexico faces substantial decreases in yields of some of its major crops, i.e. maize and pulses. Figure 4.1 shows that substantially less water is subtracted from aquifers in the counterfactual scenario compared to the baseline – due to the depletion of these aquifers. However, this water bottleneck has some knock-on effects; i.e. these yield changes induce an increase in agricultural land to compensate for production losses in order to retain the regional agricultural production. Similarly, South Africa faces yield decreases of some crops. Its main crop maize is cultivated mainly rainfed and therefore yield losses in maize are small. However, temperate cereals are more often irrigated and more substantial yield losses are therefore projected for this crop. Similar to Mexico, the imposed water bottleneck also impacts land use; i.e. these yield changes necessitate an increase in agricultural land in order to maintain regional production.

North Africa and the Middle East are severely affected by the imposed bottleneck. Figure 4.1 shows a severe reduction in the projected share of non-renewable groundwater in overall irrigation water in the counterfactual scenario with the imposed bottleneck. The bottleneck hence results in significant agricultural production losses in these regions. The dominant crop in both regions is temperate cereals, which is predominantly rainfed but there is also some irrigation of temperate cereals. Imposing the groundwater bottleneck affects the yield of temperate cereals in North Africa and the Middle East only a little, but it does heavily impact the other irrigated crops maize and rice. Moreover, land and surface water resources are so constrained in these regions that no alternative suitable locations are available for these irrigated crops; i.e. the regional demand for these irrigated crops cannot be met without increasing imports (see also Section 4.2). Clearly, the groundwater bottleneck severely contributes to land competition in these regions.

China has a substantial irrigated agricultural area and partially relies on non-renewable groundwater withdrawals for irrigation, which are reduced in the counterfactual scenario due to the imposed bottleneck. Nonetheless, agricultural yields in China are only modestly affected by the imposed bottleneck. Following the assumptions discussed in Section 2.4, relatively fewer aquifers are projected to become depleted than in most other Asian countries. Also, the aquifers that become depleted in China have a modest contribution to overall agricultural production and it is fairly easy to adjust the land use system to absorb the shocks posed by the depleted aquifers. The projected agricultural yield losses do induce an increase in agricultural land to compensate for the production losses, but this increase is also very modest.

Imposing the groundwater bottleneck results in most European countries in much smaller shares of non-renewable groundwater in overall irrigation water withdrawals than in the baseline. This translates into yield losses in these regions. Projected yield losses for some crops in the various European (sub-) regions at first glance seem quite dramatic (Table 4.1). However, these yield losses often concern crops that have very minor production volumes in these regions. An example is rice, which shows huge yield losses in EU non-OECD countries where it covers only 0.1% of the current cropland. Moreover, most of the EU non OECD countries (e.g. mainly Romania and Bulgaria) have aquifers that are depleted in the counterfactual scenario (or they are northerly countries), which means that very few alternative locations are available for irrigated rice. In EU non-OECD countries, the main crops (respective cropland shares: temperate cereals: 51%; maize: 20%; oil crops: 20%) show yield decreases but these are small compared to the yield losses of rice (i.e. yield losses ranging from -0.4 to -0.8%). As a result, the increase in agricultural land to compensate for production losses is also very small in this region, and impacts on land competition are negligible.

Substantial yield losses (up to -26%) are also found in maize, pulses, and roots and tubers in the OECD EU countries and in Other OECD Europe. But these crops occupy only a limited share of the cropland in these countries while temperate cereals and oil crops occupy together almost 90% of harvested cropland in these countries. Yield losses projected for these latter crops are much smaller than the yield losses for pulses and roots and tubers. These yield losses mostly occur in the Mediterranean countries (Iberian Peninsula, Greece) of this region. Overall, the combined yield losses of these crops do induce an increase (of around + 4.5%) in agricultural land to compensate for production losses. This bottleneck therefore does seem to exacerbate land competition in the European OECD countries.

The impacts on foodcrop area are very different for the regions, subject to local conditions and water resources available; see Figure 4.2. For the world in total, the foodcrop area increases by 2.4%, large enough to have noticeable impact on natural areas, with consequences for biodiversity. The impact on (pristine) forests remain limited, as many of the arid regions with more substantial losses do not have a lot of forest cover in the first place.

Figure 4.2. **Changes in land use change between 2015 and 2060
in the water bottleneck scenario**

(Change from baseline in thousand square kilometres)

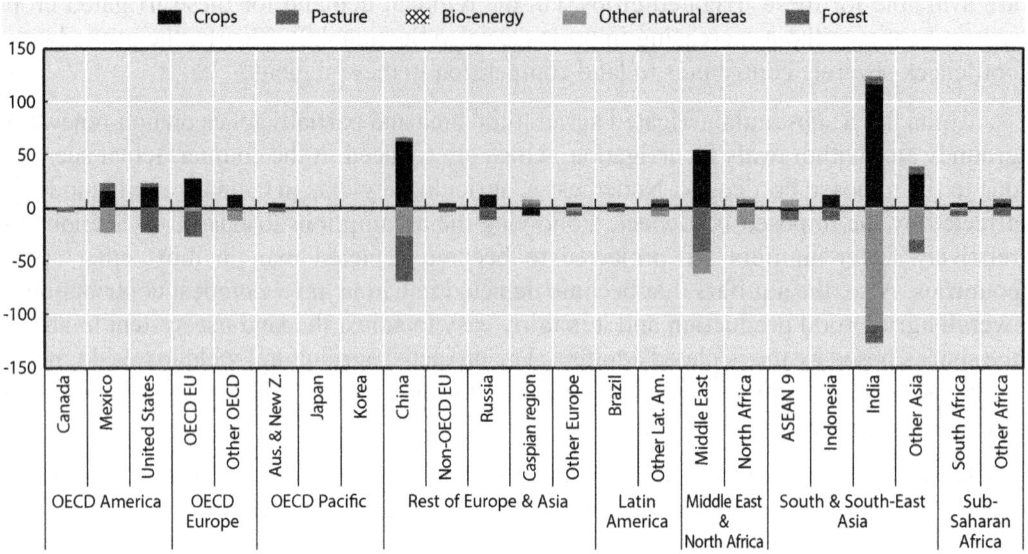

StatLink ᴍᴬᴾ http://dx.doi.org/10.1787/888933554772

Note: Figure depicts absolute deviation from baseline in the amount of land use change between 2015 and 2060.

Source: IMAGE model.

Economic consequences

The changes in crop yields, as outlined above, do not translate proportionately into economic losses. There are several mechanisms that influence the resulting change in agricultural and macroeconomic activity. First, in some regions the lower yields due to water shortages can be more easily compensated by expanding agricultural land (extensification) than in other regions. Secondly, in some regions the agricultural sector is a small part of the economy, while in others it represents a significant share of GDP and exports. Thirdly, the ability to absorb shocks domestically differs between regions. This is – at least partially – captured through the variation in changes in food prices. Fourthly, competitiveness of domestic agricultural and food producers on the domestic and international markets depends not on the absolute changes in production costs, but on the size of the shock relative to competitors. This can be illustrated through changes in import shares and net trade volumes. Each of this mechanism is investigated in detail below.

The re-allocation of agricultural production between countries will imply that the global agriculture value added loss is very moderate (less than 1%).[1] The region-specific results for agricultural production in Panel A of Figure 4.3 show that the large reductions in the contribution of agriculture to the economy are projected to occur in Middle East, India and North Africa. The panel also clearly shows that the ease with which new agricultural land can be taken into production drives the land use response: in roughly half the regions, the yield loss is more than compensated by increases in land use, thereby boosting agricultural production (as measured by value added generated in the agricultural sector, i.e. the contribution of agriculture to GDP). In the other regions, and at the global level, the increase in agricultural land use is insufficient to fully compensate for the yield loss, and agricultural value added is projected to decline below baseline levels. Unfortunately, the potential to increase total land devoted to agricultural activities remains very limited in the same countries that are the most strongly affected by the limited groundwater access: the Middle Eastern and North African countries and India where fertile arable land is scarce and expensive, and land markets are sometimes heavily regulated. In contrast, in e.g. Sub-Saharan Africa extensification can more than compensate for the yield losses. This scenario thus illustrates the close interactions between the land and water resources: changes in land use can sometimes compensate for water bottleneck but only when it is amply available, so both aspects need to be understood when drawing conclusions on the economic consequences.

Figure 4.3. **Changes in agricultural and macroeconomic activity in 2060 in the water bottleneck scenario**

(Percentage change from baseline)

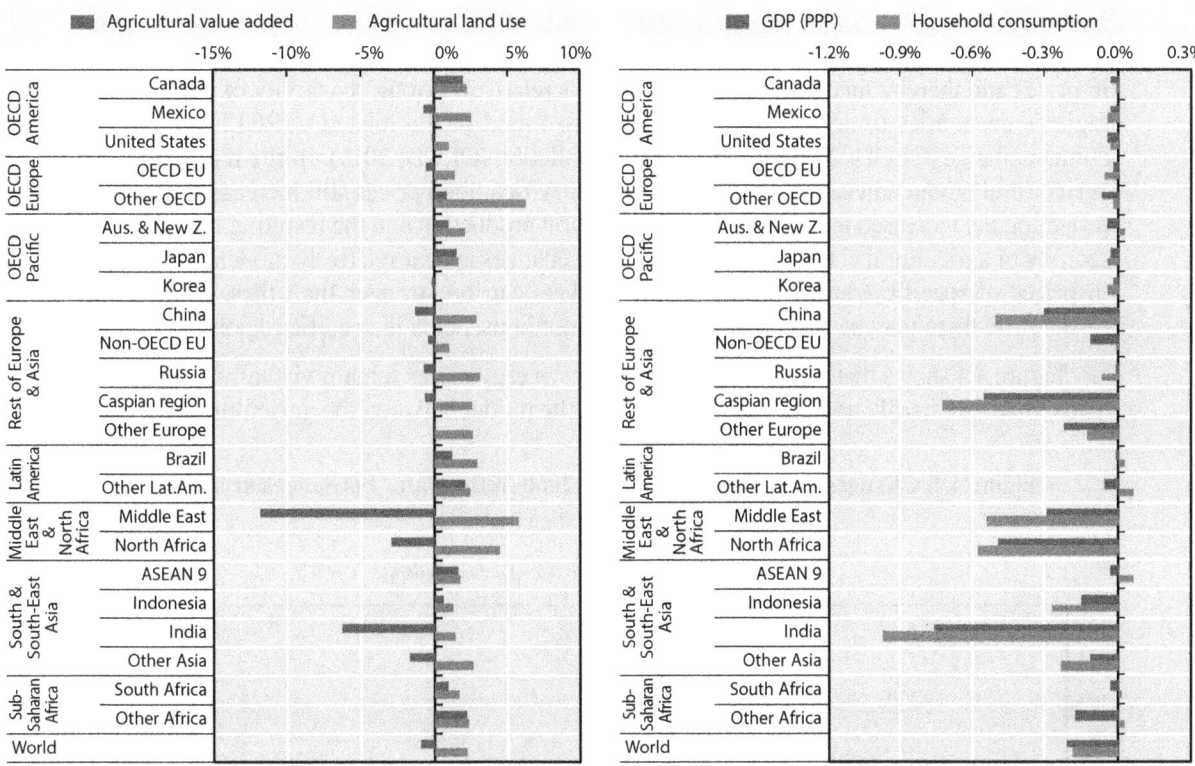

StatLink http://dx.doi.org/10.1787/888933554791

Note: In Panel A, agriculture refers to all crop sectors and the livestock sector.

Source: ENV-Linkages model.

Panel B of Figure 4.3 shows the consequences of the water bottleneck at the macroeconomic level. In almost all regions, GDP in 2060 is (sometimes slightly) below the baseline level. The global loss amounts to 0.2%, highlighting that this specific water bottleneck will have only limited consequences for the global economy. There are several regions where the losses are more significant, however, although GDP losses are remain below 1% for all regions. These are especially China, the Caspian region, the Middle East, North Africa and India. For the latter three, this is in line with the severe yield shocks and changes in the agricultural sector highlighted above. For China and the Caspian region, the economic repercussions of relatively modest yield shocks are stronger as firstly the agricultural sector comprises a relatively large share of the economy and secondly these regions are food importers and thus lose from increasing global food prices (see Figure 3.4).[2]

In many regions, household consumption follows the trend of GDP, although results are often more negative for those countries that are severely affected by the shock, and less negative or even positive for less affected countries. The countries that hardly rely on non-renewable ground water can benefit (at least in terms of their consumption level) from increasing their share on the global agricultural markets. In general, regions that are not directly affected by the water bottleneck would have a chance to increase their market share, and thus benefit from the bottleneck, despite unchanged or even worsening domestic conditions.

The increased agricultural production costs resulting from degraded yields also translate into increases in regional household prices for food (Figure 4.4).[3] Although food is internationally traded, and the global food market price will adjust to all the regional changes, regional prices can deviate from the world market price. Not surprisingly, the food price increases are largest in India, Middle East and North Africa, but also in China and the Caspian region. In the latter case, a relatively small yield reduction produces a more significant increase in prices and thereby macroeconomic losses. This relatively strong sensitivity of the Caspian region's economies to agricultural shocks is also found in the related CIRCLE reports on climate change (OECD, 2015) and outdoor air pollution (OECD, 2016). In the regions where agricultural production can expand, such as Other Africa, food prices still increase somewhat, reflecting the increased marginal cost of agricultural production and the resulting larger global scarcity of agricultural commodities. While these changes appear relatively moderate, changes in prices of specific commodities in local markets can be stronger than these aggregated results, and there may be significant effects for poor households in specific regions.

Figure 4.4 shows that in the model simulations energy prices remain virtually unchanged. Thus, there are hardly any interaction effects in the model between the agricultural changes

Figure 4.4. **Changes in consumer prices in 2060 in the water bottleneck scenario**

(Percentage change from baseline)

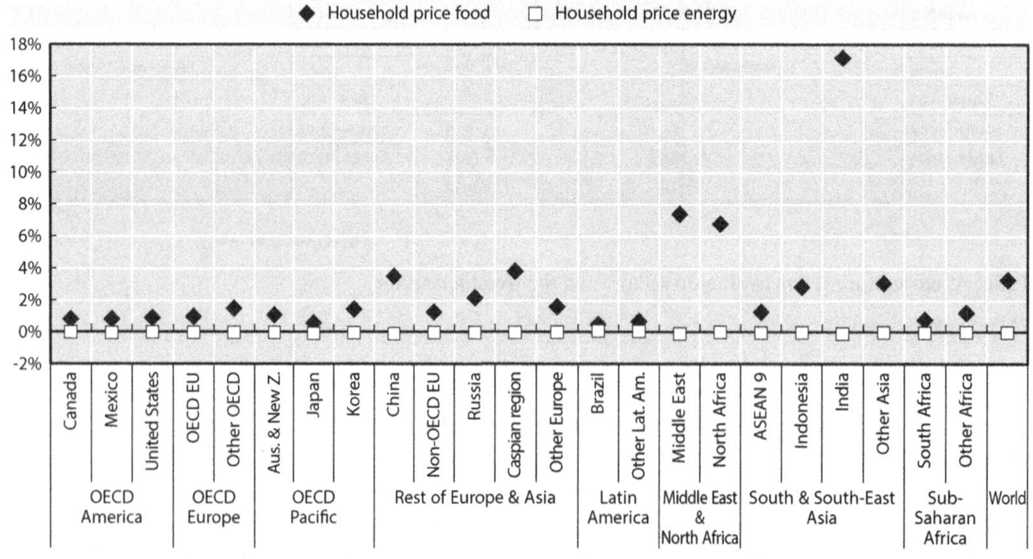

StatLink ⌨🖳 http://dx.doi.org/10.1787/888933554810

Note: Food prices reflect a weighted average of all crops, livestock and food products; energy prices reflect a weighted average of coal, oil, gas and electricity.

Source: ENV-Linkages model.

induced by the water bottleneck and the energy system. This is however driven by the absence of a direct shock of the water bottleneck on energy supply. In reality, water scarcity may also affect the energy sector; this could not be incorporated in the modelling, but is explored in Annex B.

Figure 4.5. **Changes in agricultural trade and food security in 2060 in the water bottleneck scenario**

(Percentage change from baseline)

Panel A. International trade in crops

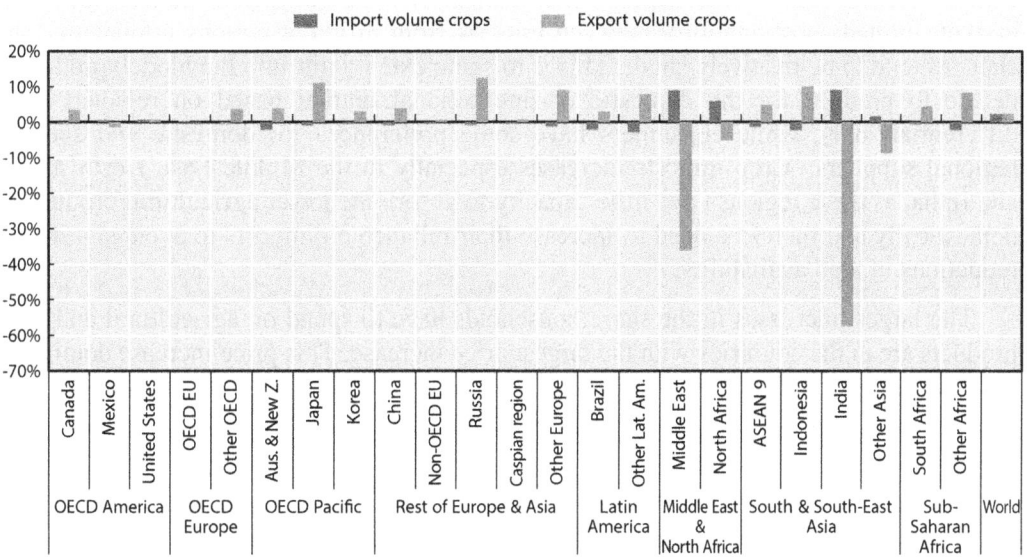

Panel B. Budget and import shares (percentage-point change)

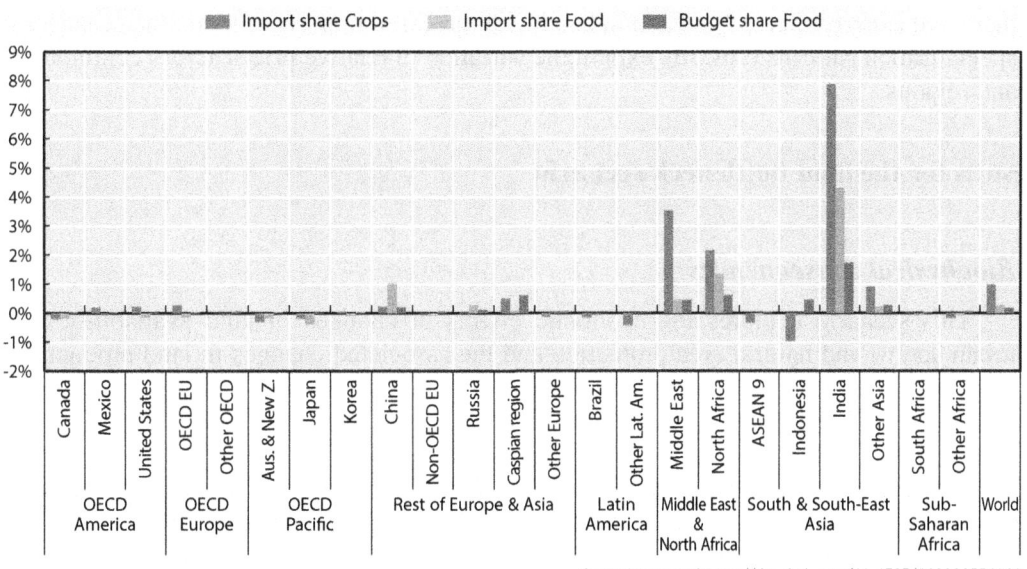

StatLink http://dx.doi.org/10.1787/888933554829

Note: In panel B, the budget share reflects consumption of all crops, livestock and food products; import shares are separated between crops and food products.

Source: ENV-Linkages model.

Figure 4.5 illustrates the consequences of the water bottleneck for international trade and food security. Russia, the regions in Eastern Europe, Latin America, Indonesia and Other Africa can all benefit from increases in their relative competitive position: they rely less on non-renewable groundwater and can take a larger share of the global market, as well as reduce their reliance on imports (i.e. increased competitiveness on their domestic market); Annex C presents the changes in trade patterns in more detail. The regions more severely hit by the water bottleneck on the other hand are projected to see their trade positions decline. This effect is relatively strong in India, as its regional competitors in South and South-East Asia are relatively better protected against the water scarcity.

Imports of crops typically have the opposite sign of exports: producers that lose competitiveness on the international market will also be out-priced on their domestic market; limited substitutability between imports from different regions implies that the changes tend to be relatively small. This is to some extent built into the model: producers decide to produce for the domestic or international market based on regional price differentials only, while consumers have some preferences for domestic and specific regional suppliers.[4] Crop imports increases especially in the Middle East, North Africa and India, as these regions have little capacity to absorb the lower agricultural production domestically and therefore need to increase their reliance on imports to avoid significant reductions in food availability.

The largest increases in the share households have to spend on agricultural and food products are in the countries with the largest price increase. This price increase dominates the change in the volume of consumption and the change in disposable income, as food products tend to be basic commodities, and consumption levels are rather insensitive to the price changes.

In China, the Middle East, North Africa and especially in India, increased imports of crops go together with increased imports of food, reflecting a reduction in the scale of agricultural sector in these regions. In contrast, the OECD Pacific regions are projected to reduce imports of both crops and food products, although the changes are very small. In between are countries such as Russia that are projected to observe a substitution effect: increased exports of crops go hand in hand with increased imports of food. Such changes in specialisation patterns typically exploit the variation in relative prices across commodities and regions.

4.2. Results for the land bottleneck scenario

Biophysical consequences

This scenario explores the economic effects of changes in land availability from urban sprawl and natural area protection and the associated changes in land productivity (i.e. yield impacts).[5] Urban sprawl can (potentially) impact land productivity if built-up areas are disproportionately often located on fertile soils and agriculture has to reallocate to other less productive locations. This can result in lower overall food crop yields and thus a larger agricultural land area to compensate for these productivity losses (to maintain regional agricultural production). Natural area protection can impact land productivity in a similar fashion, in particular where very suitable land would become unavailable for agricultural uses.

In the IMAGE model the potential productivity of crops, a function of climate and soil quality, is just one factor in the attractiveness of grid cells for agricultural production.

Other factors include the proximity of existing urban and agricultural areas, accessibility (roads, water bodies) and slope. As a consequence, the impact can also go in the other direction if agriculture is relocated to other parts of the region with higher productivity, that were not selected in the baseline due to the other spatial allocation factors. Table 4.2 shows the resulting yield changes in 2060 and illustrates that the impact on food crop yields varies considerably between regions, but also between crops within regions. Additional analyses (not shown) indicate that in almost all regions the yield impact of natural area protection is much smaller than urban sprawl, which indicates that nature reserves typically will not occupy grid cells more suitable for agriculture; therefore the following discussion will mainly focus on the impact of urban sprawl.

Table 4.2. **Changes in crop yields in 2060 in the land bottleneck scenario**

(Percentage change from baseline)

		Temperate cereals	Rice	Maize	Tropical cereals	Pulses	Roots & tubers	Oil crops
OECD America	Canada	0%		-4%	7%	1%	-6%	-2%
	Mexico	-7%	-1%	-1%	-4%	-5%	-4%	-2%
	United States	1%	-2%	0%	0%	1%	0%	0%
OECD Europe	OECD EU	1%	-9%	-13%	-6%	-1%	-5%	-1%
	Other OECD	-1%	11%	-5%	-1%	-9%	-2%	0%
OECD Pacific	Australia & New Zealand	0%	0%	0%	-11%	3%	-9%	0%
	Japan	1%	6%			1%	0%	-1%
	Korea		-3%	-1%	-1%	3%	0%	2%
Rest of Europe & Asia	China	0%	-5%	-1%	-1%	2%	0%	-3%
	Non-OECD EU	0%	-56%	2%	3%	-1%	-2%	1%
	Russia	-1%	6%	0%	0%	0%	-1%	0%
	Caspian region	0%	1%	-1%	1%	-1%	0%	-1%
	Other Europe	0%	-1%	-1%	-6%	4%	0%	-1%
Latin America	Brazil	-2%	-1%	-1%	-1%	-2%	-3%	-2%
	Other Latin America	-1%	1%	-1%	-2%	-1%	1%	0%
Middle East & North Africa	Middle East	-2%	-5%	3%	-1%	0%	-15%	-5%
	North Africa	2%	-4%	-1%	-2%	-2%	2%	2%
South & South-East Asia	ASEAN 9	0%	2%	2%	2%	3%	2%	5%
	Indonesia		1%	0%	-1%	1%	1%	0%
	India	0%	0%	0%	1%	-7%	2%	3%
	Other Asia	-1%	2%	-2%	-1%	-3%	2%	-1%
Sub-Saharan Africa	South Africa	2%	0%	2%	1%	3%	2%	3%
	Other Africa	0%	1%	1%	0%	0%	0%	-1%

StatLink ⧉ http://dx.doi.org/10.1787/888933555342

Note: Averages over irrigated and rainfed production are shown. Temperate cereals comprise wheat, rye, oats and barley. Empty cells reflect situations where no significant production of those crops takes place.

Source: IMAGE model.

With relatively few exceptions, the yield impact per crop type in most regions is relatively limited. As argued above, the sign of the impact can differ between crops. Higher yields can be the result of shift towards more productive land, see above, but also reallocation within the region can lead to some crops experiencing a lower yield and others a higher yield. Some deviations from the baseline are more significant: e.g. tropical cereals in Canada, Australia and New Zealand; rice in non-OECD EU; and roots and tubers in Middle East, but these typically concern less important crops in those regions and the numbers may represent "noise" rather than "signal". In OECD-EU and Mexico the impact exceeds 4% loss for several crops, including important ones: in OECD-EU including maize (-13%), rice (-9%) and roots and tubers (-5%); in Mexico temperate cereals (-7%), pulses (-5%) and roots and tubers (-4%).

In the United States, Other Africa and the Caspian region there is little effect on land productivity. In Other Africa – despite a significant increase due to population and urbanisation trends in the baseline – and in the Caspian region, the urban area is small compared to the total area in 2060, even in the land bottleneck scenario: 2.7% and 1.7%. However, this is not the case in the United States where built-up land makes up 11% of the total surface in the land bottleneck scenario. Besides the share of built-up land it also matters if plenty alternative locations are available suitable for food crop production. As a consequence, agricultural yields in these regions are hardly affected by the imposed land bottlenecks and the agricultural land area also does not differ between counterfactual and baseline scenario.

Impacts on net agricultural land area are thus very small in these regions. Still, biodiversity and carbon stocks can be affected as relocation also plays a role here. If agriculture shifts to previously unused natural land, the conversion is bound to release much of the carbon stock. And the loss of natural quality and biodiversity is instantaneous on the new agricultural land, but only recovers with delay on the land converted from agriculture to nature. In Mexico, Brazil, EU OECD 4 Larger countries, Other OECD Eurasia, EU non-OECD countries, Russia, Middle East, Other Asia and China there is a small yield effect; i.e. crop yields are lower – albeit sometimes marginally – in the counterfactual than in the baseline scenario. As stated, additional analyses indicate that the effect of urban sprawl is generally larger than natural area protection. This also applies to these regions, and most of the yield impact should thus be attributed to urban sprawl. Nonetheless, the yield impacts of urban sprawl still remain very modest in most of these regions (Mexico, Brazil, EU OECD 4 Larger countries, EU non-OECD countries, Middle East) and is almost negligible in some others (Other OECD Eurasia, Russia, Other Asia). In most cases, crop yields decrease only a few percent although some minor crops show a more substantial decrease. These small yield losses mean that the agricultural area differs only marginally between the counterfactual scenario and the baseline.

In ASEAN 9 countries all crop yields are (marginally) higher in the counterfactual than in the baseline scenario. The reason for this must be that the new sites are more suitable than the current sites. The positive yield impacts translate into a smaller food crop area in the counterfactual scenario than in the baseline.

In several regions (Canada, Russia, Other Latin America, Indonesia, India and Other Asia), food crop yields respond in mixed positive and negative directions to urban sprawl and natural area protection. In these regions some crops have slightly lower yields, whereas other crops slightly higher yields in the counterfactual scenario compared to the baseline. But the overall, net impact of these yield impacts remains negligible; i.e. the yield gains and losses in the counterfactual scenario offset each other and the agricultural area is therefore hardly different from the baseline; see Figure 4.6.

Figure 4.6. **Changes in land use change between 2015 and 2060
in the land bottleneck scenario**

(Change from baseline in thousand square kilometres)

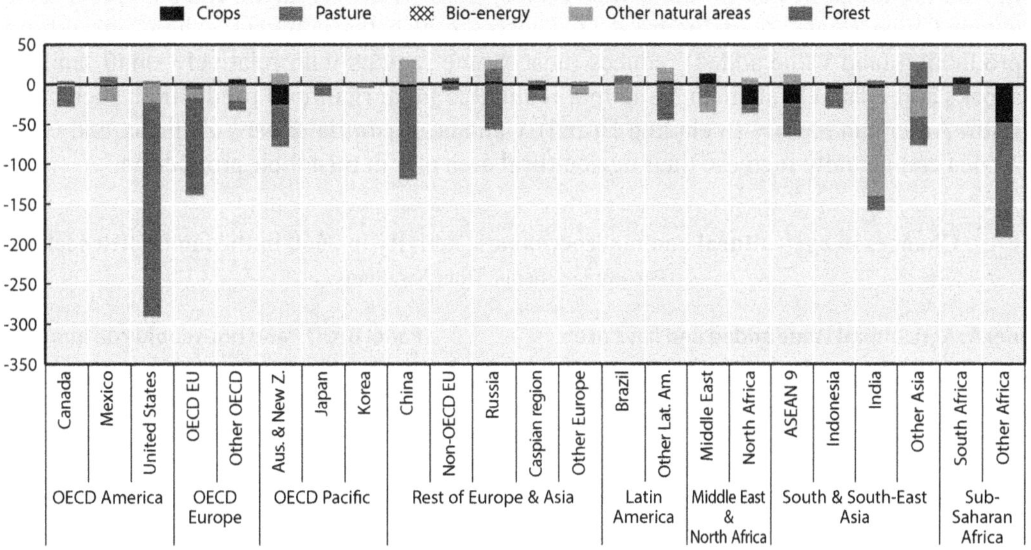

Note: Figure depicts absolute deviation from baseline in the amount of land use change between 2015 and 2060.

Source: IMAGE model.

While the impact on the net foodcrop area is relatively limited, in particular the larger urban area assumed in the land bottleneck scenario has a much more significant effect on the forest area; see Figure 4.6. The percentage change in pristine forest area refers to the change from 2015 to 2060 observed in the baseline and the counterfactual, rather than the state in 2060. This indicator is chosen because the land bottleneck already changes landcover in 2015. The United States present an interesting example, with no change in total foodcrop area, yet 16% more loss of pristine forest than the baseline. Compared with the baseline, the relocation induced by more urban sprawl and nature protection occurs at the expense of land not used in the baseline.

For the world as a whole, the foodcrop area remains almost unchanged from the baseline, while the pristine forest area decreases by 3%-points more than the baseline trend from 2015 to 2060.

Economic consequences

In this scenario, the IMAGE model results provide two inputs for ENV-Linkages: a change in yields for different crops in different regions, and a change in the potential supply of land for agricultural production. As the IMAGE results discussed above have shown, a typical response to the forced reallocation of agricultural activity is to intensify production of certain crops on highly productive lands to ensure sufficient production of food on a limited amount of land. Nonetheless, the land bottleneck can have significant effects in countries where land reallocation is less of an option.

The reduction in land that is available for agriculture ranges from -2% to -14% (see Figure 4.6). However, countries that are closer to their maximum potential land will not be able to accommodate the land shock as easily as countries that have more room for land conversion (potentially at the expense of other policy objectives, such as those for biodiversity and maintenance of ecosystems, as discussed above). The largest reductions in land use are projected for the United States, OECD Europe, Japan, India and to a lesser extent China (Panel A of Figure 4.7). These are also the countries where agricultural production (and value added) reduces most. Some regions with relatively small land use shocks and relatively abundant land that is suitable for agricultural production, such as the Latin American regions (including Brazil), Canada, Australia & New Zealand, and Other Africa can actually increase their agricultural area and in turn their production.

Figure 4.7. Changes in agricultural and macroeconomic activity in 2060 in the land bottleneck scenario
(Percentage change from baseline)

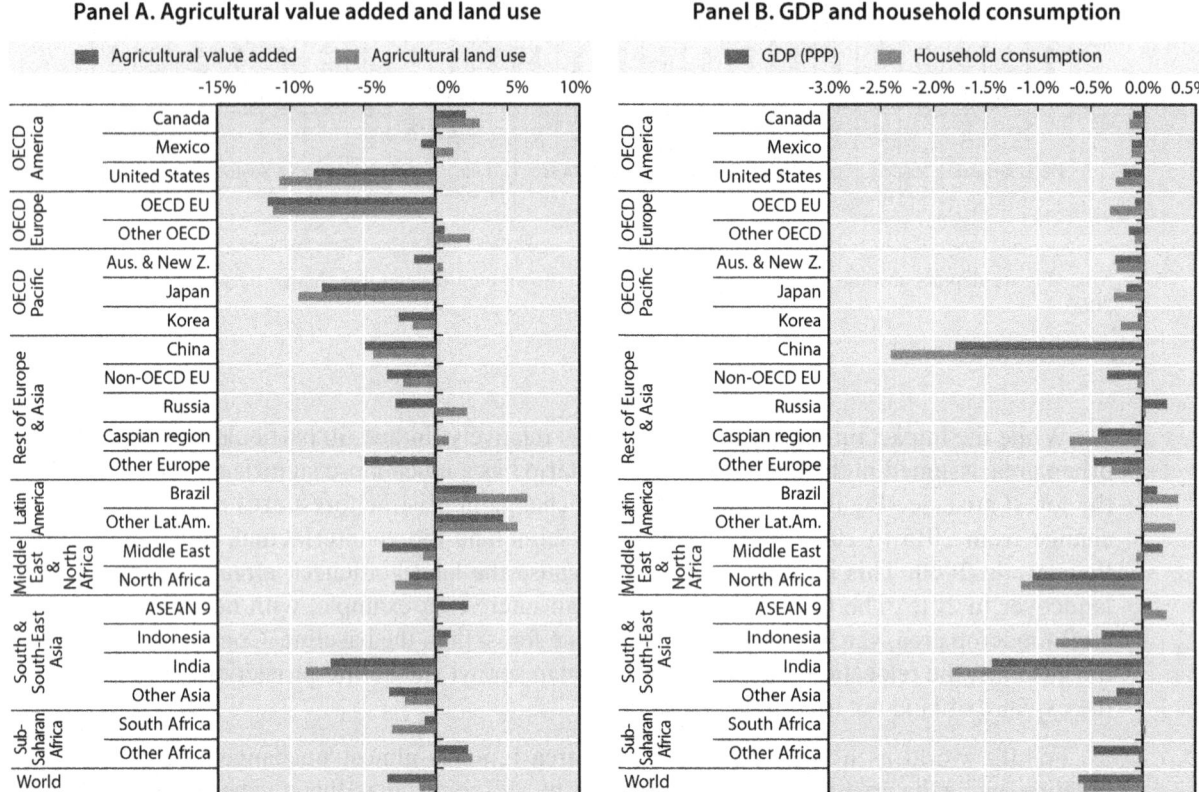

Note: In Panel A, agriculture refers to all crop sectors and the livestock sector.

Source: ENV-Linkages model.

In macroeconomic terms, the major losses from the land scenario arise in China, India and North Africa, as shown in Panel B of Figure 4.7. Small gains can be reaped in Latin America (including Brazil), the ASEAN region and – at least in GDP terms – Russia and the Middle East. In the OECD regions, the relatively small share of agriculture in GDP (see Figure 3.4) prevents large macroeconomic repercussions. Furthermore, the United States and Japan manage to keep agricultural production losses smaller than land use reductions, i.e. they intensify agricultural production (see Table 4.2). In contrast, in China the more modest land use reductions translate into larger agricultural production losses, not least because average yields decline by around 2%.

Regardless of the opportunity to reallocate agricultural land, the pressure on the land markets increases, agricultural production becomes more expensive and consumer prices for food increase (Figure 4.8). The effect is the strongest in China and India, which combine relatively large yield losses for essential crops with significant reductions in agricultural land.

Figure 4.8. **Changes in consumer prices in 2060 in the land bottleneck scenario**

(Percentage change from baseline)

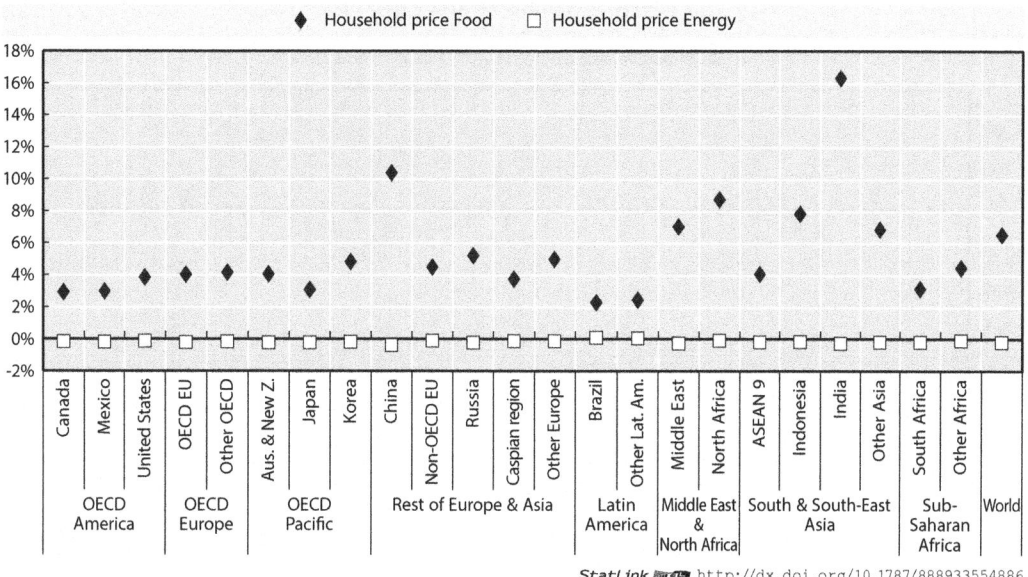

StatLink http://dx.doi.org/10.1787/888933554886

Note: Food prices reflect a weighted average of all crops, livestock and food products; energy prices reflect a weighted average of coal, oil, gas and electricity.

Source: ENV-Linkages model.

Most regions slightly reduce their import shares of crops, in line with the global contraction of agricultural trade (see Panel A of Figure 4.9 for changes in trade patterns). Main exceptions are the United States, OECD EU and India, for whom the large reduction in domestic production needs to be compensated by additional imports to avoid large reductions in food consumption. Figure 4.9 also shows that India also increases the import share of food (crops and food products together), while this hardly happens in the United States and OECD EU.

Apart from India, the other regions that start to significantly increase the share of food that is imported are China and North Africa. This is driven by increased imports of food products, to compensate for the reduced supply of food by domestic producers, which is in turn driven by the loss of crop production and increased domestic production costs. In several OECD countries, not least Canada and Japan, the share of imports in total food demand is projected to decrease below baseline levels. For most of these regions, increased domestic production is the main driver for this result, but in Japan, it reflects a partial withdrawal from the international market: domestic production decreases, and in the model simulations this triggers a more than proportionate reduction in exports, combined with a small reduction in imports.

As the costs of production go up in India, Indonesia and other countries, the budget share that households have to spend on food increases as well. As explained above, the increased food budget share in India primarily reflects the larger domestic production costs. In regions such as Indonesia, where agricultural production can expand, the increased budget share comes mostly from the increased world market price for crops and food products, which also influences local prices.

Figure 4.9. **Changes in agricultural trade and food security in 2060 in the land bottleneck scenario**
(Percentage change from baseline)

Panel A. International trade in crops

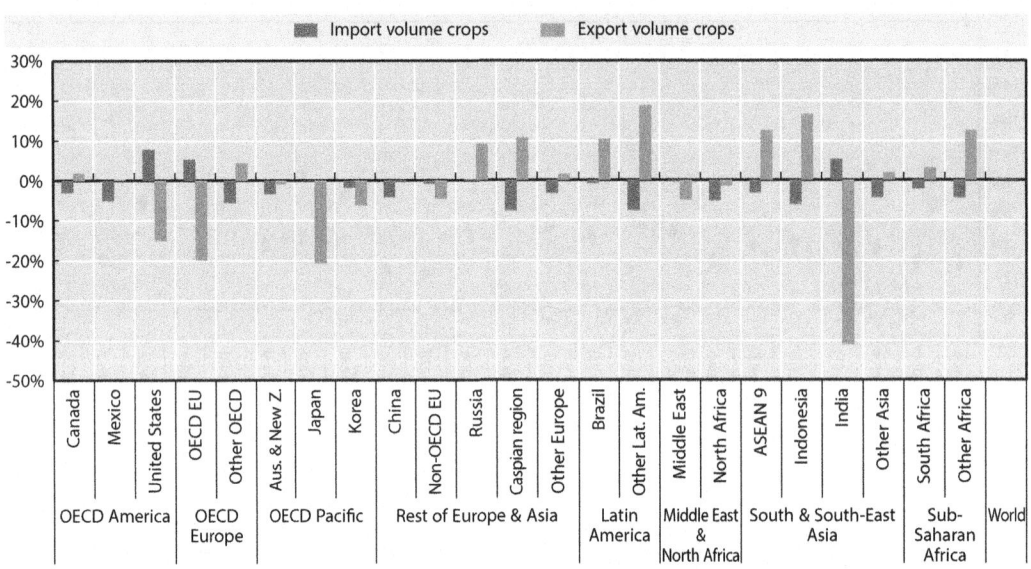

Panel B. Budget and import shares (percentage-point change)

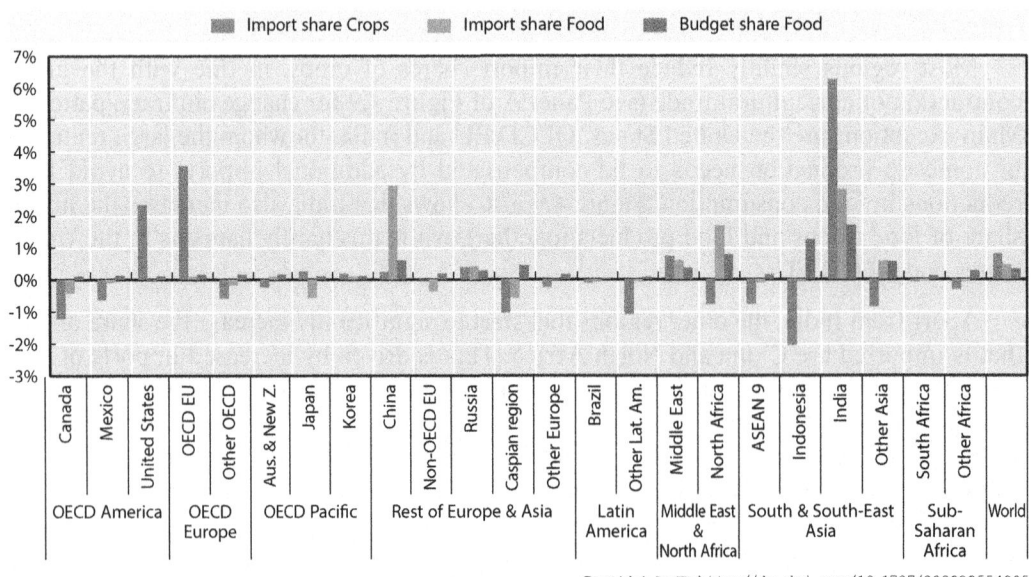

StatLink http://dx.doi.org/10.1787/888933554905

Note: In panel B, the budget share reflects consumption of all crops, livestock and food products; import shares are separated between crops and food products.

Source: ENV-Linkages model.

4.3. Results for the energy bottleneck scenario

Biophysical consequences

As described in Section 2.4, the energy bottleneck scenario focusses on large-scale production of energy carriers from biomass, commonly referred to as biofuels. The main nexus issue arising is the land required to produce biomass feedstock that can be converted into biofuels, either at or close to the place of production, or near the place of consumption of the fuels. Land availability to sustain the biomass production is often not adjacent to major consuming locations. This holds at different scales: cities are major consumers, but land in the immediate surroundings is subject to competing claims, therefore scarce and costly. At larger scales, suitable land is mostly more available in countries and regions of limited energy demand. Trade of feedstock or energy products will balance supply and demand within regions.

At the global scale, more than 5.5 million km² land is needed to produce woody and non-woody (grasses, etc.) feedstock in short rotation and annual cycles. Currently prevailing practices to produce energy from food crops such as maize, wheat, sunflower and palm oil, are deemed inefficient in the longer term and are not considered here. Although limited quantities of these foodcrop based products may continue to be grown at specific locations, here the focus is on the so-called second-generation supply chains using dedicated woody and non-woody crops, such as coppice, miscanthus and other high-yielding species. As illustrated in Figure 4.10, the energy crop area is distributed over pretty much all countries and regions, though very unevenly. Production is concentrated in Latin America (Brazil and other Latin America), in South-East Asia (Indonesia and ASEAN 9) and in Other Africa. The large area in Oceania results from the regional demand-supply balancing algorithm in the model. The result should be treated with caution, as it may be a model construct rather than a plausible prospect, warranting further investigation.

Figure 4.10. **Changes in land use change between 2015 and 2060
in the energy bottleneck scenario**

(Change from baseline in thousand square kilometres)

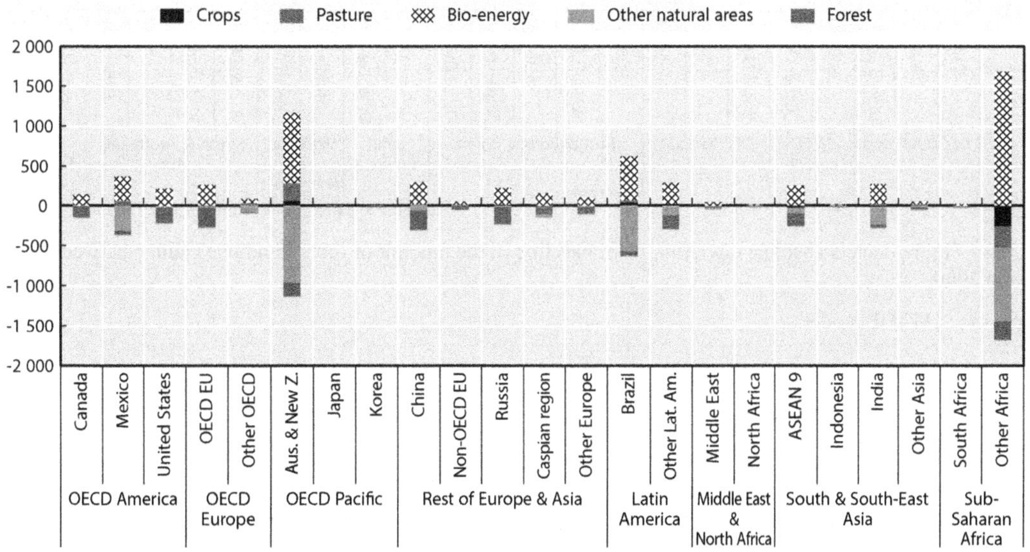

StatLink ᴍᴤᴳ http://dx.doi.org/10.1787/888933554924

Note: Figure depicts absolute deviation from baseline in the amount of land use change between 2015 and 2060.

Source: IMAGE model.

In the IMAGE model in this case, the additional land to grow energy crops goes at the expense of cropland used to grow food and feed, see also the economic consequences below. However, given the allocation rules that apply to all crop types, the cropland area for food production is not affected much. By construction, forest land for nature conservation and ecosystem service provisioning purposes is protected; losses are projected to be concentrated in particular in regions with limited supply of suitable, untapped resources of other natural land comprising savannah, scrubland and natural grassland, Hence, the dominant conversion concerns the other natural land types. Partly, the loss of forest land in the energy bottleneck scenario compared with the baseline projection is explained by the choices made for abandoned land in the IMAGE model. If forests are cut for conversion to agricultural land or for timber production, the areas are open for new purposes, such as growing bio-energy crops. So, less former forest land is left to regrow gradually to reach a (semi-) natural state decades later. Until the re-growing forests reach a more mature state, they are considered to be managed. Hence, in the energy bottleneck case the managed forest area is smaller than in the baseline, but in addition unmanaged forest is also affected; see also Figure 4.11.

Figure 4.11. **Change in mature and managed forest area in 2060 in the energy bottleneck scenario**

(Change from baseline in thousand square kilometres)

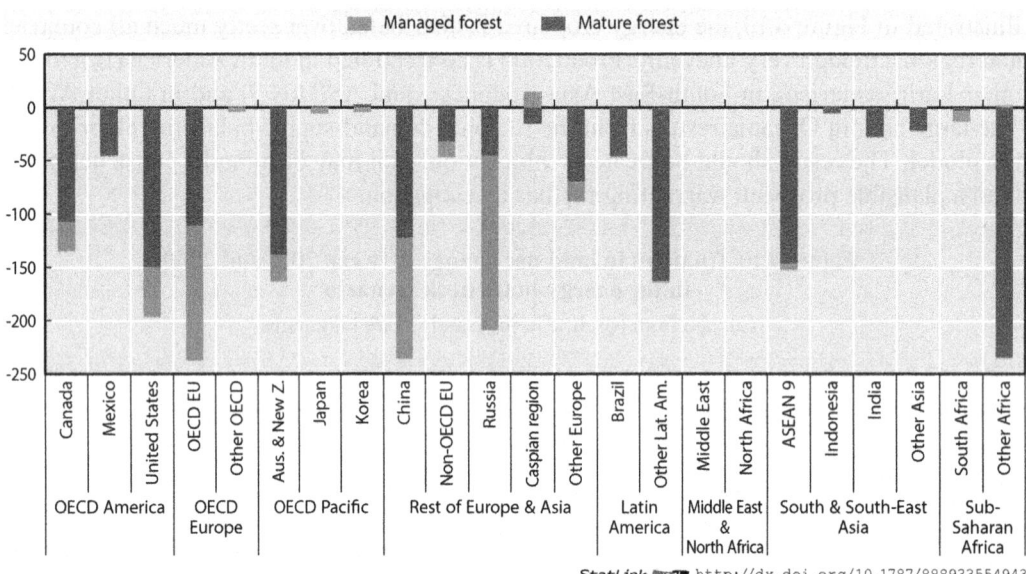

StatLink http://dx.doi.org/10.1787/888933554943

Note: Figure depicts absolute deviation from baseline in the amount of forest land use change between 2015 and 2060.

Source: IMAGE model.

As confirmed, the land occupied by foodcrops changes due to reallocation of land to find land to produce energy crops. Depending on the availability of new land and the productivity thereof, the sign can go either way, as is shown in Table 4.3. Whether the net effect is more food crop area or less, see Figure 4.10, depends on the impact per crop and the share of each crop in the total area. Russia is an example where yield positive and negative impacts occur, and the net effect on the area is limited. For most crops and in most regions the difference is relatively small, but in some instances the change in yield is significant. In Australia and New Zealand, almost all crops have much lower yields except rice and maize, which suggests food crops are shifted to less favourable land. And in Other OECD a lot of additional natural land is taken into production to compensate the large production of bio-energy crops, and on average the new land is less productive. As indicated earlier, the energy bottleneck scenario results for this region warrant further scrutiny and must be treated with caution.

Table 4.3. **Changes in crop yields in 2060 in the energy bottleneck scenario**

(Percentage change from baseline)

		Temperate cereals	Rice	Maize	Tropical cereals	Pulses	Roots & tubers	Oil crops
OECD America	Canada	0%		0%	0%	2%	1%	0%
	Mexico	0%	0%	-1%	-1%	-4%	-4%	1%
	United States	0%	0%	0%	0%	0%	2%	0%
OECD Europe	OECD EU	0%	-1%	-1%	-4%	-3%	-3%	-1%
	Other OECD	0%	4%	0%	0%	-17%	0%	0%
OECD Pacific	Australia & New Zealand	-19%	0%	3%	-14%	-18%	-27%	-28%
	Japan	-1%	0%			-2%	0%	-2%
	Korea		0%	0%	0%	1%	0%	0%
Rest of Europe & Asia	China	0%	0%	0%	0%	1%	-1%	0%
	Non-OECD EU	0%	0%	1%	4%	8%	2%	1%
	Russia	-1%	4%	5%	-9%	4%	-1%	0%
	Caspian region	-1%	-3%	0%	2%	2%	1%	-18%
	Other Europe	0%	4%	-1%	-3%	8%	1%	0%
Latin America	Brazil	-4%	-2%	-2%	-2%	-5%	-7%	-5%
	Other Latin America	-1%	0%	-1%	-1%	-2%	0%	-2%
Middle East & North Africa	Middle East	0%	-1%	0%	0%	3%	-1%	1%
	North Africa	0%	0%	0%	0%	-1%	7%	0%
South & South-East Asia	ASEAN 9	0%	2%	2%	2%	5%	2%	5%
	Indonesia		0%	0%	-1%	1%	-1%	1%
	India	-1%	-1%	0%	1%	-1%	1%	1%
	Other Asia	0%	-1%	-3%	-2%	0%	0%	-5%
Sub-Saharan Africa	South Africa	0%	0%	3%	1%	0%	0%	4%
	Other Africa	-1%	-2%	-1%	-1%	0%	0%	-3%

StatLink ⟨⟩ http://dx.doi.org/10.1787/888933555361

Note: Averages over irrigated and rainfed production are shown. Temperate cereals comprise wheat, rye, oats and barley. Empty cells reflect situations where no significant production of those crops takes place.

Source: IMAGE model.

The loss of forest, both managed and unmanaged, and other natural land is associated with major losses of natural quality, biodiversity and a range of ecosystem services they could have provided. The latter include water- and (local) climate regulation, tourism, habitat for endangered species and others. The change in land-use also gives rise to reductions in carbons stocks in living and dead biomass and soils. In the case of forests it is less of a loss, than an opportunity foregone to store carbon in the re-growing forests.

Recognising the specifically high nature value of forests, and their important contributions to providing ecosystem services, the development of forest area can be considered a relevant proxy for the state of the natural environment. Particularly relevant are the so-called mature forests, which are not affected by large-scale human activities (although potentially affected by lower impact activities such as hunting and gathering, hiking, etc.). In the baseline projection, the total global forest area declines only slightly by just over 1% between 2015 and 2060. However, this is net effect from expansion in most OECD regions, Russia and China and losses in other regions including Latin America, ASEAN and Other Asia, and Other Africa due to expansion of cropland. As discussed above, in the energy bottleneck scenario the net forest area decreases in all countries and regions, and compared to the baseline projection in 2060 it shrinks by 5.2%. In line with the energy crop production areas, biggest losses in absolute terms occur in Latin America, ASEAN and Other Africa; see Figure 4.10. In relative terms, the percentage loss is particularly high in Mexico (-21%), Europe (EU-OECD -11%; other EU and other OECD: -15/-22%), ASEAN 9 (-15%) and Other Africa (-10%).

As the managed forest area expands in the baseline due to increased demand for timber, the mature forest area declines more than the total forest area: -4.5% versus -1.2%. In the energy bottleneck case another 4.5% of mature forest is lost, substantially more than managed forest. This is partially explained by the fact that part of the additional area needed to accommodate energy crops on top of food crops is established on the land that in the baseline is converted into managed forest.

From a climate change perspective, the changes in carbon stocks imply that the emissions from land-use end up higher than in the baseline projection. This is a transient phenomenon, peaking in the 2025-30 period at around 1.5 GtC/year, as shown in Figure 4.12. Because less forest is regrowing after harvest, they sequester and store less carbon in biomass and soils. Also, additional land is deforested with loss of carbon stocks as a consequence. And finally, growing energy and foodcrops on other natural land can also have effects for the carbon stocks and flows. As a net result, over the time horizon 2015-60 the remaining carbon stock in the energy bottleneck scenario is around 24 GtC

Figure 4.12. **Land-use related carbon emissions in 2060 in the baseline and energy bottleneck scenarios**

(Megatonnes carbon)

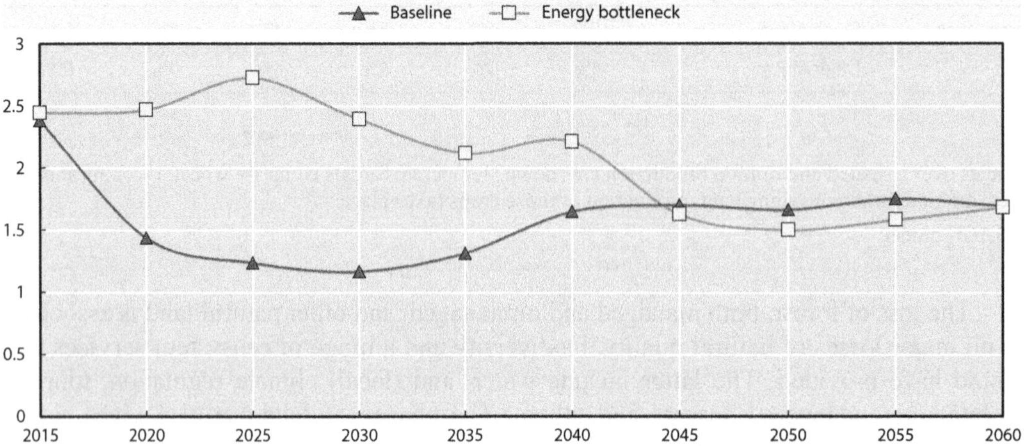

Source: IMAGE model.

smaller than in the baseline. In terms of GHG emissions, relevant for climatic change, this amounts to 88 Gt CO_2 more in the atmosphere over the period 2015 to 2060 as a result of the bioenergy shock.

Obviously, at the point of use biofuels substitute for fossil fuels and thereby avoid the associated CO_2 emissions. This is explored in the section on economic consequences below, which shows that there is a significant rebound effect such that avoided fuel combustion emissions are substantially smaller than the volume of biofuels may at first glance indicate.

Economic consequences

As discussed above, the joint modelling framework cannot capture the full extent of energy bottlenecks in the nexus. Core linkages between energy and water, i.e. energy requirements for water supply and water requirements for energy supply, are discussed qualitatively in Annex B, but the focus of the quantitative analysis presented here is on the potential pressure on the land system from an ambitious biofuel production scenario. This is purely meant as an illustrative example of how the agricultural and energy sectors interact, and how these interactions affect the rest of the economy. The regional allocation of biofuel production is also exogenously determined, based on an assessment in IMAGE of the land that is potentially available for biofuel production (see Chapter 2), rather than on minimising the macroeconomic effects.

Figure 4.13 presents the volume of additional biofuel production by region; this is the input to the ENV-Linkages model. The markets for liquid fuel (oil) then respond to the increased supply by lowering oil prices and reducing the production of existing oil and biofuel (in short, "existing oil production"). The model projects that in most regions, on balance total liquid fuel production increases moderately (globally around 240 Mtoe, less than 3% of the projected global production). However, there are two major exceptions: Brazil and the Middle East. These are two large producers in the baseline, and therefore the ones with the most to lose from the new biofuel supply. In Brazil, this is compensated by a

Figure 4.13. **Changes in liquid fuel production in 2060 in the energy bottleneck scenario**
(Change from baseline in mtoe)

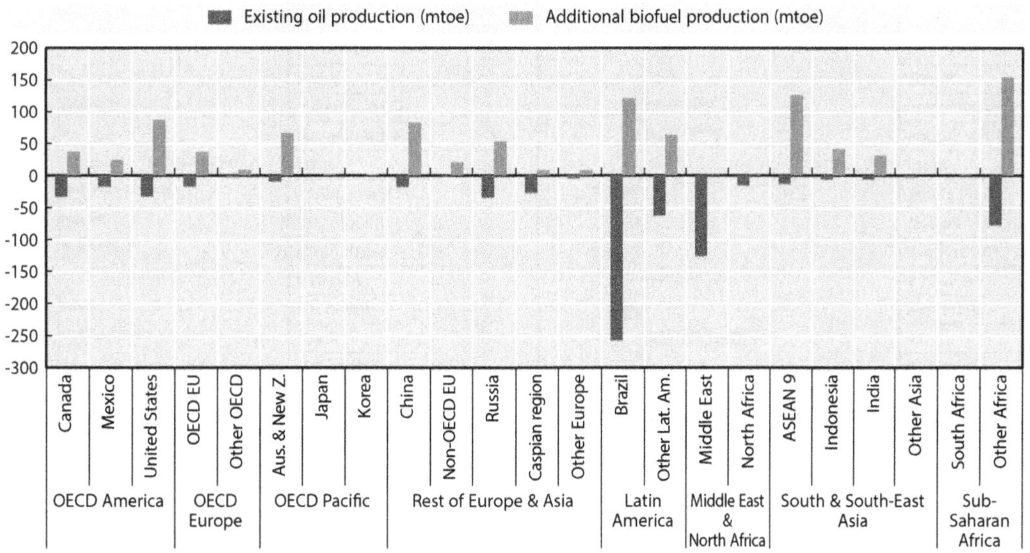

Source: ENV-Linkages model.

significant biofuel production, but the capacity for biofuels is much smaller in the Middle East, and therefore hardly any biofuel production is projected there.

The agricultural systems also undergo important transformations. The expansion of the biofuel sector is detrimental to food crop production due to reduced land availability (and some induced effects on yields) and therefore agricultural value added decreases in many regions, as highlighted in Panel A of Figure 4.14. Losses are especially large in Australia and New Zealand. The crowding out effect of the new biofuel production is relatively strong there. But although the percentage losses in agricultural production are largest in these countries, the contribution of the agricultural sector to the economy is larger in some of the other affected regions, especially the Caspian region. Hence, the moderate agricultural sector losses there translate into more significant macroeconomic losses.

In the energy sector, the additional biofuel production crowds out some existing energy production (Panel B of Figure 4.14). Losses are largest in Brazil, in line with the significant reduction in oil production in this region. But the contribution of the energy sector to the economy is also reduced in e.g. India, not least due to a decline in overall economic activity. The reduction in oil production in most countries leads to lower value added generated in the energy sector, despite the rebound effect of the policy on energy

Figure 4.14. **Changes in sectoral economic activity in 2060 in the energy bottleneck scenario**
(Percentage change from baseline)

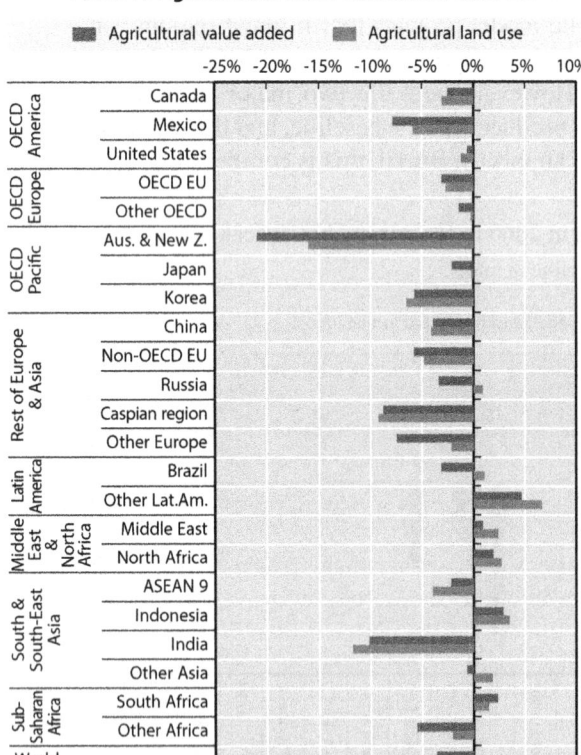

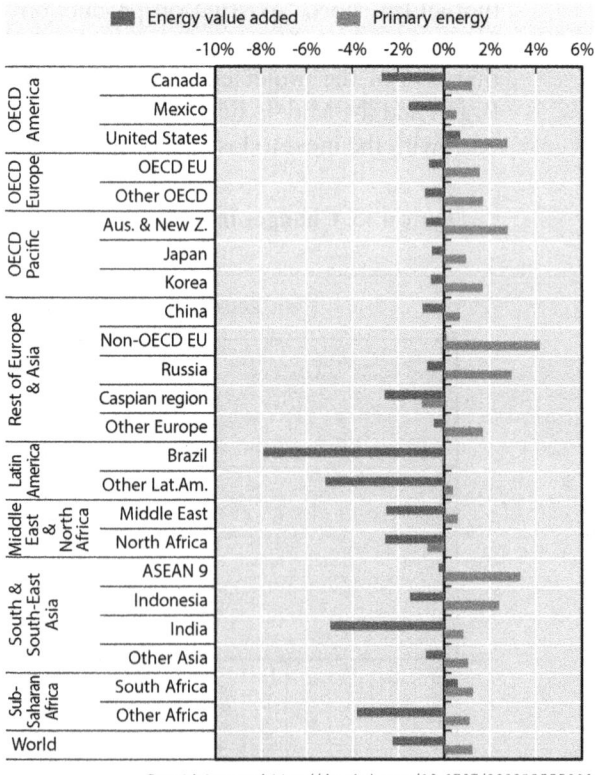

Panel A. Agricultural value added and land use

Panel B. Energy sector value added and primary energy demand

StatLink http://dx.doi.org/10.1787/888933555000

Note: In Panel A, agriculture refers to all crop sectors and the livestock sector; in Panel B, energy refers to coal, oil, gas and electricity; energy sector value added excludes additional biomass production.

Source: ENV-Linkages model.

production in general. There are a few small exceptions, however, most notably the United States, where the increase in economic activity extends to other energy sectors, not least electricity production.

The additional fuel production is detrimental to the existing oil exporters. As the global economy is boosted, however, global demand for energy increases. Not only oil markets are boosted, but the global gas market is also stimulated (not shown in Figure 4.13; for gas production, the substitution effect to oil is smaller than the scale effect from increased energy production). The net effect on total primary energy production is positive in all regions, and especially energy exporters can benefit from this.

Panel A of Figure 4.15 shows that Russia, the ASEAN region (including Indonesia), Australia, New Zealand and the United States are projected to be able to increase their GDP and consumption levels in this bottleneck scenario significantly. The largest GDP gains are in Russia with roughly 3%; smaller gains are projected for several other regions. GDP losses are concentrated in China, the Caspian region, North Africa, India and Other Africa, i.e. the regions that rely most on agriculture. The expansion of the global energy markets particularly boosts Russia, which increases its gas exports; Russia also increases its total import volume. The smaller than expected GDP losses in e.g. the Middle East, which suffers from reduced oil exports and lower energy prices, is driven to a large extent by increased exports of industrial products in combination with reduced imports.[6]

Figure 4.15. **Changes in macroeconomic economic activity in 2060 in the energy bottleneck scenario**
(Percentage change from baseline)

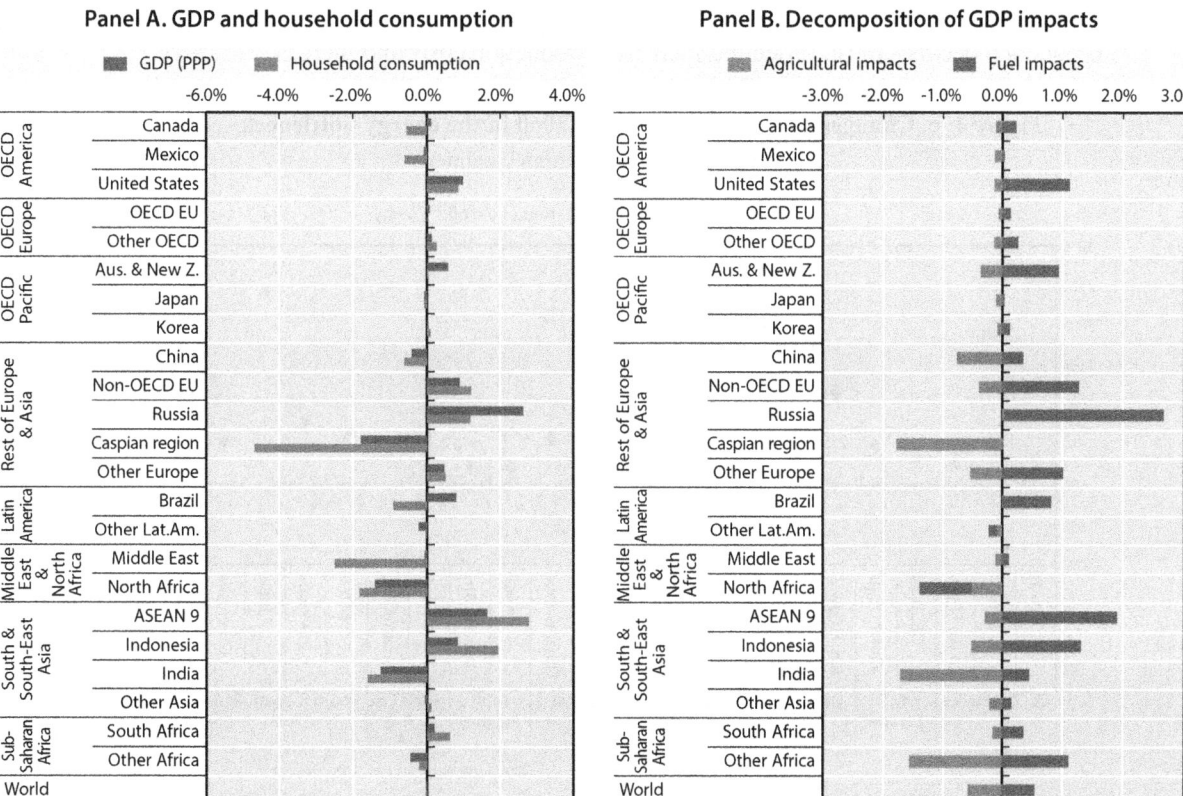

StatLink ᐧᐧᐧᐧᐧ http://dx.doi.org/10.1787/888933555019

Source: ENV-Linkages model.

The large oil production losses in Brazil and in the Middle East reduce consumption levels in these countries significantly more than GDP levels. In part, this is caused by the international trade effects explained above, and in part it reflects the negative pressure on income from a slowdown of capital accumulation.

The new biofuel production increases economic activity and in itself leads to macroeconomic gains. However, the biofuel production at least partially crowds out agricultural land use (as discussed above). Therefore, the agricultural impacts are mostly negative, and the net effect on the macro economy is mixed. Panel B of Figure 4.15 decomposes the total GDP effect into contributions of the shock to the energy system through the increased production of liquid fuel, and the shock to the agricultural system through changes in crop yields and available land for crop production.

The panel clearly shows the trade-off: virtually all the gains in GDP can be attributed to the effects of the increased biofuel production, whilst most of the losses are connected to the reduced agricultural yields and land use. There are a few exceptions, however: in a few countries, most notably North Africa, there are losses from the energy shock, as new biofuel production crowds out existing oil production. For a few regions, such as Russia, competitiveness gains from the agricultural shock compensate for the direct agricultural losses, following the international reallocation of agricultural production, along the lines discussed for the other bottlenecks.

Given the expansion of the energy sector and contraction of agriculture compared to the baseline projection, it is not surprising to see in Figure 4.16 that household prices of food increase and prices of energy decrease. The variation in food prices between countries is larger, reflecting the closer harmonisation of international prices for energy, and the more local markets for food. The largest increases in food prices occur in the regions where agricultural production declines most, reflecting increased production costs and increased scarcity.

Figure 4.16. **Changes in consumer prices in 2060 in the energy bottleneck scenario**

(Percentage change from baseline)

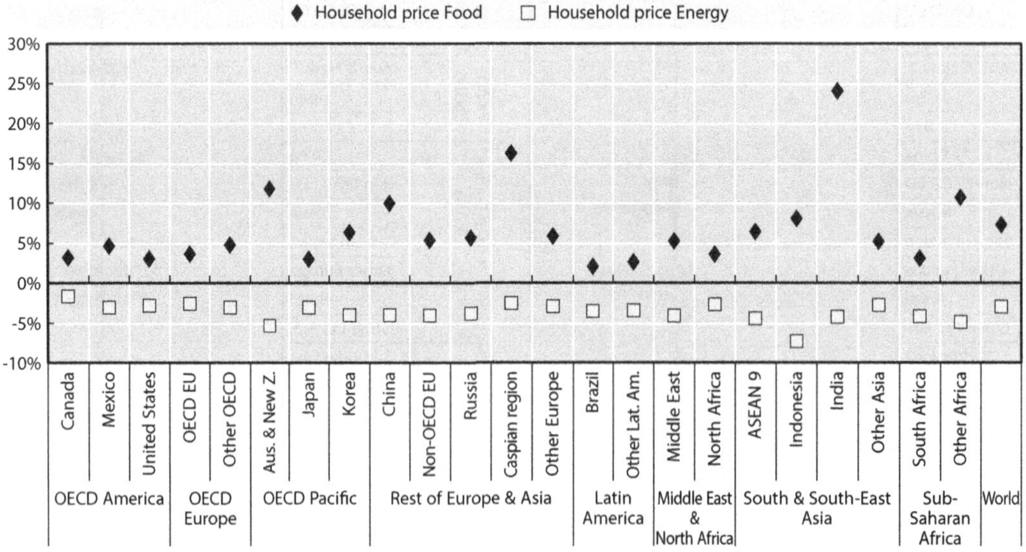

StatLink ⬛ http://dx.doi.org/10.1787/888933555038

Note: Food prices reflect a weighted average of all crops, livestock and food products; energy prices reflect a weighted average of coal, oil, gas and electricity.

Source: ENV-Linkages model.

Global international agricultural trade remains roughly at the baseline level, but with shifts between regions (Figure 4.17). India, Australia and New Zealand are on one side of the spectrum, with increased imports and reduced exports of agricultural commodities. For these countries, the biofuel production crowds out agricultural production, leading

Figure 4.17. **Changes in international trade for selected sectors in 2060 in the energy bottleneck scenario**

(Percentage change from baseline)

Panel A. Crops

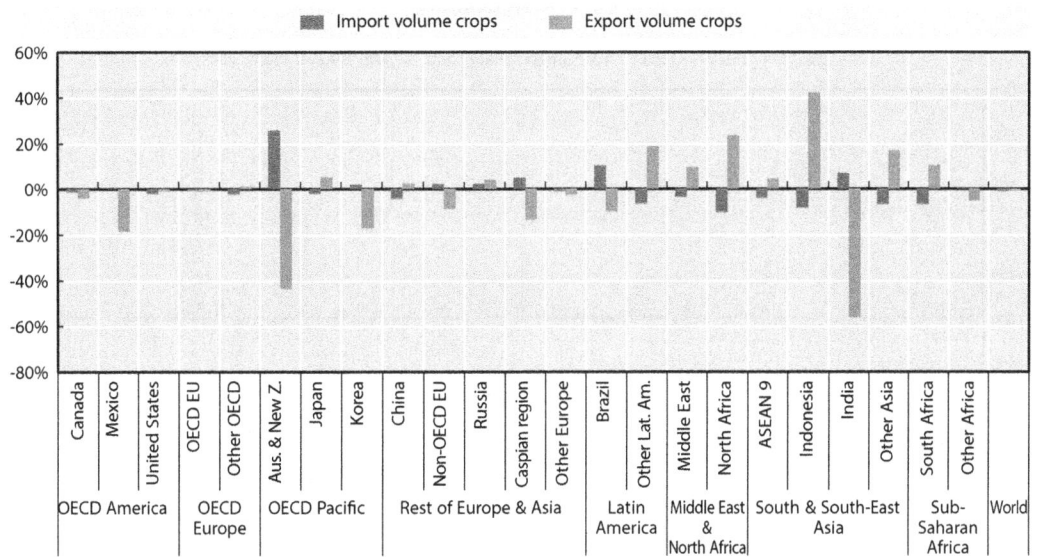

Panel B. Energy

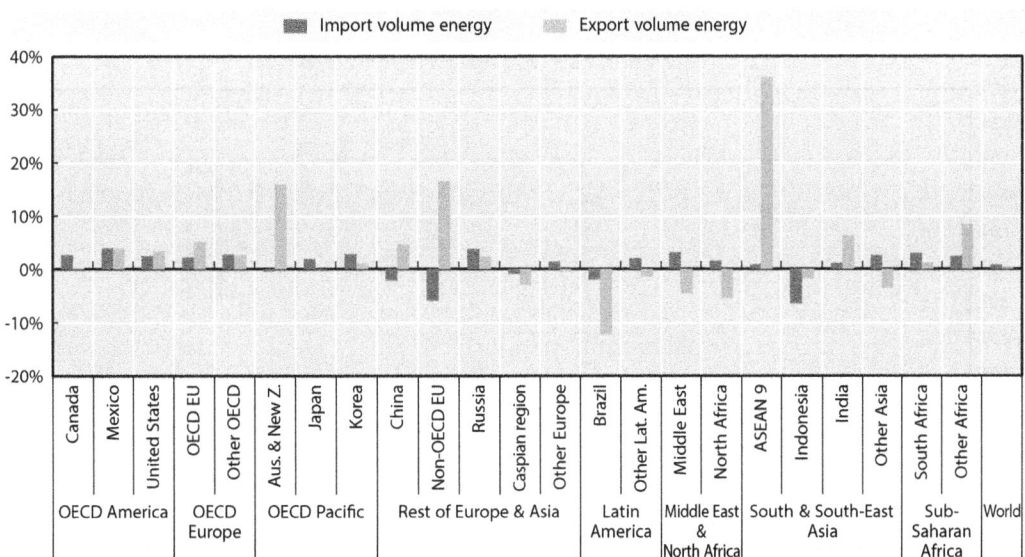

StatLink http://dx.doi.org/10.1787/888933555057

Note: In Panel A, crops refers to all crop sectors combined; in Panel B, energy refers to coal, oil, gas and electricity.

Source: ENV-Linkages model.

to lower domestic production and increased reliance on imports. Indonesia, North Africa and Latin America are at the other extreme, with significant increases in exports. In these regions, the land use requirements for biofuel production can easily be absorbed by taking new land into production; and in the case of North Africa there is virtually no additional biofuel production. Thus, agricultural production is not limited, and the competitiveness of their crop producers on the international market is improved.

Figure 4.18. **Changes in budget and import shares for selected sectors in 2060 in the energy bottleneck scenario**

(Percentage point change from baseline)

Panel A. Agriculture

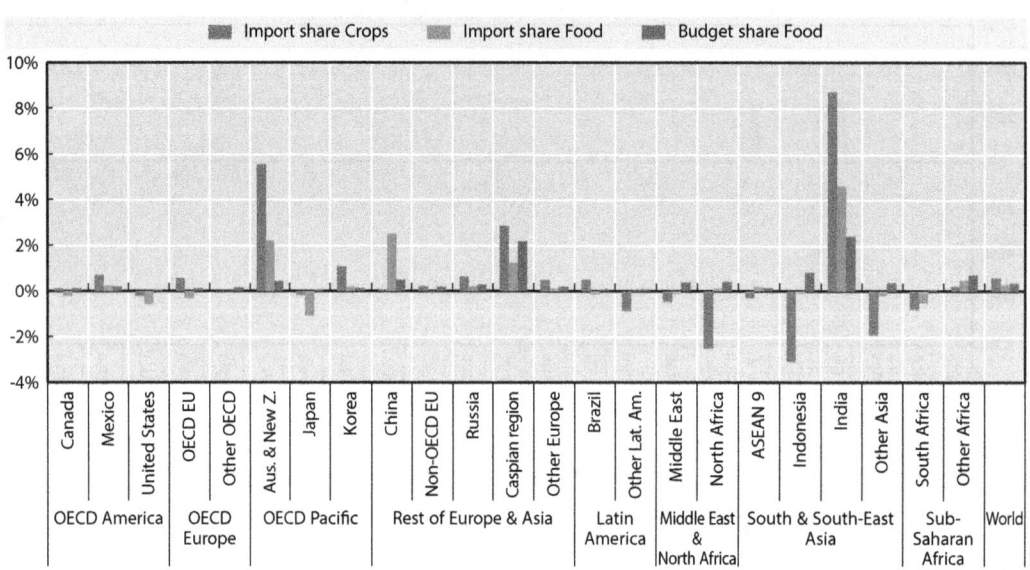

Panel B. Energy

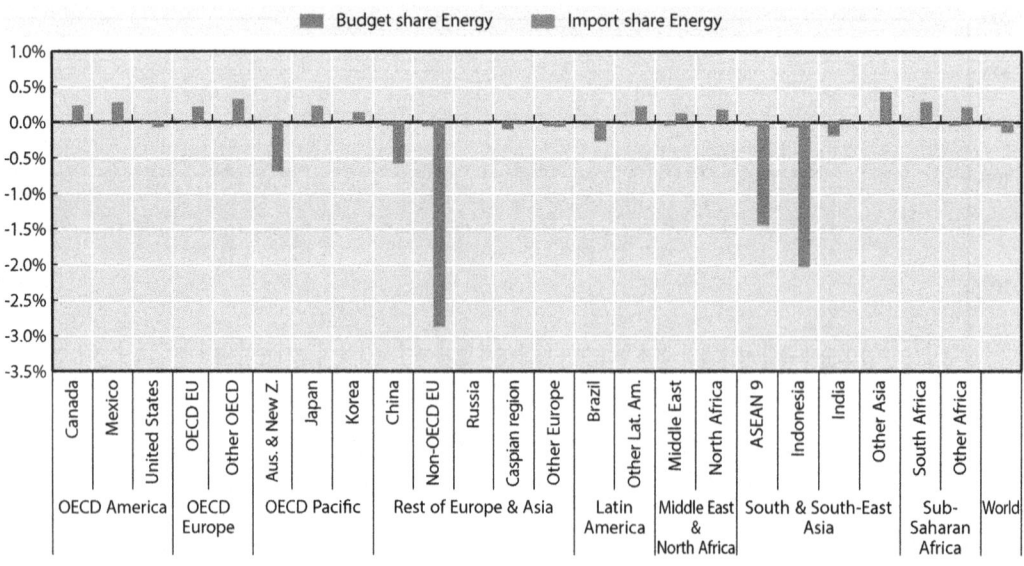

StatLink ⌐⌐⌐⌐ http://dx.doi.org/10.1787/888933555076

Note: In Panel A, the budget share reflects consumption of all crops, livestock and food products; import shares are separated between crops and food products; in Panel B energy refers to coal, oil, gas and electricity.

Source: ENV-Linkages model.

The changes in food products largely confirm these findings. Panel A of Figure 4.18 shows that in Australia and New Zealand, China, India and a few other regions both the food budget shares and the food import shares increase slightly. The increase in food budget shares is more pronounced in the regions where food prices increase the most. The United States and Japan, and to a lesser extent some other regions, can in contrast increase food self-sufficiency.

Panel B of Figures 4.17 and 4.18 highlight that the international trade effects for energy are in many regions opposite to those for crops. The budget shares for energy are virtually unchanged. Although energy prices are lower than in the baseline, there is a significant additional supply of liquid fuel that boosts energy consumption. The import shares of Non-OECD EU, the ASEAN regions (including Indonesia) and, to a lesser extent, Australia and New Zealand, China and Brazil, are reduced. These regions can improve their competitive position on both the domestic and international market: reduce imports and increase exports of energy. In most other regions, the import share increases slightly (less than half a percent-point) as the global energy market expands and total demand declines.

4.4. Results for the combined bottlenecks scenario

This section presents the results for a scenario combining the three types of nexus bottlenecks corresponding to land, water, and energy. It aims at answering how the various bottlenecks combine into a joint shock on the biophysical and economic system; and whether they reinforce or mitigate each other in terms of crop yields, agricultural land use, economic activity and the policy objectives, not least food security.

Biophysical consequences

The combined bottlenecks scenario aims to show how the three bottlenecks interact and add-up. While the previous scenarios each analysed the impact of a single type of bottlenecks (i.e. water bottleneck scenario, land bottleneck scenario and energy bottleneck scenario), the combined bottlenecks scenario implements all three simultaneously. Especially interesting is whether the combined impact of these bottlenecks is additive, or whether there is an interaction effect; i.e. is the combined impact of these bottlenecks simply the sum of its' components, or is it more or less? The multiple nexus interactions imply that the impact of bottlenecks in land-water-energy resources may not be fully captured if not taking all the elements of the nexus together. It is important to note that many of the interactions within the land-water-energy nexus are captured in the IMAGE modelling framework. Even though some important interactions are not represented in the current model, it still makes for a useful tool to study these interaction effects.

The element shared by all bottlenecks is their effect on availability of land to grow food and feed crops, accounting for suitability to sustain yields. Moving food production to other locations than in the baseline is thus bound to have effects on productivity, as shown in the preceding sections. The total effect of all bottlenecks together could simply be the sum of the three bottlenecks, which implies they are largely independent. If, however, a shift of crop land from one bottleneck would overlap geographically with the shift from other bottlenecks, the combined effect can be smaller. For example, if a grid cell depending on unsustainable groundwater would be unsuited due to the water constraint, but that grid cell would also fall within the boundaries of a protected nature site in the land constraint case, the effect would not add up as the grid cell can only be excluded from production once. In contrast, agriculture could shift to a new location due to failing supply of water in the water bottleneck case and move to a location close to an urban area or to an existing nature reserve. If in the combined case that new location would become unavailable also due to urban or nature reserve expansion (the land constraint), the total effect can become bigger than the sum as agriculture has to move to a more remote location, with possibly lower yields.

Table 4.4 shows the impacts of the combined bottlenecks on food crop yields in the various regions. Compared with those of the individual bottleneck scenarios (see Tables 4.1, 4.2, and 4.3), in many regions food crop yields are most affected in the combined bottlenecks scenario. In these regions (e.g. Mexico, Other Latin America, China), the impacts of the individual bottlenecks are negative in all scenarios and their combined impact thus results in the largest impact in the combined bottlenecks scenario. For instance, in China, the water bottleneck leads to 7% reduction in rice yields (Table 4.1), 5% reduction in the land bottleneck scenario (Table 4.4) and no change in the energy bottleneck scenario

Table 4.4. **Changes in crop yields in 2060 in the combined bottlenecks scenario**

(Percentage change from baseline)

		Temperate cereals	Rice	Maize	Tropical cereals	Pulses	Roots & tubers	Oil crops
OECD America	Canada	0%		-3%	13%	2%	-5%	-2%
	Mexico	-27%	-28%	-6%	-13%	-16%	-5%	-5%
	United States	-1%	-18%	-2%	-3%	-2%	-6%	0%
OECD Europe	OECD EU	0%	-6%	-6%	-3%	-12%	-22%	-1%
	Other OECD	-3%	22%	-20%	-2%	-35%	-19%	-1%
OECD Pacific	Australia & New Zealand	-22%	-3%	2%	-15%	-25%	-29%	-35%
	Japan	1%	6%			2%	-1%	0%
	Korea		-3%	-3%	-2%	0%	0%	2%
Rest of Europe & Asia	China	-3%	-9%	-3%	-6%	-4%	-4%	-10%
	Non-OECD EU	1%	-76%	2%	3%	4%	-2%	1%
	Russia	-1%	-4%	1%	-10%	5%	-2%	-2%
	Caspian region	-6%	-18%	-13%	2%	-16%	-16%	-24%
	Other Europe	-1%	0%	-4%	4%	3%	-1%	-1%
Latin America	Brazil	-7%	-3%	-3%	-4%	-8%	-10%	-7%
	Other Latin America	-2%	0%	-3%	-3%	-3%	-1%	-1%
Middle East & North Africa	Middle East	-24%	-39%	1%	-25%	-18%	-14%	-4%
	North Africa	-1%	-33%	-22%	-49%	-10%	-7%	0%
South & South-East Asia	ASEAN 9	-1%	3%	3%	2%	5%	3%	5%
	Indonesia		1%	0%	-1%	0%	1%	-1%
	India	-19%	-22%	-20%	2%	-15%	2%	4%
	Other Asia	-12%	0%	-4%	-12%	-6%	-1%	-7%
Sub-Saharan Africa	South Africa	-3%	0%	-6%	-8%	4%	3%	1%
	Other Africa	-6%	-3%	-1%	-1%	-1%	0%	-4%

StatLink ⟪⟫ http://dx.doi.org/10.1787/888933555380

Note: Averages over irrigated and rainfed production are shown. Temperate cereals comprise wheat, rye, oats and barley. Empty cells reflect situations where no significant production of those crops takes place.

Source: IMAGE model.

(Table 4.3); Table 4.4 shows that the water and land bottlenecks reinforce each other and lead to a combined yield loss of 9%. In other regions, the impacts are not negative in all scenarios. As positive and negative impacts of the individual bottlenecks operate in different directions, they can cancel each other's effects out. As a result, their combined impact in the combined bottlenecks scenario is not the largest and food crop yields are thus more affected in some of the individual bottleneck scenarios. Also, as observed for individual bottlenecks, the high losses found in the combined bottlenecks scenario for yields of some crops in some regions often concern less important crops where small absolute changes can appear as large percentage changes, and their impact on total food crop area remains limited.

Figure 4.19. **Changes in land use change between 2015 and 2060 in the individual and combined bottlenecks scenarios**

(Change from baseline in thousand square kilometres)

Panel A. Land use change in the combined bottlenecks scenario

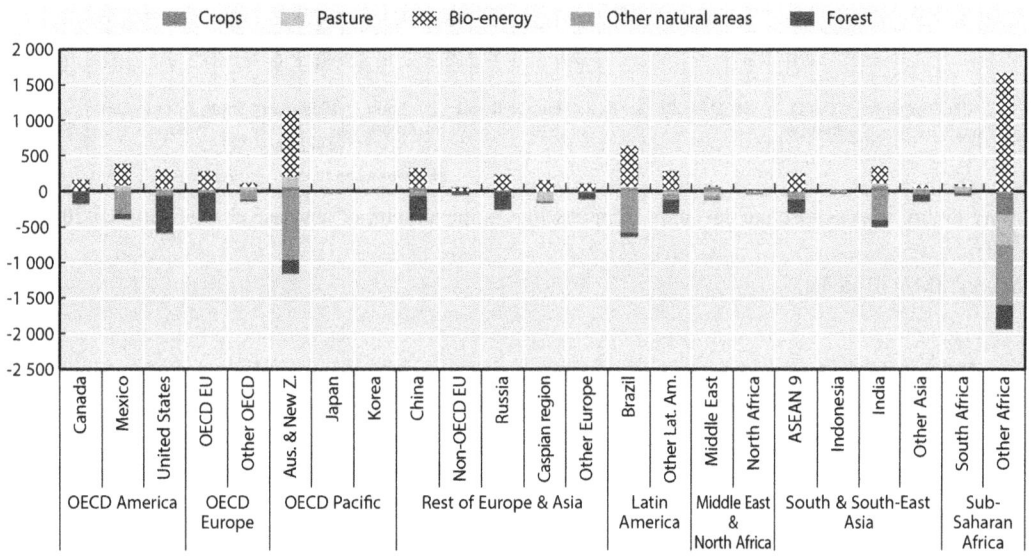

Panel B. Crop land change in the various scenarios

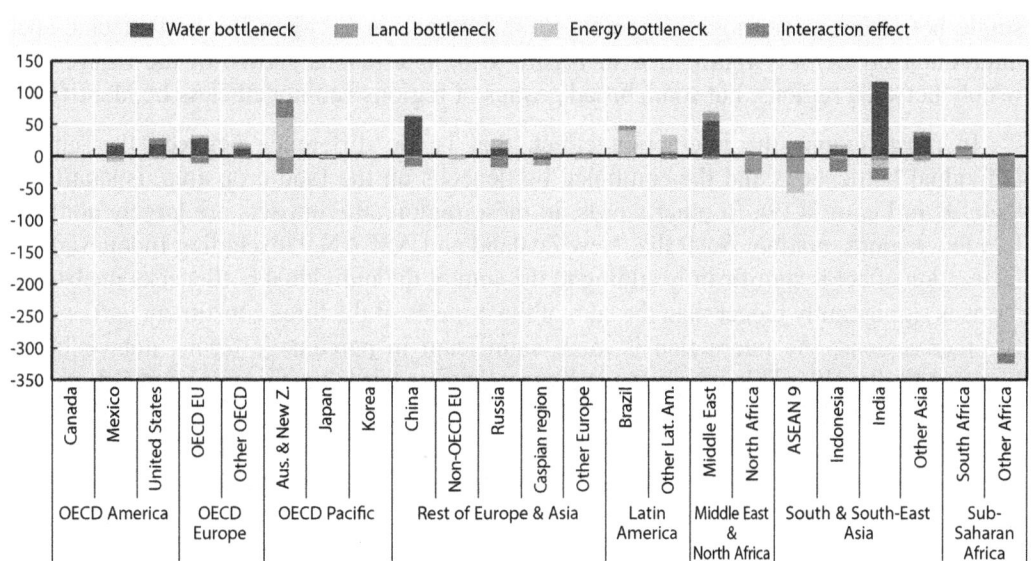

Figure 4.19. **Changes in land use change between 2015 and 2060 in the individual and combined bottlenecks scenarios** *(continued)*

Panel C. Forest land change in the various scenarios

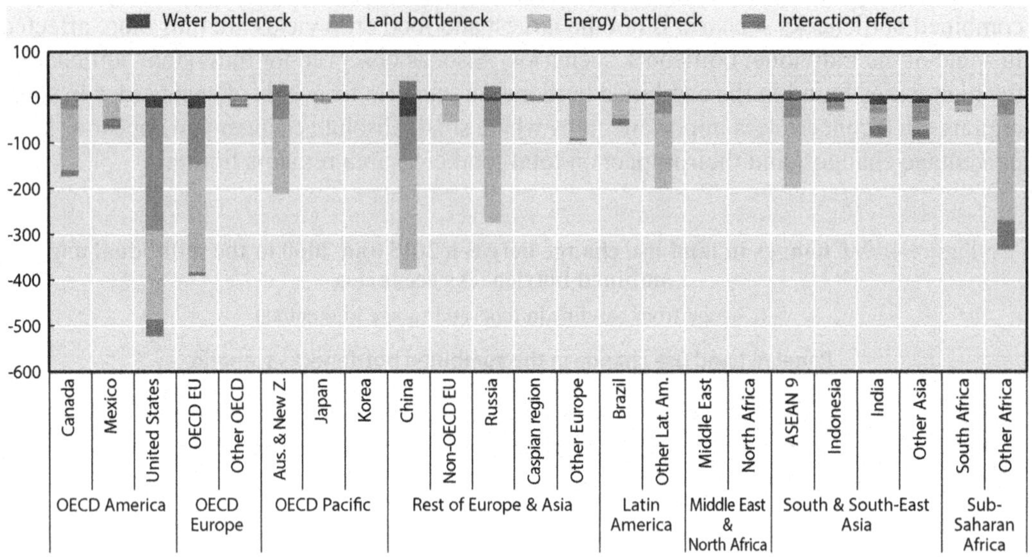

Note: Figure depicts absolute deviation from baseline in the amount of land use change between 2015 and 2060.

Source: IMAGE model.

Figure 4.19 shows the changes in land use change per world region for the single bottleneck scenarios as well as the combined bottlenecks scenario (all in comparison to the baseline). In IMAGE, lower food crop yields induce an increase in agricultural land (and vice versa) to compensate for the production losses and to maintain regional agricultural production (Panel A). Therefore, the food crop area in the combined bottlenecks scenario should simply be the sum of the food crop area changes of the three single bottleneck scenario if there is no interaction effect. However, if food crop area changes in the combined bottlenecks scenario are conspicuously higher/lower than the sum of the three single bottleneck scenarios, this points to an interaction between the bottlenecks; such interaction effects are highlighted in Figure 4.18. The results shown in the figure vary widely between regions, but some broad groups of regions can nonetheless be identified.

In most regions the interaction effect, that is the difference between the sum of individual bottlenecks and the combined bottlenecks on the food crop area, is small (see Panel B in Figure 4.19). In other words, in these regions the impacts are largely additive. In a few regions, notably Australia, New Zealand and ASEAN 9 (excluding Indonesia), the interaction effect is significantly adding to the sum of the individual bottlenecks in absolute terms is significantly bigger than the sum of the impacts of the three constituent bottlenecks. In other regions, the interaction is more significant in percentage terms, not visible in Figure 4.18, Panel B. This is the case in Korea, South Africa, North Africa and Other Asia. In quite a few regions, the absolute interaction effect is just negative and decreases the sum of the three bottlenecks slightly as the individual scenarios overlap. In relative terms the biggest interaction effects occur in Indonesia, India, Middle East and Other Europe. At the level of the total world, the interaction effect is slightly positive: 0.2%, the limited impact understandable given the varying positive and negative results at the regional level.

In all regions, the changes in land use lead to a decrease in total forest cover; see Figure 4.19, Panel C. The energy bottleneck is the main contributor, followed by the land bottleneck, but the size of the two impacts varies between regions. Regions where the interaction effect compensates some of the loss of forest cover are Australia and New Zealand, China, Russia and, to a lesser extent, also Other Latin America, ASEAN 9 and Indonesia. In other regions, the interaction effect adds to the sum of the three individual bottlenecks: United States, Other Africa, India, Other Asia and, to a smaller degree, Canada, Mexico and Brazil.

The interaction effects with regards to food crop area and forest cover play a role in close to all regions, in either positive (compensating in part the individual bottlenecks) or negative direction. As the magnitude of the interaction is small for the world total and for many of the regions, this underlines that considering the nexus in an integral sense when looking at impacts and policies is mostly relevant for hotspots only, but less so at the larger scale.

Economic consequences

The macroeconomic effects of the combined bottlenecks are in most regions close to the sum of the effects for the individual bottlenecks, as shown in Figure 4.20. For agricultural value added (Panel A), the models try to find the best land allocation to accommodate the different shocks together, and such "optimisation" works better than when the three individual bottlenecks are not considered simultaneously. But while this may help limit the reduction in crop yields, in many regions the capacity to deploy additional land for agriculture is limited, and it becomes more than proportionately costly to extensify agricultural production. Especially in a region such as Japan this leads to increased pressure on agricultural land use. Thus, in most regions the effect of the combined bottlenecks on agricultural value added is quite strongly negative.

Figure 4.20. **Changes in agricultural and macroeconomic activity in 2060 in the individual and combined bottlenecks scenarios**

(Percentage change from baseline)

Panel A. Agricultural value added

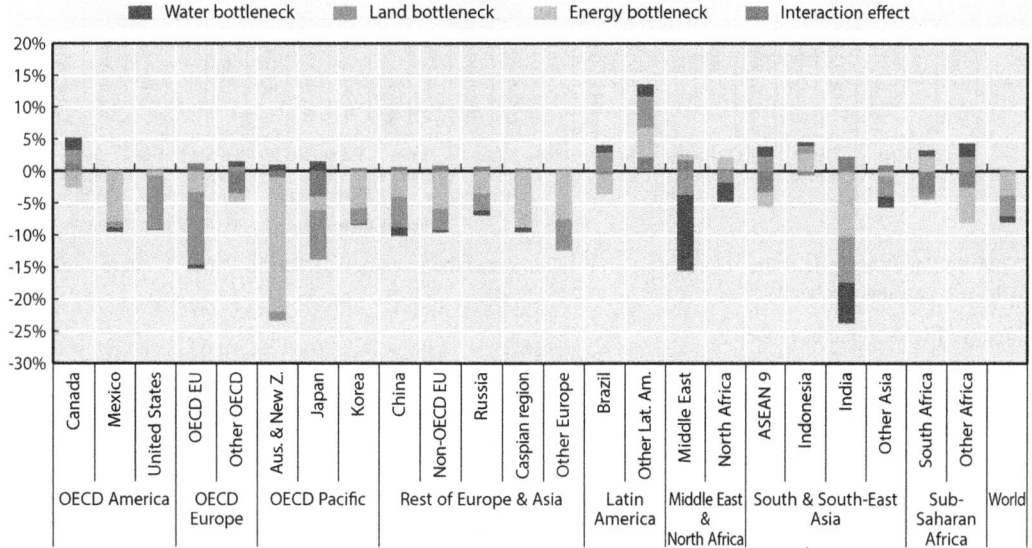

Figure 4.20. **Changes in agricultural and macroeconomic activity in 2060 in the individual and combined bottlenecks scenarios** *(continued)*

Panel B. Energy sector value added (excl. additional biomass production)

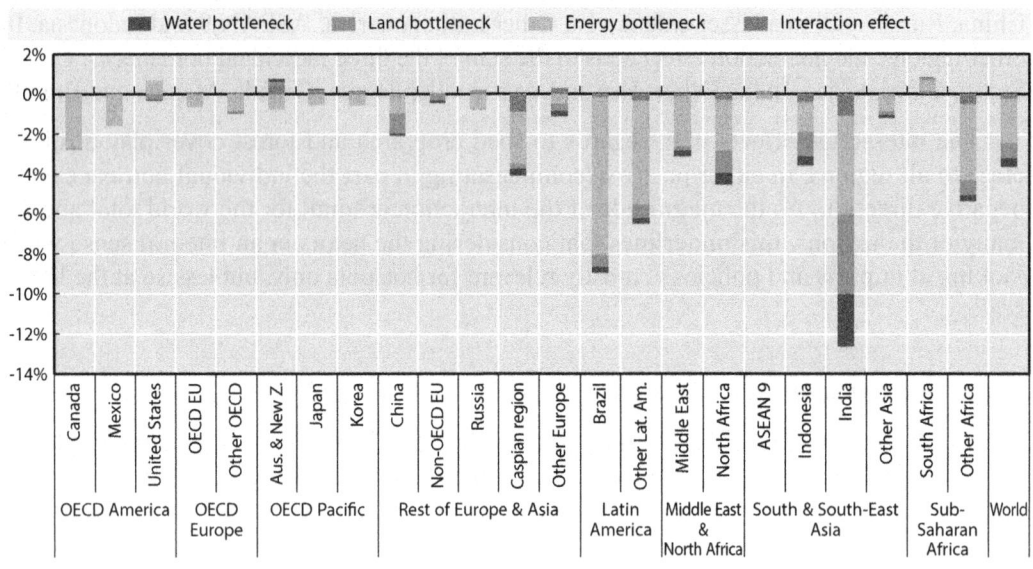

Panel C. GDP

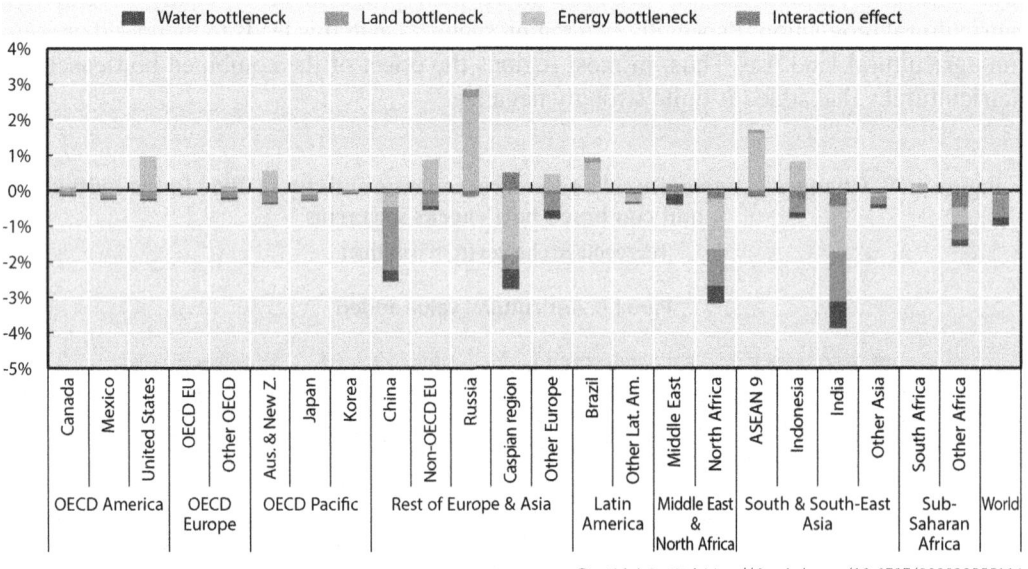

StatLink http://dx.doi.org/10.1787/888933555114

Note: In Panel A, agriculture refers to all crop sectors and the livestock sector; in Panel B, energy refers to coal, oil, gas and electricity.

Source: ENV-Linkages model.

The effect on value added generated in the "traditional" energy sector, i.e. excluding the new biomass production, is dominated by the energy shock, as expected (Panel B); these results have been explained in Section 4.3. In a few regions, there are significant indirect effects of a general economic slowdown caused by the water and land bottlenecks that imply a reduced demand for energy. This is most prominent in India.

In some regions, not least Russia, the GDP effects are dominated by the gains from the energy shock (Panel C), and the combined bottlenecks lead to a projected increase in GDP above baseline levels. But there are also regions where the negative pressures on the economy from the different shocks amplify each other, and the combined bottlenecks scenario projects a worse GDP result than the sum of the individual bottlenecks. Such negative interaction effects on GDP are especially visible in North Africa, India and Other

Figure 4.21. Changes in consumer prices in 2060 in the individual and combined bottlenecks scenarios

(Percentage change from baseline)

Panel A. Food

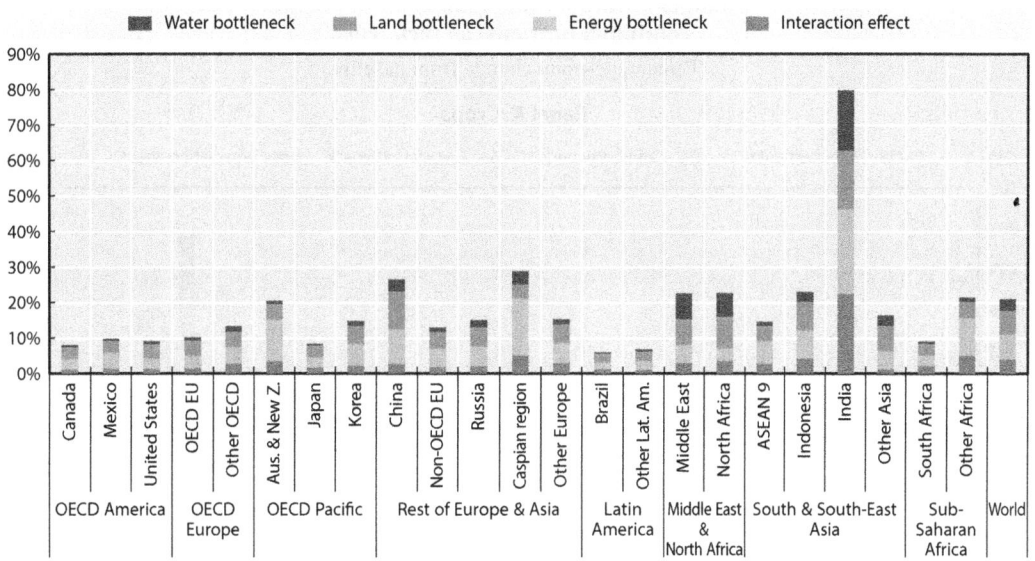

Panel B. Energy

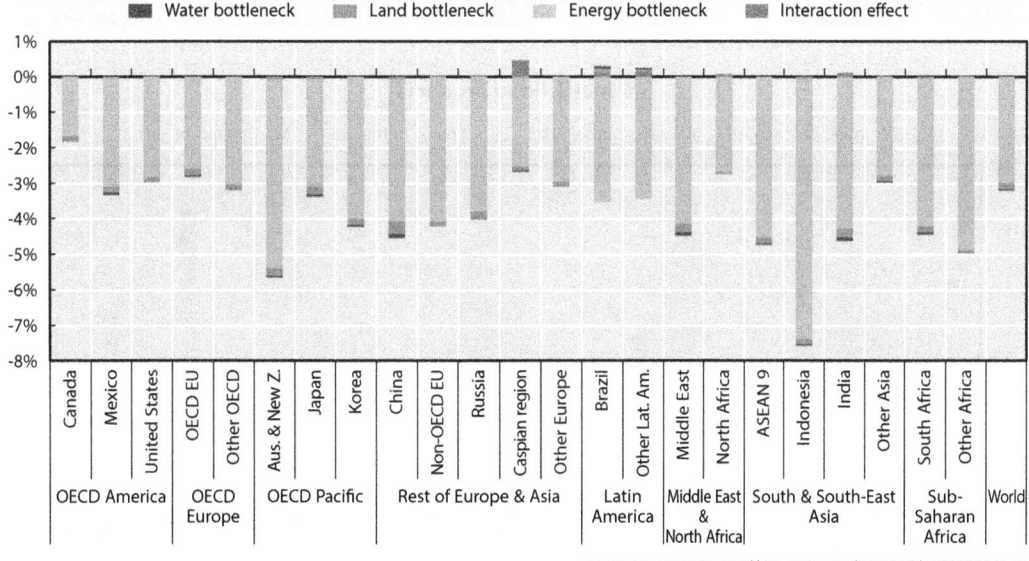

StatLink http://dx.doi.org/10.1787/888933555133

Note: Food prices reflect a weighted average of all crops, livestock and food products; energy prices reflect a weighted average of coal, oil, gas and electricity.

Source: ENV-Linkages model.

Africa. This highlights the logic that small shocks can be accommodated in the economy more easily than large shocks. Thus, large negative shocks caused by the nexus bottlenecks tend to strengthen each other. In contrast, there is a positive interaction effect in the Caspian region, where trade effects are relatively strong, and the trade implications of the combined bottlenecks differ from the sum of the individual bottlenecks.

Food prices for households, as shown in Figure 4.21, follow the same trends as observed for the individual bottlenecks and increase in all regions. On top, there tends to be an interaction effect between the policies that further drives up food prices, especially in India, as the different bottlenecks reinforce each other. For energy prices, the changes of opposite sign, but are much smaller, as only the energy scenario has a significant effect.

Figure 4.22. **Changes in import shares in 2060 in the individual and combined bottlenecks scenarios**

(Percentage-point change from baseline)

Panel A. Crops

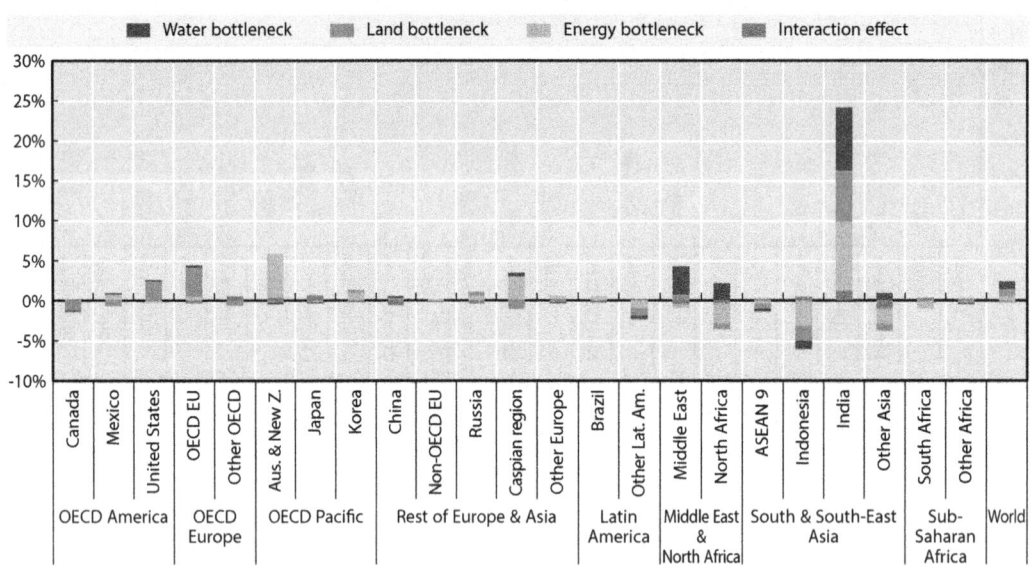

Panel B. Food products

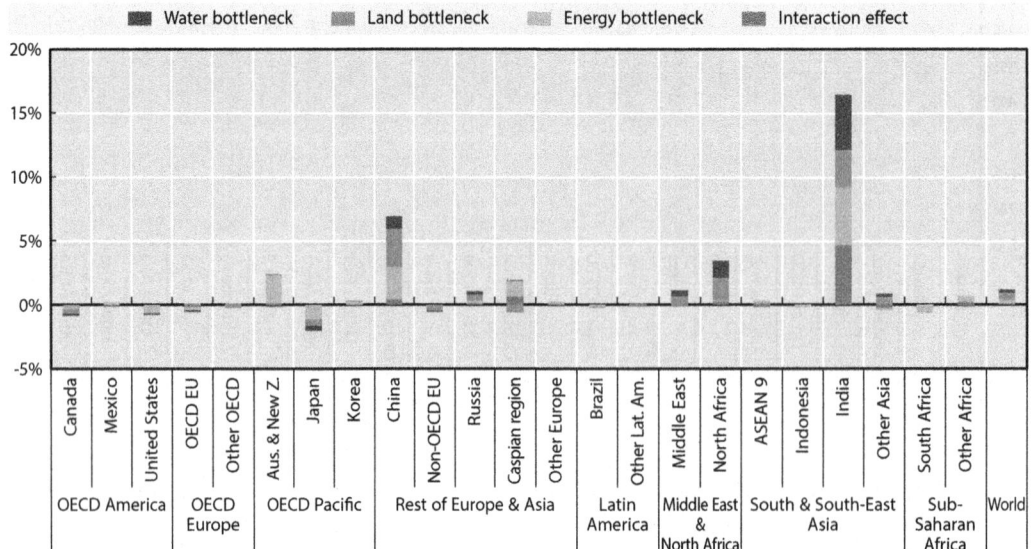

Figure 4.22. **Changes in import shares in 2060 in the individual and combined bottlenecks scenarios** *(continued)*

Panel C. Energy

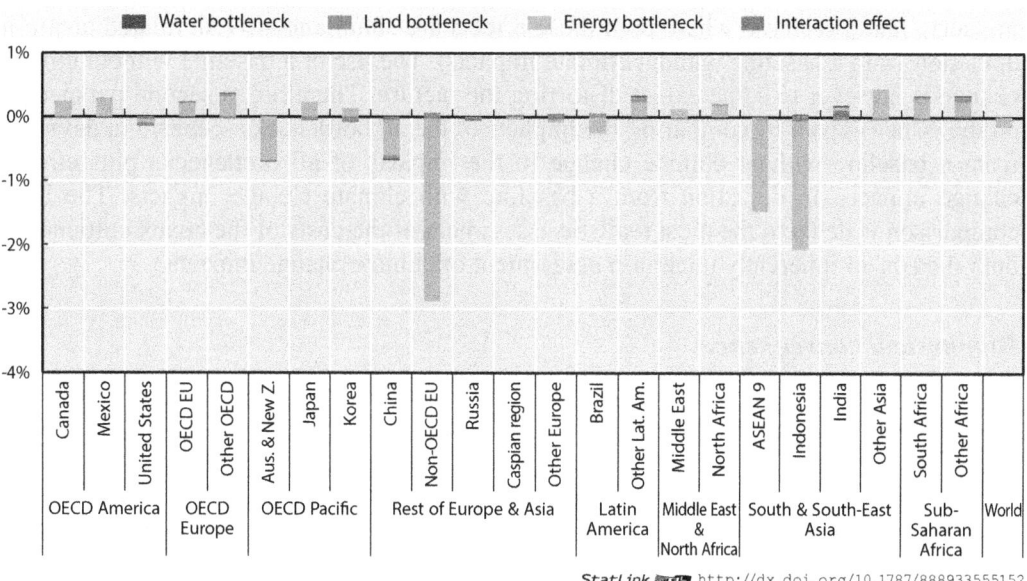

StatLink http://dx.doi.org/10.1787/888933555152

Note: In Panel A, crops refers to all crop sectors combined; in Panel B, food products refers to the food production sector only; in Panel C, energy refers to coal, oil, gas and electricity.

Source: ENV-Linkages model.

Finally, the changes in import shares shown in Figure 4.22 can shed further light on the consequences of the nexus bottlenecks on food and energy security. In line with the results discussed above, the problems are strongest in India, where the various bottlenecks add up to a significant increase in dependence on crop and food imports. China is also projected to increase the share of imports in total food demand, through a sum of small effects for the various bottlenecks. Interaction effects between the various bottlenecks are small in all regions except India (due to the scale effect of compounded bottlenecks).

Import shares for energy are much more mixed and dominated by the energy bottleneck scenario. As explained in Section 4.3, in many regions there is a small increase in import dependence due to the shifting relative prices, while in a few concentrated regions – Australia, New Zealand, China, Non-OECD EU, Brazil, ASEAN9 and Indonesia – import dependency decreases significantly.

4.5. Sensitivity of the results to climate change: Combined bottlenecks with climate change

The modelling analysis presented above ignores potential future effects of climate change on the agricultural and economic systems. This section considers climate change impacts on agriculture and land use, as projected by IMAGE.[7] The climate change scenario is in itself not a nexus analysis. Rather, it is a preparatory step to investigate the combined bottlenecks plus climate change scenario. The main purpose of this section is to identify to what extent the analysis above is influenced by overlaying trends in climate change impacts in agriculture. This could clarify where there are significant reinforcing effects, and where different mechanisms can mitigate each other.

There are two different presentations of the effects of climate change on assessment of the consequences of the combined nexus bottlenecks. First, the changes stemming from climate change (in deviation from a baseline without climate impacts) can be compared with those of the bottleneck scenarios (also in deviation from a baseline without climate impacts), and a scenario where both these effects are simultaneously simulated (again in deviation from a baseline without climate impacts). The use of a baseline without climate change is however to some extent distorting the picture. Therefore, a second perspective on the issue is given by comparing the impacts of the all bottlenecks scenario in deviation from a baseline without climate change to the impacts of all bottlenecks plus climate change impacts, in deviation from a baseline with climate change impacts. The latter comparison is de facto the most realistic assessment of the costs of the nexus bottlenecks, but relies on an inherently uncertain assessment of climate change impacts.

Biophysical consequences

In the preceding sections, the impacts of the nexus bottlenecks, individually and combined, are compared against the baseline, assuming no future climate change occurs. So, all projections assume that climate parameters such as temperature, precipitation and atmospheric greenhouse gas concentrations remain as they were in 2015. For example, the global average temperature remains constant at 1°C over the entire period until 2060.

To put the nexus related impacts in perspective, the baseline and combined bottlenecks scenario are also analysed assuming climate change continues into the future to reach the 3°C mark by 2060, slightly higher than the central case assumed in the OECD CIRCLE report on climate change (OECD, 2015). Changes in local, monthly temperature and precipitation are used to explore climate change impacts on yields of food crops in the IMAGE model. In line with what was assumed in earlier analyses of climate change on agriculture (OECD, 2015; Valin et al., 2014), any effect of higher CO_2 emissions on crop growth, the so-called CO_2 fertilisation, was not taken into account here. Impacts differ between regions, but also within regions between the various crop types. This illustrates that the sensitivity of crop types for changes in climate conditions is different, but in addition crops may be grown in different locations within a region, and the spatial and temporal climate change effect is not distributed uniformly either; see Table 4.5.

For all crops the negative climate change impact on the productivity of food crops is quite substantial in many regions, ranging from a few percent to 44% reduction. On the whole, more moderate climate zones tend to have less negative impacts than (sub-)tropical regions, where losses in crop yield exceed to -10% mark for all crop groups considered here (Brazil -16% to -26%; ASEAN 9 -11% to -44%; Indonesia -14% to -27%; India -10% to -21%; and Other Asia -11 to -21%). How important such impacts per crop type are depends also their share in the diet and production in the regions. In that respect the outcome for rice is worth noting: substantial losses of -11% to -20% in Asian regions where rice is a major staple food (Korea, ASEAN 9, Indonesia, India and Other Asia).

On the other hand, several crops show enhanced yields, such as temperate cereals (United States +2%, China +7% and Russia +20%), and maize (Canada +15%, OECD-EU +9%, Australia and New Zealand +5%). Also here the positive impact on the agricultural sector depends on the share of the crops in total production, the examples listed above all concern important regional crops. Another striking example is tropical cereals in Other OECD with 44% higher yield, but this is grown on less than 0.5% of the foodcrop area only.

Table 4.5. **Changes in crop yields in 2060 in the climate change scenario**

(Percentage change from baseline)

		Temperate cereals	Rice	Maize	Tropical cereals	Pulses	Roots & tubers	Oil crops
OECD America	Canada	-2%		15%	-1%	-12%	4%	4%
	Mexico	-19%	0%	-1%	-18%	-26%	-4%	-4%
	United States	2%	0%	-3%	-5%	-6%	0%	0%
OECD Europe	OECD EU	-5%	-19%	9%	-1%	-5%	-8%	-8%
	Other OECD	-6%		-16%	44%	-6%	-12%	-12%
OECD Pacific	Australia & New Zealand	1%	4%	5%	-19%	5%	-8%	-8%
	Japan	1%	7%			-8%	2%	2%
	Korea		-14%	0%	-5%	0%	2%	2%
Rest of Europe & Asia	China	7%	-5%	-6%	-6%	-3%	4%	4%
	Non-OECD EU	-5%	-41%	-14%	-17%	-25%	-12%	-12%
	Russia	10%	-34%	-4%	-27%	-5%	8%	8%
	Caspian region	0%	-17%	2%	-3%	-11%	-3%	-3%
	Other Europe	-6%	-12%	-10%	-3%	-12%	-11%	-11%
Latin America	Brazil	-20%	-20%	-16%	-18%	-20%	-26%	-26%
	Other Latin America	-4%	-10%	-13%	-12%	-15%	-14%	-14%
Middle East & North Africa	Middle East	-10%	0%	-6%	-35%	-1%	-6%	-6%
	North Africa	-19%	-4%	7%	-3%	-15%	-18%	-18%
South & South-East Asia	ASEAN 9	-44%	-19%	-15%	-11%	-12%	-18%	-18%
	Indonesia		-20%	-16%	-14%	-27%	-20%	-20%
	India	-15%	-11%	-10%	-13%	-17%	-21%	-21%
	Other Asia	-12%	-11%	-14%	-12%	-20%	-21%	-21%
Sub-Saharan Africa	South Africa	-16%	-23%	-2%	-16%	-12%	-15%	-15%
	Other Africa	-22%	-19%	-15%	-15%	-22%	-24%	-24%

StatLink ᴍ⏴ᴍ http://dx.doi.org/10.1787/888933555399

Note: Averages over irrigated and rainfed production are shown. Temperate cereals comprise wheat, rye, oats and barley. Empty cells reflect situations where no significant production of those crops takes place.

Source: IMAGE model.

As IMAGE on its own does not account for feedback effects of commodity prices on consumption or trade, lower yields induce in each region an expansion of agricultural land to compensate for lower yields.[8] Where all crop types, or at least all major crops, in a region are affected strongly, substantial expansion is the result. As can be seen in the first column of Figure 4.23, the climate effect in the baseline ranges from (very) small to very substantial impacts on food crop area in the world regions.

For the global total, 14% more land would be needed to offset the loss of agricultural productivity. In line with the findings for yield impacts, foodcrop area expands in all regions with just one exception: Japan. The expansion in regions in more moderate climate zones, such as OECD (except Europe, Korea and Mexico), China and Russia, the impact is relatively limited to an expansion up to 2%. The remaining more developed and emerging economies in moderate climate zones expand between 7% and 11%, while all (sub-)tropical regions in Latin America, Africa and Asia would require anywhere between 13% and 31% additional land to grow crops.

Figure 4.23 illustrates that for the world in total the effect of climate change appears much bigger than for the combined bottlenecks addressed in this report. The relative importance of the two issues climate change and LWE nexus, however, varies strongly

Figure 4.23. **Changes in food crop area between 2015 and 2060 in the combined bottlenecks scenario with and without climate change**

(Change from baseline in thousand square kilometres)

Panel A. Baseline without climate change

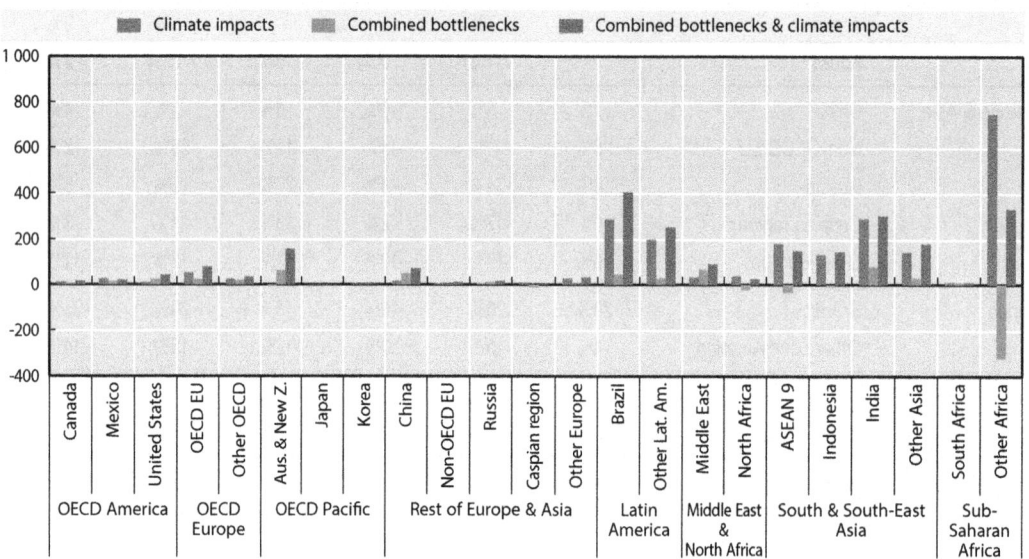

Panel B. Climate change in both baseline and combined bottlenecks scenario

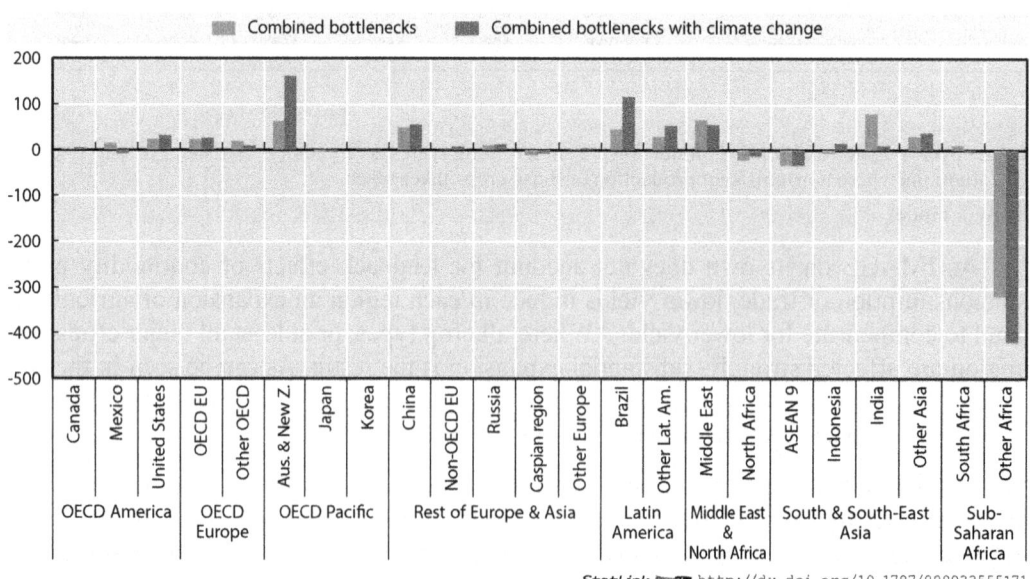

StatLink http://dx.doi.org/10.1787/888933555171

Note: Figure depicts absolute deviation from baseline in the amount of land use change between 2015 and 2060.

Source: IMAGE model.

between regions. Firstly because in the combined bottlenecks scenario more regions show a negative sign than in the climate scenario (where only Japan has a negative sign). In other regions the climate change impact is much smaller than the nexus bottlenecks (Australia and New Zealand, China, Caspian region and Middle East). If the climate change effect is factored into both the baseline and the combined bottlenecks scenario (Panel B of Figure 4.23), it turns out that the effect of the bottlenecks on food crop area varies somewhat at the regional level, but global effects are still very small.

Economic consequences

Figure 4.24 shows the two different perspectives on the influence of climate change impacts. Panel A presents the first perspective. Climate impacts can boost the agricultural sector in some OECD countries (and the Caspian region). This stems from the fact that the competitive position of the agricultural sector on the domestic and world markets depends not only on the domestic impacts of climate change, but also on the relative impact vis-a-vis the closest competitors. Thus, countries that are hurt by climate change, but less so than other countries, can exploit that relative difference and increase market share. Such effects are in line with – and further explored by – Dellink et al. (2017), who use the ENV-Linkages model to tease out the international trade consequences of a wider set of climate change damages to the economy.

Figure 4.24. **Changes in agricultural value added in 2060 in the combined bottlenecks scenario with and without climate change**

(Percentage change from baseline)

Panel A. Baseline without climate change

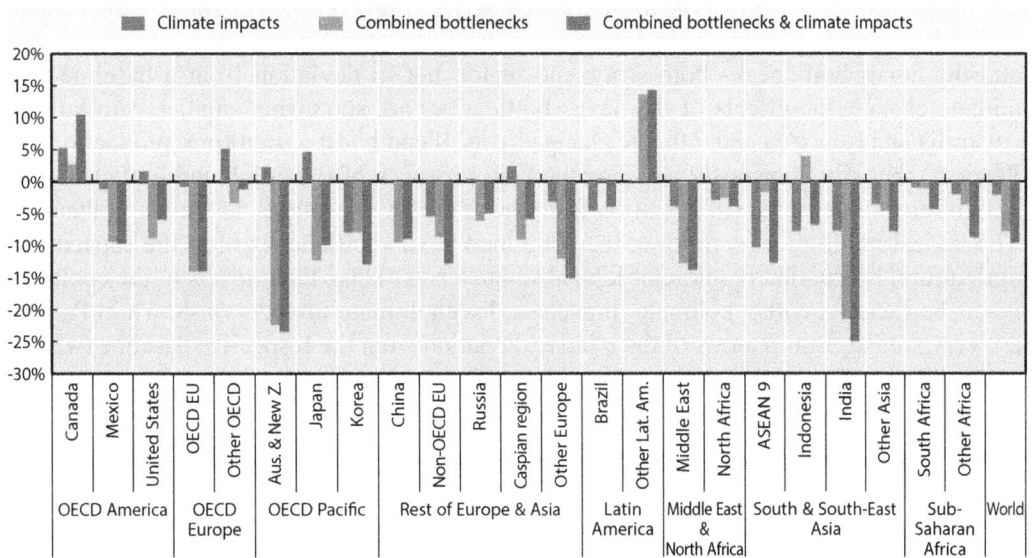

Figure 4.24. **Changes in agricultural value added in 2060 in the combined bottlenecks scenario with and without climate change** *(continued)*

Panel B. Climate change in both baseline and combined bottlenecks scenario

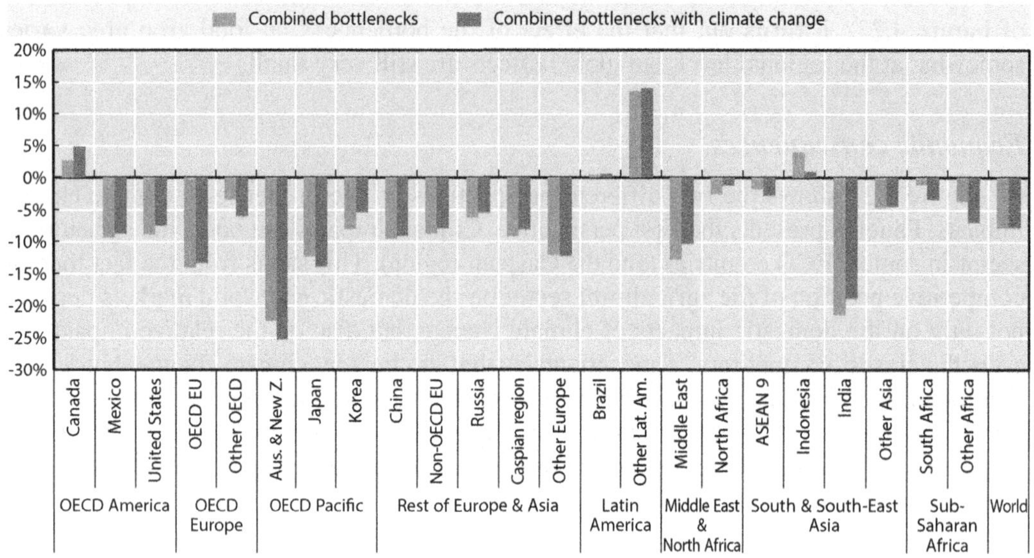

StatLink ⬛⬛⬛ http://dx.doi.org/10.1787/888933555190

Note: Agriculture refers to all crop sectors and the livestock sector.

Source: ENV-Linkages model.

For the two regions with the most affected agricultural sectors, Australia, New Zealand and India, the complexity of the interactions are illustrated: in the latter, climate change and the nexus bottlenecks both strain the sector, but in deviation from a baseline with climate change, the effects of the nexus bottlenecks are somewhat smaller. Similarly, in Australia and New Zealand, climate change by itself can boost agricultural production (see Panel A), but simultaneously worsens the consequences of the combined bottlenecks on agricultural value added (in deviation from the respective baselines, as shown in Panel B). The logical intuition is as follows: the combined nexus bottlenecks limit the capacity for agricultural production in (more or less) absolute terms. Thus, the impacts of the combined nexus bottlenecks without climate impacts and with climate impacts as shown in Panel A are very similar. But in terms of the relative deviation from the respective baseline (without and with climate change), this implies that effects with climate change are stronger in Australia and New Zealand, while they are relatively smaller in India.

In line with the analysis in earlier sections, the GDP impacts are to a large extent driven by the consequences for the agricultural sector. Figure 4.25 highlights that projected climate impacts on agriculture have only minor consequences for GDP in the OECD countries, but that negative effects are stronger in Asia and Africa, especially India. As a consequence, climate change impacts strengthen the negative effect of the nexus bottlenecks on these economies. Partly, this stems from the negative consequences of climate change on agricultural yields directly. But there are also potentially strong indirect effects, as relatively easy adaptation options to accommodate one shock (either climate change or the nexus bottlenecks) can only be employed once, and two negative shocks are thus more than proportionately hurting these economies. This effect is especially strong in India and Other Africa. Furthermore, the combination of both shocks affects international trade patterns and hampers the smoothing of domestic shocks through increased reliance on trade by either boosting exports to generate alternative revenues, or importing cheaply to avoid large price spikes. This is especially visible for Indonesia: by themselves the combined nexus bottlenecks have only very minor consequences for GDP, but when climate change is added, negative consequences start to dominate.

These effects are more easily seen in Panel B of Figure 4.25, which compares the consequences of the combined bottlenecks from the second perspective, i.e. with climate change in both the baseline and the bottleneck scenario. The panel confirms that at least by 2060, climate change impacts are not dominating the results, but do worsen the negative consequences of the combined nexus bottlenecks, especially in those regions that are most severely affected.

Figure 4.25. **Changes in GDP in 2060 in the combined bottlenecks scenario with and without climate change**

(Percentage change from baseline)

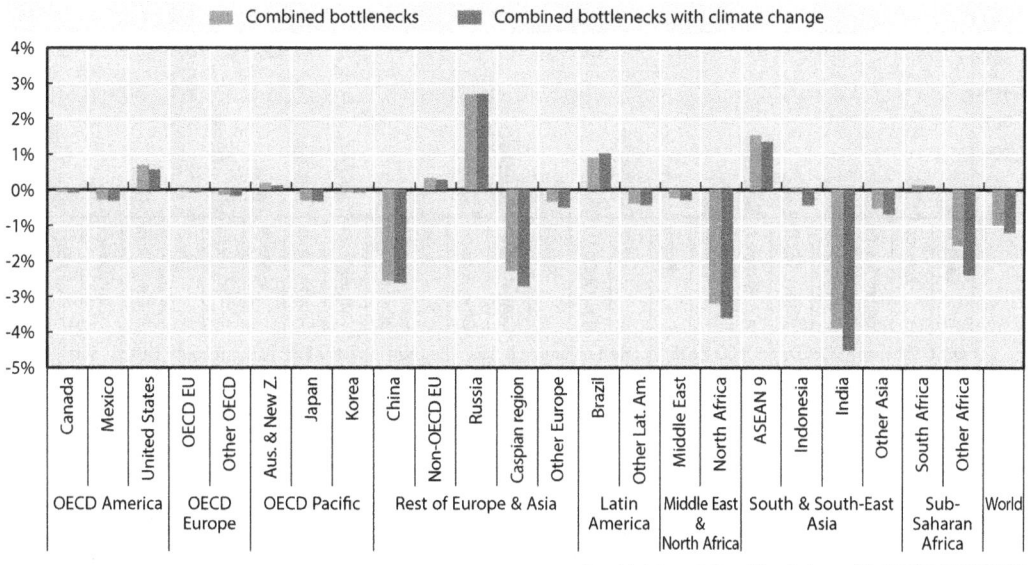

StatLink ⫶ http://dx.doi.org/10.1787/888933555209

Source: ENV-Linkages model.

These nuanced differences notwithstanding, the overall conclusion from Figures 4.24 and 4.25 has to be that the qualitative conclusions about the macroeconomic consequences of the nexus bottlenecks are quite robust against the assumptions on climate change impacts. Figure 4.26 confirms this: changes in consumer prices for food and energy are very similar, irrespective of the inclusion of climate change impacts on the agricultural system.

The sensitivity of the results for import shares of various commodities to the assumptions on climate change is a bit more pronounced, at least in some of the most affected regions. This reflects that relatively small price differentials between regions can lead to significant realignments of international trade patterns for the most heavily traded commodities, which include crops, food and energy. The dampening effect of climate change on agricultural production in India is also visible in Figure 4.27, Panel A, as the simulation with climate impacts projects a slightly smaller increase in import dependency for crops, although the qualitative conclusion that import dependency increases far more in India than in other regions still stands. In Indonesia, the reduction in import dependency when including climate impacts does not stem from increased (read: smaller reductions) domestic production, but rather from the fact that climate change has a strong negative effect on crop production. When this is included in the baseline, there is less opportunity for Indonesia to reduce its import dependency in response to the nexus bottlenecks.

Figure 4.26. **Changes in consumer prices in 2060 in the combined bottlenecks scenario with and without climate change**

(Percentage change; climate change in both baseline and combined bottlenecks scenario)

Panel A. Food

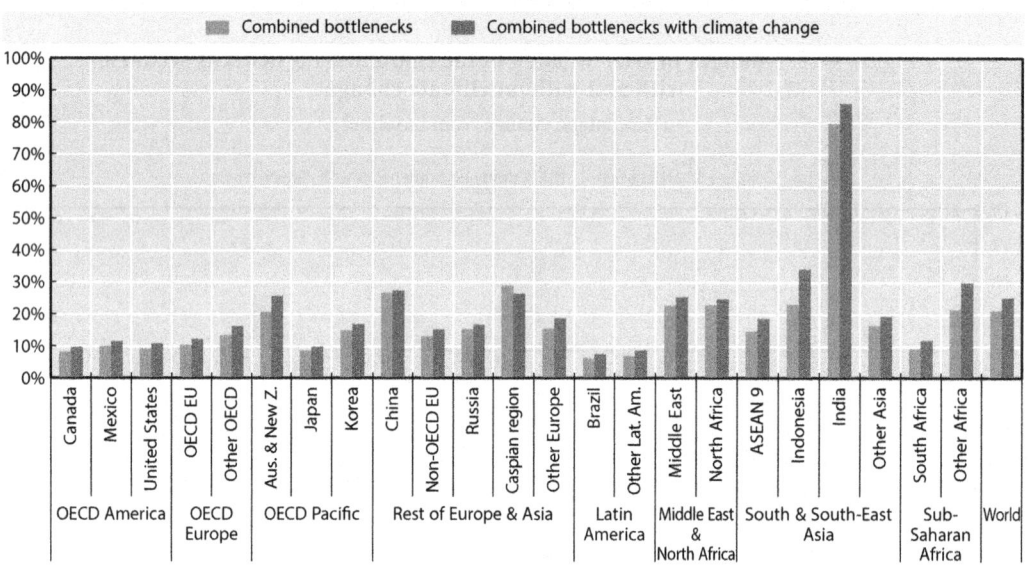

Panel B. Energy

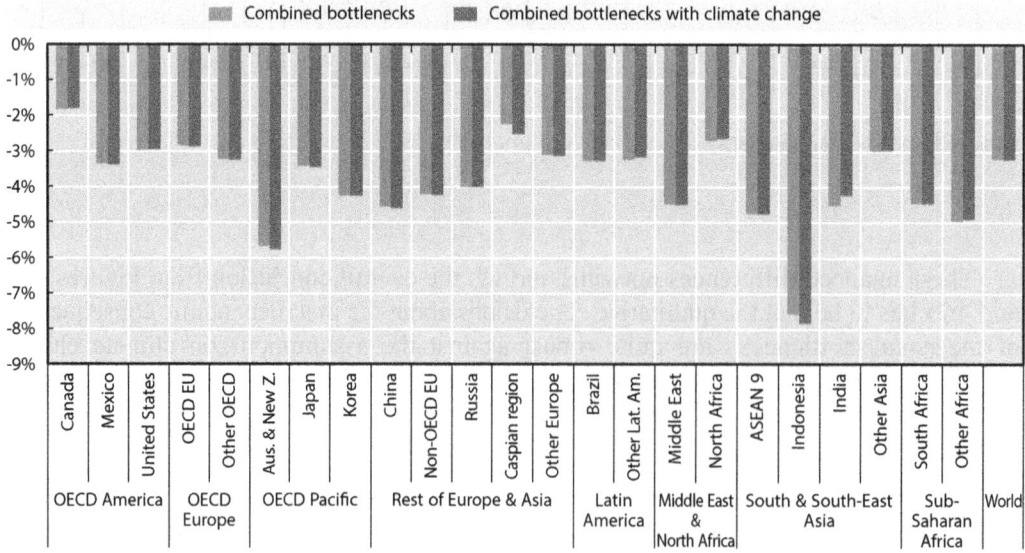

StatLink http://dx.doi.org/10.1787/888933555228

Note: Food prices reflect a weighted average of all crops, livestock and food products; energy prices reflect a weighted average of coal, oil, gas and electricity.

Source: ENV-Linkages model.

Figure 4.27. **Changes in import shares in 2060 in the combined bottlenecks scenario with and without climate change**

(Percentage-point change; climate change in both baseline and combined bottlenecks scenario)

Panel A. Crops

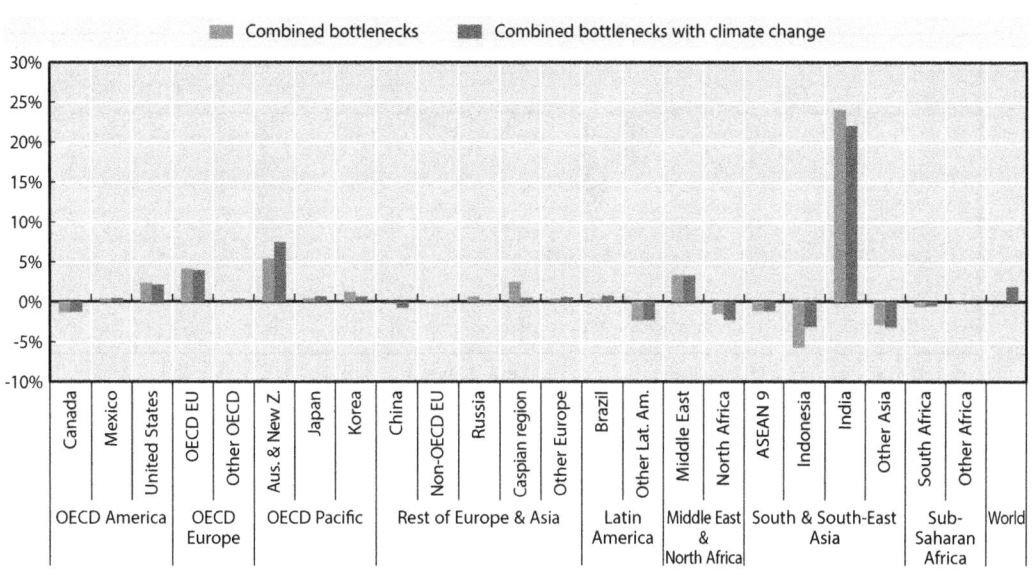

Panel B. Food products

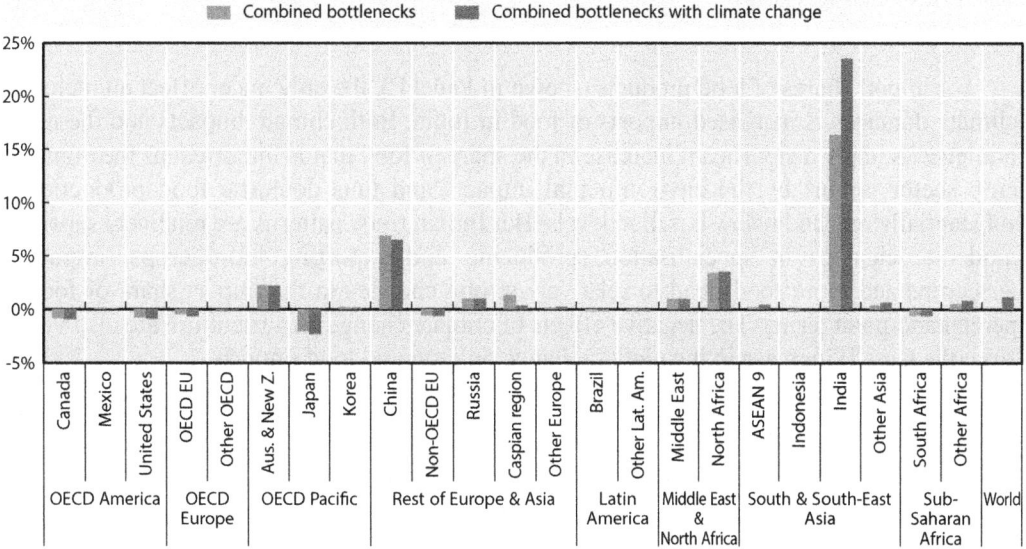

Figure 4.27. **Changes in import shares in 2060 in the combined bottlenecks scenario with and without climate change** *(continued)*

Panel C. Energy

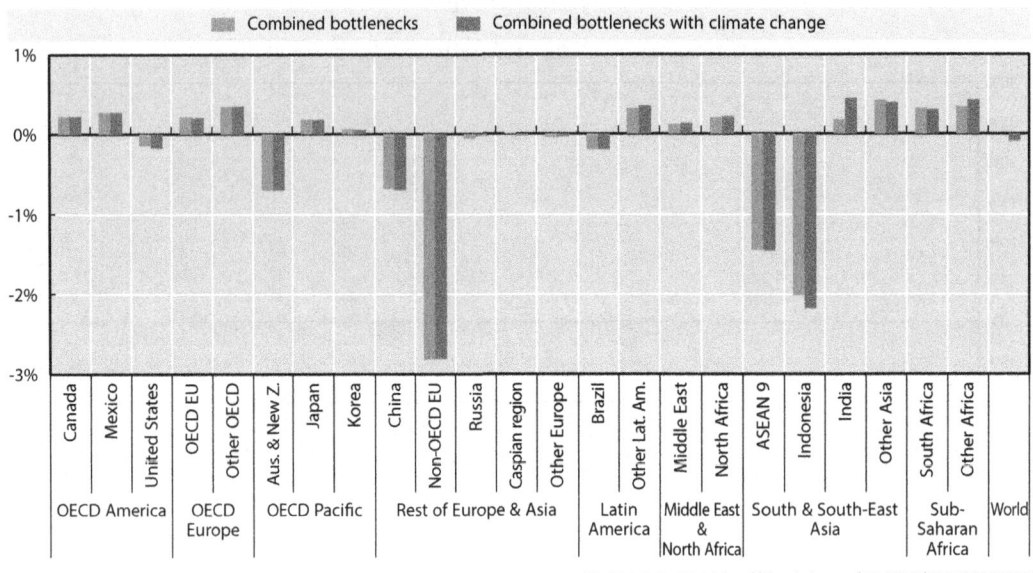

StatLink ⣿⣿ http://dx.doi.org/10.1787/888933555247

Note: In Panel A, crops refers to all crop sectors combined; in Panel B, food products refers to the food production sector only; energy refers to coal, oil, gas and electricity.

Source: ENV-Linkages model.

For import shares of food products (shown in Panel B), the only major effect on including climate damages is increased imports of food in India. Both climate impacts and the nexus bottlenecks imply a significant increase in the share of food that is imported, as the domestic crop sector is hurt by the environmental impacts and thus domestic food production is substantially reduced below baseline levels. But Indian trade patterns are relatively sensitive: moderate changes in specialisation (producing and exporting more crops, importing less crops and more food) lead to relatively strong changes in the import share of food in percentage-point terms. The negative effects of climate change on agriculture are also visible from the (small) increase in the global reliance on crop and food imports.

Finally, the changes in import shares of energy as a consequence of the combined nexus bottlenecks (Panel C) are quite robust against the assumption on climate change. Again, the Indian and Indonesian economies are most sensitive to the climate change impacts, but the effects are very small in comparison with the impacts on crops and food products.

Notes

1. Note that the model endogenously handles change in trade volumes, but does not allow the creation of trade from or to places where none exist currently.

2. Furthermore, regions with large exports, e.g. the Middle Eastern countries with their oil exports, can more easily absorb a change in imports of food and agricultural products without significantly worsening their terms of trade.

3. This reflects the average of household prices for agricultural commodities and food products, weighted by their consumption volume.

4. This is governed in the model through the Armington assumption, and is based on empirical observations of bilateral trade patterns.

5. Other important effects of urban sprawl, such as those on water and energy, are potentially also significant, especially in terms of costs of provision and access to the resource; these could, however, not be included in the modelling analysis due to a lack of robust data.

6. Changes in relative prices ensure that these shifts occur under the constraint of a fixed trade balance.

7. These impacts are not identical to broader assessment of the economic consequences of climate change as presented in the earlier CIRCLE report (OECD, 2015). Full implementation of all climate damages in ENV-Linkages would however muddle the assessment of the impacts of the nexus bottlenecks and is therefore not considered in this section.

8. As explained in Chapter 2, there are further price feedback effects in ENV-Linkages, such that effective land use is determined to follow economic principles.

References

Dellink, R.B. et al. (2017), "The international trade consequences of climate change", *OECD Trade and Environment Working Papers*, No. 2017/01, OECD Publishing, Paris.

OECD (2016), *The Economic Consequences of Outdoor Air Pollution*, OECD Publishing, Paris, http://dx.doi.org/10.1787/9789264257474-en.

OECD (2015), *The Economic Consequences of Climate Change*, OECD Publishing, Paris, http://dx.doi.org/10.1787/9789264235410-en.

Valin, H. et al. (2014), "The future of food demand: understanding differences in global economic models," *Agricultural Economics* 45, pp. 51-67.

Chapter 5

An integrated look at the nexus bottlenecks

This chapter first identifies general patterns that emerge in the way the bottlenecks affect the different policy objectives laid out in Chapter 1. It then discusses the major trade-offs and synergies between the bottlenecks at the regional level. The chapter ends with putting the analysis in this report into context, including a discussion of the robustness of the results.

5.1. An integrated look at the nexus for the various policy objectives

This section looks at the different policy objectives laid out in Section 1.2 and especially Figure 1.1: welfare, environmental quality, food security, water security and energy security. The aim is to identify general patterns that emerge across the different bottlenecks in the way the bottlenecks affect these objectives.

Welfare

In terms of the welfare effects of the nexus bottlenecks, it is clear that the constraints posed by the bottlenecks tend to lead on balance to relatively modest negative effects at the global level, depressing GDP and consumption levels to somewhat below their baseline level. But there are always some countries which can benefit from the changes in international competitiveness of countries. Especially the ASEAN economies and countries in Latin America can benefit from the fact that their competitive position is less affected than that of their major trading partners. Thus, they can reap a larger share of the global market. This is not least driven by the fact that these countries are capable of expanding their land use at relatively low costs to accommodate the bottlenecks and thus avoid major price increases.

At the other end of the spectrum are the countries that rely heavily on the scarce resources. This is especially the case for the water resource in India and the land resource in China. The various bottlenecks also strengthen the negative welfare effect in India, highlighting the role of this region as a fragile hotspot. Section 5.2 teases out these regional effects in more detail. The quantitative analysis also illustrates how the exploitation of the least critical (or scarce) resource can overcome the negative economic consequences of the other resources.

Although the modelling assessment cannot quantify the effects on different household groups, the increasing food prices (see also the discussion on food security below) that result from all three nexus bottlenecks, suggest that the welfare of the poorest households may be especially adversely affected. Especially in the countries with a negative effect on consumption will increases in food prices and the associated increase in the budget share of households spent on food lead to equity concerns that warrant further investigation.

Environmental quality

Two main effects of nexus bottlenecks on the environmental quality of the land surface are changes in pristine forest cover and the carbon stock. Pristine (or mature) forest in the biophysical modelling context concerns forest lands not drastically impacted by human activities.[1] In the baseline, pristine forest global cover decreases by around 4.5% between 2015 and 2060, the land bottleneck adds some 2.5%, the energy bottleneck doubles the loss and all bottlenecks combined go at the expense of 8% more loss than the baseline. Many environmental services are provided by pristine forests such as habitat for species, genetic resources, local and regional water and climate regulation, carbon sequestration and tourism. Hence the loss means these services are seriously affected in particular in the biggest loser regions and countries.

The other key quality of land is the carbon stocks it contains in soils and in living and dead biomass. Conversion of natural land to other purposes such as crop land or clearing for timber, tends to release important shares of these stocks and hence contribute to a net release to the atmosphere where it raises the atmospheric concentration of CO_2, the biggest contributor to man-made climate change. As new plants and trees start to grow on the once natural land, these start to rebuild carbon stocks, but a slow rate and in any cases not close to the original level, certainly not within many decades, Under current climate conditions, retained until 2060 in the baseline and the nexus bottleneck scenarios, the terrestrial biosphere loses some 70 Gt of carbon; the land and energy bottlenecks add 12% and 33%, respectively, to that volume.

Food security

Food security is one of the key policy objectives that is threatened by the nexus bottlenecks. All three bottleneck scenario lead to deteriorations in food security as reflected in increasing food prices and increased budget shares spent on food. Furthermore, in most regions the import share of food increases, indicating increased pressure on self-sufficiency. The consequences are especially pronounced in India, and the land bottleneck (primarily the effect of urban sprawl), which directly takes away fertile agricultural land, poses the biggest threat. The combination of all bottlenecks further amplifies the increase in food prices, while climate change further increases food budget shares and reliance on food imports, especially in India and Indonesia.

This effect of the nexus bottlenecks on food security can also have important social repercussions. It is likely that especially the poorest households are hurt by the nexus bottlenecks. As discussed above, this can lead to equity issues and loss of welfare for these groups. Of course, this has to be seen in a context of a baseline where food production rises significantly in the coming decades, as do per capita incomes. Thus, the negative effects are mostly in deviation from baseline, not with respect to 2015 levels.

The potential productivity of agriculture per unit of area depends strongly on local climate conditions, soil quality and availability of water. In practice, actual yields also depend on the intensity and adequacy of land management, including fertiliser application, pest and disease controls, seed quality, irrigation, mechanisation, etc. In order to maximise farm income, using the most productive, accessible land offers the best prospects. Good land may be un-accessible for a variety of reasons: it may be out-competed by other uses than food production; it may be remote from existing settlements, roads or waterways; its use may be restricted due to nature conservation concerns, etc. In the baseline, all these considerations play a role in determining where agriculture is located and what that implies for average yields.

The water bottleneck reduces the growth on those parts of irrigated land for which less or no water can be sourced. In order to make up for the loss, more rainfed production is needed and this affects the average productivity. For the world as a whole the negative impact on yields is small, as the biggest share of production is not affected by the reduced water availability and well-managed rainfed yields are close to those of irrigated crops. For a small set of regions, however, the yield reductions are more serious. In particular where alternative sites are scarce, total food production can get under pressure with implications for food security and self-sufficiency.

Water security

Water security is a key condition for human development. Water is indispensable to sustain food and fodder production, human settlements, industries, electric power production and ecosystem requirements. At the global level the average annual amount of renewable fresh water, that is the surplus of precipitation minus evaporation and transpiration to the atmosphere, exceeds the demand. But the spatial allocation, seasonal and inter-annual variability and uneven distribution of population density over the land surface make that large parts of the human population are confronted with periods of water scarcity. Over and above the quantitative aspect addressed here, widespread water pollution adds to the problem as it reduces the usability of water unless large-scale treatment is applied. Many people live under severe water stress, which implies a high likelihood of facing periods of shortages.

Agricultural production to feed local people and contribute to exports depends strongly on irrigation to make up for insufficient precipitation, and in many areas irrigation relies critically on non-renewable aquifers. Even though the projected increase in total irrigation water demand is very moderate, depletion of non-renewable sources is bound to reduce future water security. Withdrawals for non-agricultural purposes are expected to increase stronger than irrigation, and an increasing number of people will face more severe water stress. The increase is concentrated in river basins already water stressed today and growth in population and economy activity per capita.

The sector shares of water demand vary strongly between the regions, but in many regions irrigation dominates in 2015. In 2060 the demand for the non-agriculture sectors increases strongly in most emerging and currently less developed regions in Asia, Africa and Latin America. In OECD regions the water demand is projected to decrease due to limited population growth, efficiency improvements and structural shifts in electric power technology and in industry towards less water-intensive sectors. The combined effect of increasing demand for non-agricultural uses, and depletion of aquifer stocks, will have serious implications for water security in many regions and countries, including India, Middle East, North Africa, Mexico and the Caspian region. Also specific parts of others regions, including Mediterranean Europe, South-west United States, and arid parts of Other Africa and Other Asia are affected.

Energy security

Finally, the implications of the nexus bottlenecks for energy security are much less clear than the implications for some of the other policy objectives. The most important interactions between water scarcity and energy security and between climate change and energy supply could not be captured in the modelling analysis. Thus, while land bottlenecks are likely to have a very minor impact on energy security, energy security threats from water bottlenecks are potentially more significant. Annex B discusses some of these potential risks and interactions.

In itself, it is clear that energy is in a strict sense not likely to be a scarce resource in the coming decades. While energy is certainly a critical resource in terms of its economic importance, the large traded volumes of energy and the availability of alternative energy sources such as wind and solar energy imply that supply risks are fairly low. A bioenergy policy could improve energy security at the national level, but the quantitative analysis shows that this comes at a trade-off with the other nexus resources, especially land, and can thus threaten other policy objectives such as food security.[2] Similarly, one can speculate that a when water scarcity becomes a significant bottleneck, advanced technologies such as desalinisation can "transfer" some of these stresses to the other resources in the nexus, in this case energy. Such a transfer would, however, likely come at the expense of other policy objectives, such as welfare.

5.2. Regional trade-offs and synergies between the nexus bottlenecks

The impacts from LWE bottlenecks vary by a great extent across regions depending on endowment, vulnerability to climate impacts, past and future socioeconomic trends. The results of the modelling analysis highlights that an assessment of the main bottlenecks in the nexus for specific regions need to focus on the local interactions between the demand and supply of food, water and energy, as these drive local bottlenecks. Therefore, for each region the insights from the modelling and scoping analysis can be brought together in an integrated perspective on the local nexus issues.

At the macro level, Canada is largely unaffected by the nexus bottlenecks; there are some small sectoral impacts from the various bottleneck scenarios, but these are small and to some extent related to the specific setup of the scenarios (e.g. on bioenergy). Mexico is slightly more affected, but the biophysical and economic repercussions of the bottlenecks remain largely limited to a reduction in yields, mostly stemming from the water bottleneck, without major repercussions for the rest of the economy as this is to a large extent compensated by an increase in cropland to preserve agricultural production.

The situation in the United States is more complex: there are significant differences between the various regions within the United States. For instance, major parts of the South West are in a state of systemic water deficit and occasionally face long periods of drought that may multiply with climate change. In these regions of the country, the nexus bottlenecks may pose critical problems at the local level. In other parts of the United States, where water is more abundant, the nexus bottlenecks are much less of a threat. Overall, the modelling analysis illustrates that the macroeconomic implications of the water bottleneck are very limited, urban sprawl (as simulated in the land bottleneck) can lead to significant reductions in agricultural value added, and the use of land for bioenergy might boost the economy. Technological developments can also influence these effects. For instance, shale gas and shale oil may put additional stress on the water system, but there is also an institutional capacity to transform the water, energy and agricultural sectors to accommodate specific shocks as they arise, and flexibility in the system allows that a bottleneck for one specific resource can be compensated by increased use of the other resources, not least using energy to increase water supply there where it is most needed.

The European OECD countries, both inside the EU and outside, operate in close international linkages between their economies. This means that specific shocks caused by the nexus to one individual country can relatively easily be compensated by changes in international trade patterns. While in several countries, especially in the south of Europe, yields are affected by the water bottleneck, and the land bottleneck affects a few countries as well, the macroeconomic repercussions for the group as a whole remain very limited.

For Australia and New Zealand, the specific bioenergy shock that is simulated in the energy bottleneck scenario has strong repercussions for agriculture as it induces a shift from exporting agricultural commodities to bioenergy, to exploit the changes in competitive position across regions and commodities. Regarding the water bottleneck, Australia is in a similar position to the United States: specific regions are very dry and vulnerable to water scarcity, but macroeconomic implications are projected to be small.

Japan and Korea may face some challenges from land scarcity and urban sprawl, as simulated in land bottleneck scenario, but on balance these countries are projected to be less affected by the developments in the nexus than most others. And while they rely on irrigation for rice production, their dependence on non-renewable water sources is very limited, and hence the impact of the water bottleneck is small.

The nexus bottlenecks are very strong in large parts of Asia, and China is no exception. To accommodate productivity losses from a lack of irrigation water for rice production in the water bottleneck scenario, land expansion is required. The land bottleneck puts even stronger pressure on land markets. This is costly in China, leading to a significant loss of GDP, around 3% for all bottlenecks together.

The non-OECD EU countries and rest of Europe region are also regions where the land bottleneck can threaten agricultural production and thus the macro economy, while increased bioenergy production might stimulate GDP. This situation is amplified in Russia: the specific bioenergy scenario projections show substantial economic gains for Russia from the increased bioenergy production, especially from improved competitive position on the international markets. To some extent, this comes at the expense of the Caspian region, where conditions are less favourable and all bottlenecks have a dampening effect on economic growth.

In Brazil, water is abundant at the country level, but there are water stressed regions in the South. Agriculture depends on surface water availability and the energy system is vulnerable to water stress. Climate change and energy security policies have boosted large-scale development of bioethanol production, thereby increasing competition for land and water. But in both Brazil and the rest of Latin America, there is economic pressure to accommodate nexus shocks by increasing land supply at the expense of forest and other natural areas. By exploiting the relatively abundant land resource, the Latin American countries can improve their trading position and reap a larger share of the global market for their exports, thereby boosting their economy, at the expense of environmental quality.

In the Middle East and North Africa, water bottlenecks are the biggest threat and can seriously threaten crop yields and agricultural value added; climate change may exacerbate this even further. The countries in the Middle East face extreme water scarcity and have developed their resource supply systems accordingly: energy is used to compensate for the lack of water. The energy consumption of the water sector has increased in recent years because of strong economic and demographic growth, subsidies to energy consumption and to agriculture production, deeper groundwater pumping and long distance transport and desalination. Land resources in the region are limited; i.e. 93.5% of all potentially suitable land is already in agricultural use in Middle East (see Chapter 3). A global surge in bioenergy production can also harm consumption levels by depressing energy exports and energy prices, although the region is more flexible in dealing with changes in fuel prices than other fuel exporters as it contains some of the lowest marginal cost producers of oil. Nonetheless, the GDP impacts of the bottlenecks remain limited in the Middle East, not least because the baseline projection entails a significant diversification of the economies in this region, making them more versatile and less sensitive to agricultural and energy shocks. Also, some countries in this region are at the forefront of using the relatively abundant resource to compensate for the scarcity of other resources, not least relieving water shortages through highly energy-intensive novel production methods. In contrast, the GDP impacts are larger in North Africa, as the economic pressure of the bottlenecks cannot as easily be accommodated by diversifying the economy.

There are interesting differences between the biophysical and economic consequences of the nexus bottlenecks for the ASEAN economies, on the one hand, and India on the other. Both rely strongly on irrigation with a big share of irrigation water provided by non-renewable resources, and both have strong demographic developments and economic growth. But the ASEAN economies can increase crop land use in response to the bottlenecks to improve their international trade position and thus boost their economy. In contrast, India, where yield losses are stronger, cannot easily accommodate the bottlenecks and is projected to have the strongest losses in agricultural value added and GDP of all regions in the world. Indonesia and the countries in the Other Asia group are intermediate cases between these extremes.

Africa is the continent facing globally the strongest demographic growth within the next decades. In addition, many African countries suffer from a lack of access to water and/or energy which results in a high vulnerability from climate change impacts. Land for agriculture is scarce in several Sub-Saharan countries, but abundant in others such as in the Congo basin. Due to the limited use of irrigation, groundwater depletion has little impact on agriculture. But important water bottlenecks can appear from the change in rainfall due to climate change. The simulated additional bioenergy production in the energy bottleneck scenario also leads to a significant reduction in forest land, and thus has negative consequences for environmental quality. Other effects might be expected from the impacts on the potential for hydropower which is a key technology for improving energy security in the region. Like in India, the strong economic growth in the baseline also makes these countries vulnerable when the growth in resource use that supports high growth is threatened. And like in India, the interaction between the different bottlenecks worsens the situation.

5.3. On the robustness of the modelling results

The analytical results presented in this report are subject to considerable uncertainty in underlying data and modelling, including the baseline projection that was used as starting point for the analysis of nexus bottlenecks impacts. The longer the time horizon, the more "known unknowns" and also "unknown unknowns" induce excursions from the baseline reported here. Uncertainties can occur in every stage of the process of calculating the biophysical and economic consequences of the land-water-energy nexus, and include:

- Uncertainties in projecting the socioeconomic drivers of economic growth (baseline);

- Uncertainties in projecting agricultural production, land use and yields (baseline);

- Uncertainties in projecting the water and energy use of agricultural and other economic activities (baseline);

- Uncertainties in specifying the policy shocks (policy scenarios);

- Uncertainties in specifying the consequences of the policy shocks on agricultural production, land use and yields (policy scenarios);

- Uncertainties in specifying the reactions of economic agents (firms and households) to the policy shocks and associated changes in the biophysical system (policy scenarios).

It is beyond the scope of this report to quantify each of these uncertainties, and they are not mutually independent (and hence very difficult to quantify). In an effort to capture some of such structural uncertainties, other studies develop a set of projections, reflecting alternative narratives of how the future could unfold (Riahi et al., 2016). By repeating nexus bottleneck assumptions for each of the alternative pathways, a range of impacts would result rather than a point estimate as in this report. For practical reasons and because multiplying the number of scenarios does not necessarily increase the clarity of the policy insights, the single CIRCLE project baseline is used in this report.

In order to reduce the reliance of the numerical results on specific baseline assumptions, all scenario results are expressed in terms of deviations from baseline. This ensures that biases and uncertainties that occur in the baseline as well as the policy scenarios are filtered out. Bottleneck deviations from the baseline are thus more robust than absolute numbers for the different scenarios. So, more than precise absolute numbers, the results indicate where a specific bottleneck hits harder than elsewhere, and which bottlenecks matter most for which world region.

Uncertainties from limited availability of authoritative data behind key variables arise at all stages. Reliable data at the appropriate disaggregation level is even more scarce, and there are limitations in which factors and relationships can be captured by the models. Regarding the baseline projection, one of the key assumptions is the evolution of agricultural productivity improvements, as summarised in yield growth for the various regions. The input data on crop yield changes (physical production per hectare) are calibrated with the utmost care, and encompass plausible regional and crop-specific trends as they are likely to evolve in the coming decades. The projections of IMAGE and ENV-Linkages are also fully harmonised on this point. One method of validating the yield projections was the participation by the modelling teams in the Agricultural Model Intercomparison Project AgMIP (Von Lampe et al., 2014). Such multi-model comparison exercises allow identification of which baseline projections are features of the model, and which assumptions need adjustment to ensure all projections are plausible. Despite ongoing efforts to enhance and expand the analytical tools with the aim to be as relevant and robust as feasible, any results can only be understood within the inherent limits posed by current capabilities.

Finally, LWE nexus bottlenecks explored represent stylised impacts of potential issues arising, for the sake of the analysis assumed to manifest themselves across all world regions in a similar fashion and at the same point in time. Results have to be viewed in this context, and they do not make it possible to assess the likelihood of their emergence in place and time as reported here. For example, in the water bottleneck all aquifers in a certain category are assumed to run out in one particular year, while in reality a much more diverse set of local and regional impacts may unfold. Nonetheless, the notion that many aquifers are being used in a way that jeopardises their continued operation makes that sooner or later consequences as presented here are bound to occur. A systematic exploration of all possible sources of uncertainty goes beyond the scope of this report. But the structural relationships implied by the combined biophysical and economic analysis make for sufficiently robust findings and implications for policy making.

5.4. Final remarks

The question is to what extent the interdependencies between each of the three constituents land, water and energy of the LWE nexus have repercussions at the macroeconomic and global level and, thus, support the urgency of promoting integrated policies for the nexus. The modelling analysis in this report does not provide an unambiguous positive answer, certainly not at the global level where bottleneck impacts are very moderate, and only a very small interaction effect emerges from the combined bottlenecks.

A multitude of convincing arguments, however, present themselves at the finer regional scale. And it seems safe to suggest that zooming to much finer scales would reveal even more striking examples where compounded problems with land, water and energy issues call for a co-ordinated, integral policy. As underlined by the stark differences in results of the modelling analysis at the regional level, different individual bottleneck challenges and different interlinkages play out in different regions of the world and in different parts of those regions. Examples include the impact of declining water supply from aquifers on yields, and thereby on agricultural land area in order to keep food security at bay. Another example is the exploitation of improved competitive position by producers that are relatively less affected by the bottlenecks than their competitors.

With this in mind, allocating vast areas to grow feedstock for biofuels, or not limiting groundwater use from non-renewable aquifers for irrigation purposes, warrants due attention in the (sub-) regions concerned. And the same holds for uncontrolled urban sprawl, and for the land needed to provide other ecosystem goods and services such as timber, water and local climate regulation, carbon storage, tourism and to reduce and eventually halt the loss of biodiversity. The bottlenecks explored here indicate that land is probably the strongest interconnector, so integral land planning approaches are important to balance the different concerns and interests.

Other feedback mechanisms between the three domains do not stand out as strongly. It is important to note that the caveats and missing links in the current study play their role in this conclusion, not least the partial treatment of the resources and their biophysical and economic linkages, and the top-down nature of the modelling exercise. In addition, the stringency of the bottlenecks that are analysed in the models affect the severity of the biophysical and economic consequences, and the more stringent the bottlenecks, the stronger the interdependencies are likely to be.

The nexus is further put in perspective by comparing it with the effects of climate change; on the whole climate change tends to add to the losses incurred by the nexus shocks. The negative consequences of climate change worsen the most vulnerable regions, not least because to some extent the regions most threatened by the nexus bottlenecks are also most at risk from climate change. But these linkages also represent potential indirect benefits for climate change policies. The energy conservation part of climate change policies induce obvious benefits due to less stress on fossil fuel resources, water withdrawal and water pollution from the energy sector. In addition, reduced electricity demand diminishes the vulnerability of the power sector to water stress. Biofuels have to be considered with their associated effects on land and water use. Supporting renewables, such as wind and solar photovoltaic technologies, often contributes to increasing water security, but may lead to new bottlenecks due to the reliance on specific scarce materials.

In around half the regions, the key results for the combined scenario fall within one percent of the sum of the individual three bottlenecks. This suggests that in these regions not much is gained from treating the issues in one overarching policy framework at the macro level, rather than pursuing each issue individually and on regional hotspots. In the other regions, highlighted in Section 5.2, the interactions from combining the bottlenecks are more pronounced and suggest that adding an overarching nexus vision to policy making has clear benefits. The finding in this report could thus help to focus future research and priorities for policy responses for addressing critical nexus resources.

Notes

1. This includes areas used by humans in earlier periods, but sufficiently long ago to have reached a semi-natural state with biodiversity largely restored. Excluded are areas completely deforested and areas in more intensive timber production schemes. Human activities which affect forests but at a smaller scale and over a relatively short time period, such as gathering and hunting and collection of firewood for local use, are not considered here. Forests as considered here consist of large, consecutive areas with close to 100% canopy cover, and thus not smaller patches of trees in biomes such as wooded tundra and savannah in IMAGE.

2. While direct competition with crop production for food is avoided when concentrating on second generation bioenergy, there is still a competition for land and thus a negative impact of bioenergy on food security.

References

Riahi, K. et al. (2016), "The shared socioeconomic pathways and their energy, land use, and greenhouse gas emissions implications: an overview", *Global Environmental Change* 42, pp. 153-168.

Von Lampe, M. et al. (2014), "Why do global long-term scenarios for agriculture differ? An overview of the AgMIP Global Economic Model Intercomparison", Agricultural Economics 45(1), pp. 3-20.

Annex A

The main socioeconomic trends underlying the analysis

The socioeconomic trends that form the basis for the baseline and counterfactual simulation projections in this report are described in OECD (2015). Here, the most relevant information is reproduced.

A baseline projection is characterised by an absence of new climate policies, the continuation of current policies for other policy domains (including energy) and plausible socio-economic developments, including demographic trends, urbanisation and globalisation trends.[1] A baseline projection is not a prediction of what will happen, but rather a plausible scenario describing a certain storyline for how these key trends affect future economic development in the absence of unexpected shocks. Chateau et al. (2011) describe the baseline calibration procedure in more detail, although the numerical calibration of the model has since been updated to reflect more recent data.

Demographic trends play a key role in determining long run economic growth. Projections of detailed movements in population by gender, age and education level determine future employment levels and human capital that drives labour productivity. While population and employment are correlated, the regional trends are differentiated by changes in participation rates for specific age groups (most prominently for people over the age of 65), changes in unemployment levels and changes in the age structure of the population (including aging).

Figure A.1 presents the baseline projection (excluding climate feedbacks) of total regional population, based on the medium variant projection of the United Nations' World Population Prospects database (UN, 2013) and EUROSTAT (2013) for European countries.[2] At global level, population will increase from around 7 billion people in 2010 to almost 10 billion people in 2060. Despite the large increase, population growth by the middle of the century is projected to be substantially lower than it currently is. While this is true in most world regions, population keeps increasing at a steep rate in Sub-Saharan Africa.

GDP growth is influenced by changes in labour, man-made capital and the use of land resources. In all cases, GDP growth is driven by a combination of increased supply of the production factors, changes in the allocation of resources across the economy, and improvements in the productivity of resource use (the efficiency of transforming production inputs into production outputs). Table A.1 shows the average GDP growth rates for the current decade (2010-20), the medium term (2020-40) and the long term (2040-60). In most countries, short-term growth is primarily driven by a variety of sources, depending on the characteristics of the current economy. These short-term projections are based on the official forecasts made by OECD (2014) and IMF (2014). In the longer run, a transition emerges towards a more balanced growth path in which labour productivity as a driver of economic growth is matched by increases in capital supply.

Figure A.1. **Trend in population by region, baseline projection**

(Billion people)

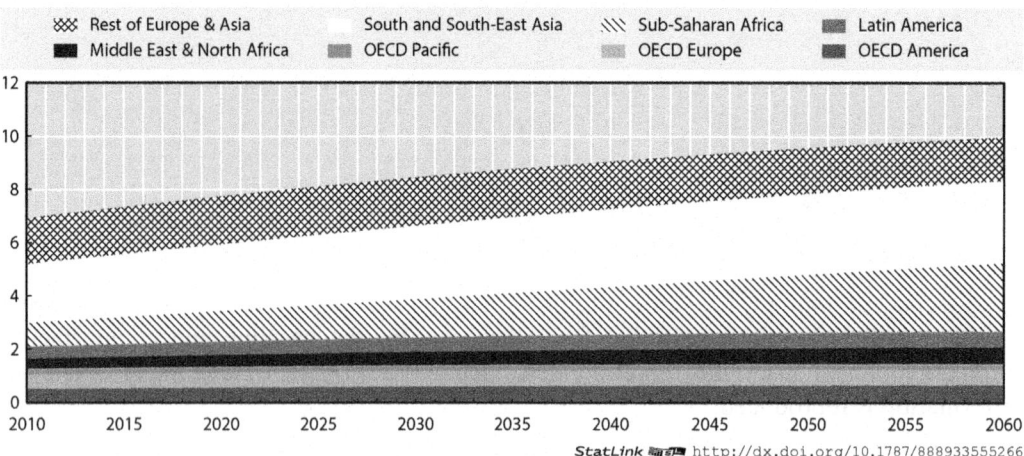

StatLink ᵃᵗᵗ http://dx.doi.org/10.1787/888933555266

Source: UN (2013) as used in the ENV-Linkages model.

Table A.1. **Economic growth over selected periods by region**

(Average annual percentage GDP growth rates)

	2010-20	2020-40	2040-60		2010-20	2020-40	2040-60
OECD America				**Rest of Europe and Asia**			
Canada	2.2	2.0	1.9	China	7.6	4.2	1.6
Chile	4.7	2.4	1.4	Non-OECD EU	2.2	2.5	1.7
Mexico	3.6	3.4	2.5	Russia	3.6	2.1	0.9
USA	2.4	1.9	1.5	Caspian region	6.3	4.8	2.6
OECD Europe				Other Europe	2.4	3.3	2.0
EU large 4	1.5	1.6	1.3	**Latin America**			
Other OECD EU	1.9	2.0	1.3	Brazil	3.3	3.0	1.8
Other OECD	3.6	2.6	1.7	Other Lat.Am.	3.6	3.7	3.1
OECD Pacific				**Middle East & North Africa**			
Aus. & New Z.	3.2	2.6	2.1	Middle East	3.4	3.7	2.3
Japan	0.9	1.0	1.1	North Africa	3.9	4.9	3.2
Korea	4.0	2.3	0.6	**South and South-East Asia**			
				ASEAN 9	4.8	4.2	3.1
				Indonesia	6.1	4.6	3.3
				India	6.6	5.8	3.6
				Other Asia	4.2	4.2	3.7
				Sub-Saharan Africa			
				South Africa	4.9	4.2	1.9
				Other Africa	5.9	6.5	6.0
OECD	2.2	1.9	1.5	**World**	3.5	3.1	2.2

StatLink ᵃᵗᵗ http://dx.doi.org/10.1787/888933555418

Source: OECD (2014) for OECD countries and ENV-Linkages model for non-OECD countries.

Table A.1 illustrates the main trends in economic development for the coming decades: continued slower growth in the OECD than in non-OECD countries (with a few exceptions), declining growth rates in emerging economies and relatively strong growth in Africa and most other developing countries.

For an understanding of the future economy, it does not suffice to look at the macro economy only. To name just a few examples, projected productivity increases vary between different sectors, increasing incomes imply a change in demand for various goods, there will also be changes in the preferences of consumers, and international trade patterns may gradually adjust to stabilise trade balances.

Figure A.2 shows how the sectoral structure in the OECD economies evolves, with the services sectors accounting for more than half of the GDP (i.e. value added) created in the future OECD economies. Generally, the shares of the various sectors in the economy tend to be relatively stable, although there are undoubtedly many fundamental changes at the sub-sectoral level that are not reflected here. The major oil exporters in the Middle East and northern Africa are projected to gradually diversify their economies and rely less on energy resources. In developing countries the trend for a decline of the importance of agriculture is projected to continue strongly. Given the high growth rates in many of these economies, this does not mean an absolute decline of agricultural production, but rather an industrialisation process, and, in many cases, a strong increase in services.

Figure A.2. Sectoral composition of GDP by region, baseline projection
(Percentage of GDP)

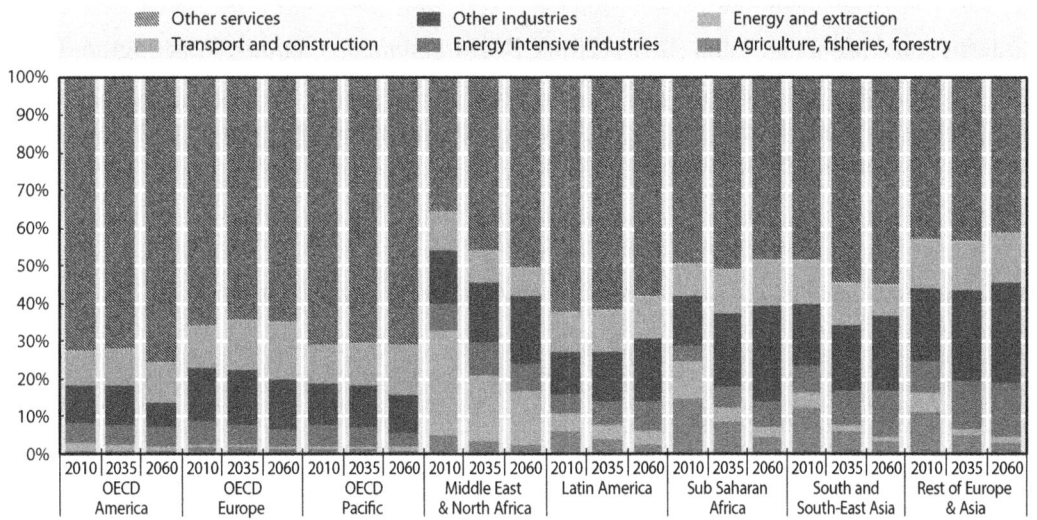

StatLink ⬛⬛⬛ http://dx.doi.org/10.1787/888933555285

Source: ENV-Linkages model.

Notes

1. More specifically, any policy that is not yet fully implemented, or that still requires an effort to be reached, is not included in the baseline. This assumption is only to provide a reference point for the assessments of the costs of inaction and the benefits of policy action, and does not reflect a view on the state of current climate policies.

2. Alternative population projections are available for the SSP scenarios (KC and Lutz, 2015); for example, in the medium SSP2 scenario, there is a stronger effect of female education on fertility than assumed here, leading to lower population levels later in the century. Using different population projections may substantially affect the numerical analysis in this chapter.

References

Chateau, J., C. Rebolledo and R. Dellink (2011), "An Economic Projection to 2050: The OECD 'ENV-Linkages' Model Baseline", *OECD Environment Working Papers*, No. 41, OECD Publishing, Paris, http://dx.doi.org/10.1787/5kg0ndkjvfhf-en.

EUROSTAT(2013), Population projection, Eurostat, the statistical office of the European Union. Online Database http://ec.europa.eu/eurostat/data/database.

International Monetary Fund (IMF) (2014), *World Economic Outlook*, Washington, DC.

KC, S. and W. Lutz (2015), "The human core of the shared socioeconomic pathways: population scenarios by age, sex and level of education for all countries to 2100", Global Environmental Change 42, pp. 181-192.

OECD (2015), *The Economic Consequences of Climate Change*, OECD Publishing, Paris, http://dx.doi.org/10.1787/9789264235410-en.

OECD (2014), *OECD Economic Outlook, Volume 2014 Issue 1*, OECD Publishing, Paris, http://dx.doi.org/10.1787/eco_outlook-v2014-1-en.

United Nations (2013), *World Population Prospects: the 2012 Revision*, UN Department of Economic and Social Affairs.

Annex B

Key linkages between water and energy

As any analysis, the quantitative assessment used in this report has limitations. In particular, it is not fit to study some of the important linkages between water and energy outlined in Chapter 1. First, the modelling tools can only capture systemic effects that are noticeable in the top-down frameworks, and ignore important local bottlenecks with severe local consequences that may occur over short time spans. Secondly, there are significant data gaps (see e.g. OECD, 2010) that prevent a full representation of all the bottlenecks in the baseline and counterfactual projections of the modelling tools. Therefore, this Annex attempts to provide further insights on the consequences of this particular linkage. Given the large data gaps, some of the key consequences of the nexus bottlenecks can only be discussed in an anecdotal way. Nonetheless, the inclusion of these consequences in the evaluation of the bottlenecks is fundamental in providing an overview of the full costs of inaction on the nexus, and therefore in the assessment of the benefits of policy action.

Water for electricity production

Water stress constrains electricity supply and thus affects the economy through three main channels. First, it can increase the cost of power generation and therefore the price paid by consumers for electricity. The macroeconomic impact of this channel is expected to be quite small given that the extra costs form a very limited share of the household's expenditures. A second possible channel is a disruption of the electric system, creating outages or blackouts with potentially very negative consequences. This is especially the case for advanced economies which are highly dependent on electrified infrastructures and information technologies. The last channel concerns regions with little access to electricity: water scarcity can be an additional obstacle to the delivery of access. This is particularly relevant for regions where the development of electricity is projected to be based to a large extent on hydropower technologies.

In general, the cost of water bottlenecks through constraining power supply for the economy is not easy to assess. On the one hand, if water bottlenecks are well managed and the change of resource availability is well anticipated, all the options available to limit the effect of water scarcity will be implemented in a cost effective way. In that case, the cost of adjusting to the bottleneck is quite low for the electricity system. On the other hand, if disruptions in the electric sector cannot be avoided, they can be very costly. Therefore one needs to take into account the cost of investments to hedge energy systems against the risk of disruption, for instance by providing more back-up generation capacity. Lastly, a major policy problem is that currently a large part of the world population has no access to electricity. Nexus bottlenecks can make the deployment of energy infrastructure more difficult, and thus hamper energy security.

Table B.1 summarises several quantitative assessments of water consumption for power generation in water-stressed areas. In general the studies provide projections for a cascade of trends. For instance economic growth drives power demand, climate change influences hydrology and exacerbates the water stress level. In turn, adaptation policies to climate change affect the choice of power generation technologies. The geographical scope is in general limited to certain countries as local circumstances matter (power generation mix, demand and hydrology). The only contributions with a global scope stem from Davies et al. (2013) and Kyle et al. (2013) but their analysis is just an assessment of future water demand from the power sector without assessing the resource constraints.

Table B.1. **Main studies of the effect of water scarcity on power generation**

Authors	Region	Scenario	Consequences
Davies et al. (2013)	World	No climate change	Adoption of better cooling technologies reduces water withdrawal of power sector by 60% at horizon 2095 with respect to baseline. But more water consumption.
Kyle et al. (2013)	World	Climate mitigation, no climate change	Stable water withdrawal at horizon 2095 despite CCS deployment, CCS and concentrating solar cost effective even with dry cooling.
Bhattacharya and Mitra (2013)	India	No mitigation, climate change causes draught and higher temperature	In 2050 20% of water withdrawal is for power generation.
Bhattacharya and Mitra (2013)	Thailand	No mitigation, climate change causes draught and higher temperature	Water scarcity is a problem for operation during dry seasons.
Rogers et al. (2013)	United States	No mitigation	Increased water withdrawal
IEA (2015)	India	No mitigation, no climate change	Slight increase in coal plant power generation costs.
IEA (2015)	China	No mitigation, no climate change	Slight increase in coal plant power generation costs.
Smart and Aspinall (2009)	Australia	No mitigation, no climate change	Increase in generation capacity in water-stressed areas (Queensland, New South Wales and Victoria)
Cervigni et al. (2015)	Part of Africa*	Hydro development, climate change: more or less runoff	In dry (wet) scenarios, over- (under-) dimensioning of new hydro capacity
Rübbelke, Stefan Vögele (2011)	EU	Less rainfall	Less thermoelectric production (focus on nuclear)
Van Vliet et al. (2012)	EU, United States	Change in hydrology	Water constraints for some power plants
Van Vliet et al. (2013)	EU	Change in hydrology, interconnections and capacities are fixed	Increase in power prices for 2030-60 with strongest increases for Slovenia (12-15%), Bulgaria (21-23%) and Romania (31-32%).
Sovacool and Sovacool (2009)	United States	No mitigation, no climate change	"Summer water deficit" and qualitative assessment of the cost for non-electricity sectors.
US DOE (2012)	South-west US	Impacts of Long-term Drought on Power Systems	Ongoing study...

*Congo, Niger, Nile, Orange, Senegal, Volta, and Zambezi river basins.

Source: Authors' compilation.

The nexus bottlenecks depend on the local circumstances. They will be aggravated by decreases in rainfall and increases in heat waves caused by climate change. The synergies with climate policies are strong. Mitigation policies can limit the stress on water resource by reducing the impact of climate change and they will also accelerate the transition from water intensive thermoelectric technologies to favour the deployment of wind and solar PV technologies which require far less water. However, low-carbon electricity does not necessarily equate to decreased water demand. Carbon Capture and Storage (CCS), hydropower, nuclear, irrigated biofuels, can all exacerbate water stress (IEA, 2016).

Even if they give good insights on the water energy part of the nexus, the studies do not quantify the cost of the nexus. Most of them just aim at identifying region of potential water deficit, i.e. hotspots for bottlenecks. They project water demand from the power sector and the water that can be supplied by the hydrological system are considered separately (Bhattacharya and Mitra, 2013; Rogers et al., 2014; Smart and Aspinall, 2009; Sovacool and Sovacool, 2009). The projected water for power generation is not constrained by water resource, and the studies merely assess the water imbalances, pointing out bottleneck without assessing how and at what cost they can be managed. Other studies take into account the power sector adjustment to water imbalance: by adjusting operation of capacity addition including the choice technologies, cooling systems and plant location or interconnections (IEA, 2015; Van Vliet et al. 2012; Rübbelke and Vögele, 2011). Few studies assess, as Van Vliet et al. (2013) and IEA (2015) the costs involved by the adjustment of the power system and therefore the impact on power prices.

One key determinant of the cost of the bottleneck which is missing in most of the studies is uncertainty. Water scarcity has to be managed by the electric sector such that there is very low risk of disruption. It means that it is necessary to invest in solutions, making the supply system resilient to extreme and rather unlikely events affecting water availability. There is a need for hedging against water stress by developing capacities that can respond to these extreme events, but that will be mostly left idle. Given the very long lifetime of the power plants, there is a high uncertainty on possible water stress and the investments for hedging against the water stress are can be very costly.

If perfectly managed by the electricity sector, water scarcity challenges can be addressed by decreasing energy demand, adjusting operation and investment in the electric supply. The differences in impacts on final prices are due to local circumstances and also to the options given to limit the dependence to the water sector. In studies where the adjustment options are limited, for instance when they do not include investment in capacity or in transmission, as in Van Vliet et al. (2013) the impact may be relatively high reaching 30% at horizon 2060 in Eastern European countries. When more options can be used, as in the IEA (2015) study on the cost of water scarcity for the coal generation technologies in China, water scarcity can be managed at a very limited cost in the coal sector (+1%) which gives reason to expect a little cost for the entire power sector.

More costly energy supply represents a loss for the whole economy. From a pure "production function" perspective, a first proxy of the GDP cost can be given by the price effect multiplied by the share of electricity expenditure in GDP. In the case of Eastern Europe, where the electricity expenditure is less than 4% of GDP, the results of Van Vliet et al. (2013) would involve a loss of GDP of around of 1.2%. In China, where electricity expenditures are less than 6% of the GDP, the IEA (2015) assessment would involve a negative GDP impact of around 0.06%. We see that the very big differences in assessments of the GDP impacts come from very different assessment of the cost for the electric system.

However, the approach mentioned above can be misleading. It doesn't take into account the additional cost required to secure against many sorts of extreme events. These costs have to reflect in higher power prices, with higher macroeconomic impacts. If the risk is not managed, disruption can happen with a very large cost for society. Finally the cost of the water constraints can be much higher than what the model of Van Vliet et al. (2013) and IEA (2015) which assume no disruption.

The economic cost of power disruption is a notion is central notion in power supply regulation. It is measured as the Value of Lost Load (VOLL) which the average cost to consumers per unit of unserved electricity due to outages (Stoft, 2002). This cost can be split into two parts: the direct damages due to the loss of assets and the indirect damages coming from the interruption of activity. For the regulator, it is the losses one wants to hedge against by investing in grid security. The VOLL is typically very high compared with power price, which reflects the importance of stable electric supply. The VOLLs, have very different values, depending largely on local circumstances, but also on the assessment method used, the time and the length of the outage. For similar approaches, the results are of similar order of magnitude. But results based on different methods are quite different, ranging from less than 20 cents per kWh to EUR 68 per kWh (Praktiknjo et al., 2011). Overall the cost of outages depends on several factors that are region specific: sectoral and geographical characteristics, duration, frequency and timing of the outage, experience and mitigation measures take. One can expect that socioeconomic trends, with GDP growth, IT technologies and increasingly complex manufacturing processes will increase reliance on electronic equipment and contribute to higher VOLLs (RAE, 2014). To our knowledge, there is no study of the VOLL with coverage sufficient to allow for a global assessment of the cost of electricity shortage.[1]

VOLL is a notion that is at first sight more fit for regions that already have a reliable power supply system and where the overnight economic cost of disruption is high. But one need to assess the economic cost of repeated outages and black outs in regions with no access to stable power supply. In this case, the power interruptions can be seen as a lack of infrastructure which creates bottlenecks for economic growth. They also induce wasteful consumptions as individual or local-level utilities need to be deployed to face the shortages. For instances, communities may need to purchase and operate small scale diesel of gasoline power generators, with as a results a power cost much higher than what could be delivered by a conventional supply system of grid and power plants.

Increased water scarcity and uncertainty about water availability created by climate change may hinder the transition towards public supply systems, in particular because in many developing countries hydro with depends on water availability is regarded as the means to improve the security of supply. But there is an uncertainty on the potential for this type of generation. For instance in West Africa, uncertainty on hydrology increase the risk of under or over investment in hydro, thus increasing the cost of hydro generation compared with a situation with less uncertainty (Cervigni et al., 2015).

Water for fossil fuel and biofuel production

Fossil fuel extraction also requires water. The water intensity of the technique varies a lot depending on the fuel and the process. The depletion of "conventional" reserves gave way to more and more water-intensive production and transformation processes. Clark et al. (2013) show that in the United States unconventional gas produced by fracking has more water consumption than conventional. Even though unconventional gas is used as transportation fuel, their water intensity is less than for conventional oil. When fuel resources are located in water scarce areas, their exploitation represents an additional claim on water use. This is for instance the case in Texas. A similar problem occurs in China where large deposits of coal and shale gas are located in very water-stressed areas.

Unconventional resources are also a threat for water quality as underlined by IEA (2016). Fossil fuel production, transportation and processing generate effluents that pollute water bodies. Fracking techniques may increase the amount of toxic effluents per unit on energy produced although the consequences are still difficult to assess.

In a world where easily accessible fossil fuel resources get depleted and where GHG emissions constraints are tight, biofuels, such as biodiesel and bioethanol can be an option for energy security. However, biofuels, if not produced from agricultural or forest residue are very water intensive (IEA, 2016) and may pressurise water resources. In addition, the competitiveness of water use will increase, in particular in regions where scarce water is also used for crops with a requirement of high amounts of water.

Energy for water supply

Water and end energy supply are also interlinked by the energy consumption for water extraction, processing and transportation. The energy intensity of water supplies depends on the structure of the water resource, the water demand as well as the need to rebalance regional demand and supply by transporting water over long distances (KAPSARC, 2015). Surface water typically requires little energy to be extracted. Also groundwater generally needs barely any intensive treatment before making it usable In contrast; extraction can be very energy intensive when deeper aquifers are used.

Water energy intensity also depends on the adequacy between zone of consumption and zone of extraction. When water resources are remote from the zones of consumption, water has to be transported over long distance which implies high energy costs. For instance, in California the State Water Project (SWP) with more than 662 miles of canals, tunnels and pipelines designed to move water from Northern California to users in the Central Valley and Southern California, is the single biggest power consumer of the state, with consumptions widely varying depending on precipitations (Trask, 2005). Note that the energy intensity of water transportation doesn't depend on the distance, but also on whether it is based on pumping or gravity.

Desalination is used in cases where water scarcity cannot be balanced by water availability in bone of the surrounding areas. This is typically the case in countries in the Gulf region. More generally, desalination increases due to urbanisation, economic growth, and especially in water stressed areas. It also increased because of the decreasing cost of desalination (Ghaffour et al., 2013). There are various options available for desalination with different energy intensities. Desalination has already been developed at a large scale in the Middle East and the United States. The increase in desalinated water capacity is also due to climate variability: in periods of drought, desalination facilities are built, but possibly not used when rain come back, which indeed has a cost for society as has been the case for the Australian desalination capacities, so there is a risk dimension.[2]

The energy intensity of the desalination process is high (Siddiqui and Fletcher, 2015) and the energy demand can be a large share of the total energy consumption. For instance, in Saudi Arabia, Siddiqui and Diaz Anadon (2011) estimate that 9% of power consumption is for water pumping and desalination for desalination. With the increasing water needs, these activities can contribute to the increase in overall increase in energy demand.

Here, the policy question is primarily about pricing of water and pricing of energy. In countries where energy prices are very low, desalination is cheap, but it induces a wasteful energy use for desalination and wasteful energy consumption. In some regions like the Gulf countries water treatment is compulsory in industries, but the water is not reused because desalinated water is relatively cheap. Another issue: give incentives to do desalination with renewable technologies. The desalination facilities could be operated when the intermittent supply is abundant (but anyway this also has a cost). So one can think about giving incentives to desalination and renewable or giving a part or the desalinated water bill to support renewable? The solution will depend on the region. In some regions, desalination may be too expensive.

The share of energy use for water related to irrigation in agriculture is important but still difficult to identify. Irrigation is important for agriculture: 16% of the world's cultivated cropland is irrigated. Most of the irrigated areas are in Asian countries. Climate change may increase the use of irrigation because irrigation reduces the climate risk on water availability. But irrigation requires big amounts of energy. Energy consumption can be high in regions where energy (power, gasoil) is still subsidised for agriculture (e.g. in India) and where there is thus no incentive to invest in efficient pumps or irrigation technique. In addition, the lower the groundwater, the deeper one needs to pump and the most one consumes energy. Plus there are difficulties to control pumping as it is still a quite uncontrolled activity. Better pricing of energy for agriculture and support for energy efficiency methods could both improve the water conservation and decrease energy consumption.

Notes

1. However, there is an online tool that calculates for most of the EU countries the costs of user defined blackout scenarios. The costs computation is based on a monograph about VOLLs (see www.blackout-simulator.com/).

2. For instance, see www.nytimes.com/2015/04/12/science/drinking-seawater-looks-ever-more-palatable-to-californians.html?_r=0.

References

Bhattacharya, A. and B.K. Mitra (2013), "Water Availability for Sustainable Energy Policy: Assessing cases in South and South East Asia", *IGES Research Report* 2013-01.

Cervigni, R. et al. (2015), *Enhancing the Climate Resilience of Africa's Infrastructure: The Power and Water Sectors. Overview booklet.* World Bank, Washington, DC.

Clark, C., R. Horner and C. Harto (2013), "Life Cycle Water Consumption for Shale Gas and Conventional Natural Gas", *Environmental Science and Technology* 47, pp. 11829-11836.

Davies, E.G.R., P. Kyle and J.A. Edmonds (2013), "An integrated assessment of global and regional water demands for electricity generation to 2095", *Advances in Water Resources* 52, pp. 296-313.

Ghaffour, N., T. Missimer and G. Amy (2013), "Technical review and evaluation of the economics of water desalination: Current and future challenges for better water supply sustainability", *Desalination*, No. 309, pp 197-207.

International Energy Agency (IEA) (2016), *World Energy Outlook 2016*, OECD publishing, Paris, http://dx.doi.org/10.1787/weo-2016-en.

International Energy Agency (IEA) (2015), *World Energy Outlook 2015*, OECD publishing, Paris, http://dx.doi.org/10.1787/weo-2015-en.

KAPSARC (2015)," Energy for Water", *KAPSARC Energy Workshop Series*, KS-1509-WB07A.

Kyle, P. et al. (2013), "Influence of climate change mitigation technology on global demands of water for electricity generation", *International Journal of Greenhouse Gas Control* 13, pp 112-123.

OECD (2010), *Coherence between water and energy policies*, OECD, Paris, www.oecd.org/officialdocuments/publicdisplaydocumentpdf/?cote=ENV/EPOC/GSP(2010)21&docLanguage=En.

Praktiknjo, A., A. Hähnel and G. Erdmann (2011), "Assessing energy supply security: outage costs in private households", *Energy Policy*, 39(12), pp. 7825-7833.

Royal Academy of Engineering (RAE) (2014), *Counting the cost: the economic and social costs of electricity shortfalls in the UK*, A report for the Council for Science and Technology.

Rogers, J. et al. (2013), *Water-smart power: Strengthening the U.S. electricity system in a warming world*, Cambridge, MA: Union of Concerned Scientists.

Rübbelke, D. and S. Vögele (2011), Impacts of climate change on European critical infrastructures: The case of the power sector, *Environmental Science & Policy* 14(1), pp. 53-63.

Siddiqi, A. and L. Diaz Anadon (2011), "The water–energy nexus in Middle East and North Africa", *Energy Policy* 39, pp. 4529-4540.

Siddiqi, A. and S. Fletcher (2015), "Energy Intensity of Water End-Us", *Current Sustainable / Renewable Energy Reports* 2(1), pp. 25-31.

Smart, A. and A. Aspinall (2009), *Water and the electricity generation industry, Implications of use*, National Water Commission of Australia,Waterlines Report Series No. 18.

Sovacool B. and K. Sovacool (2009), "Identifying future electricity–water tradeoffs in the United States", *Energy Policy* 37(7), pp. 2763-2773.

Stoft, S. (2002), *Power System Economics: Designing Markets for Electricity*, Wiley-IEEE Press, Piscataway.

Trask, M. (2005), "Water Energy Relationship", *California Energy Commission Staff Paper* CEC-700-2005-011.

US Department of Energy (US-DOE) (2012), "Impacts of Long-term Drought on Power Systems in the U.S. Southwest", presentation prepared for the US DOE Office of Electric Delivery and Energy Reliability, Infrastructure Security and Energy Restoration Division.

Van Vliet et al. (2012), "Vulnerability of US and European electricity supply to climate change," *Nature Climate Change* 9, pp. 676-681.

Van Vliet, M.T.H, S. Vögele and D. Rübbelke (2013), "Water constraints on European power supply under climate change: impacts on electricity prices", *Environmental Research Letters* 8.

ORGANISATION FOR ECONOMIC CO-OPERATION AND DEVELOPMENT

The OECD is a unique forum where governments work together to address the economic, social and environmental challenges of globalisation. The OECD is also at the forefront of efforts to understand and to help governments respond to new developments and concerns, such as corporate governance, the information economy and the challenges of an ageing population. The Organisation provides a setting where governments can compare policy experiences, seek answers to common problems, identify good practice and work to co-ordinate domestic and international policies.

The OECD member countries are: Australia, Austria, Belgium, Canada, Chile, the Czech Republic, Denmark, Estonia, Finland, France, Germany, Greece, Hungary, Iceland, Ireland, Israel, Italy, Japan, Korea, Latvia, Luxembourg, Mexico, the Netherlands, New Zealand, Norway, Poland, Portugal, the Slovak Republic, Slovenia, Spain, Sweden, Switzerland, Turkey, the United Kingdom and the United States. The European Union takes part in the work of the OECD.

OECD Publishing disseminates widely the results of the Organisation's statistics gathering and research on economic, social and environmental issues, as well as the conventions, guidelines and standards agreed by its members.

OECD PUBLISHING, 2, rue André-Pascal, 75775 PARIS CEDEX 16
(97 2017 41 1 P) ISBN 978-92-64-27933-9 – 2017